CLAMP

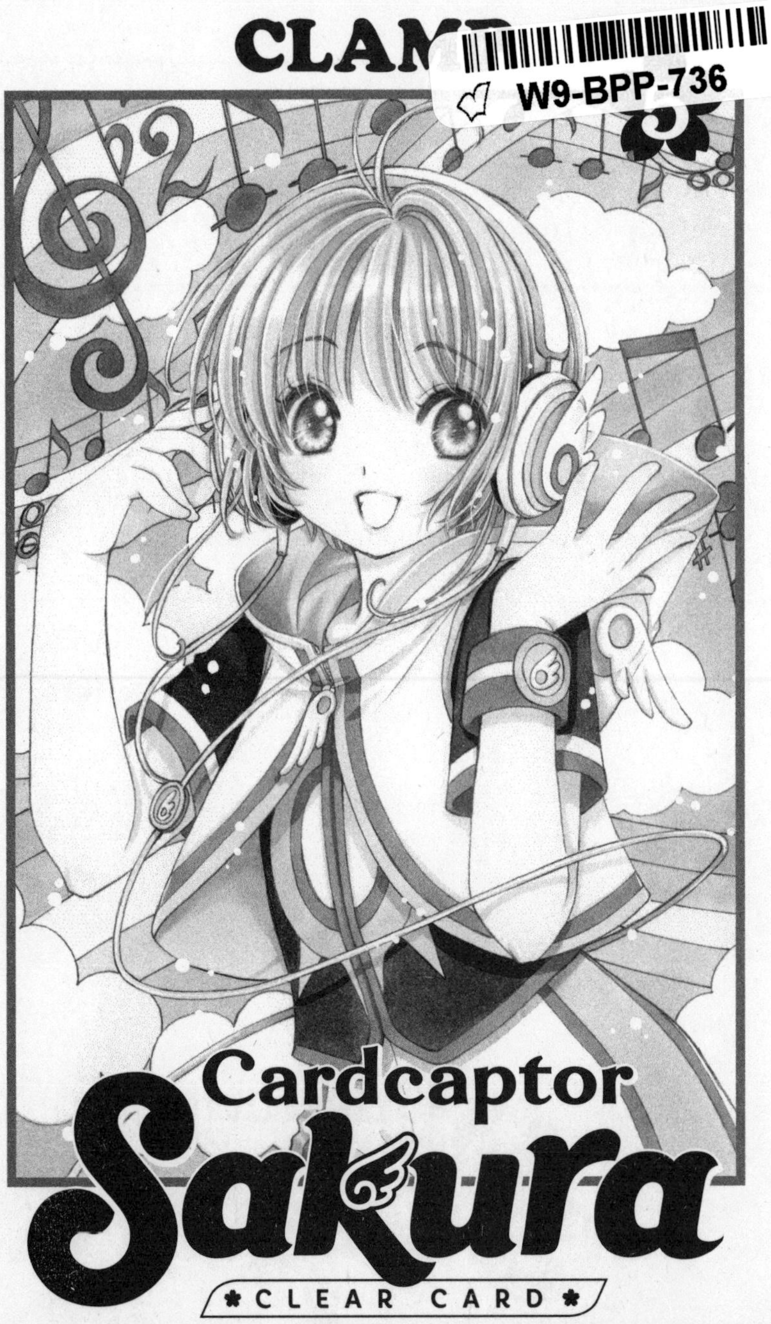
3

Cardcaptor Sakura

CLEAR CARD

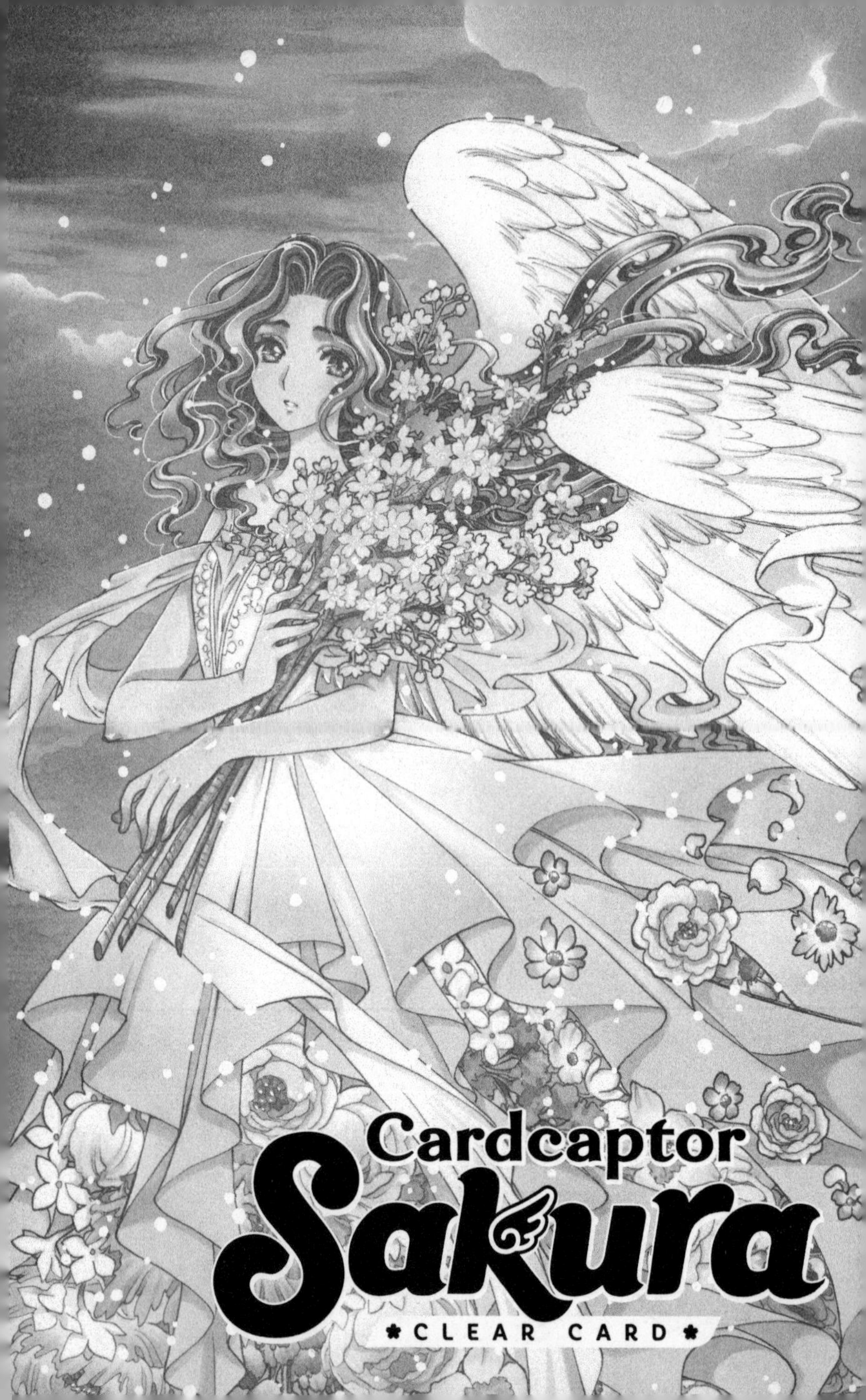
Cardcaptor
Sakura
CLEAR CARD

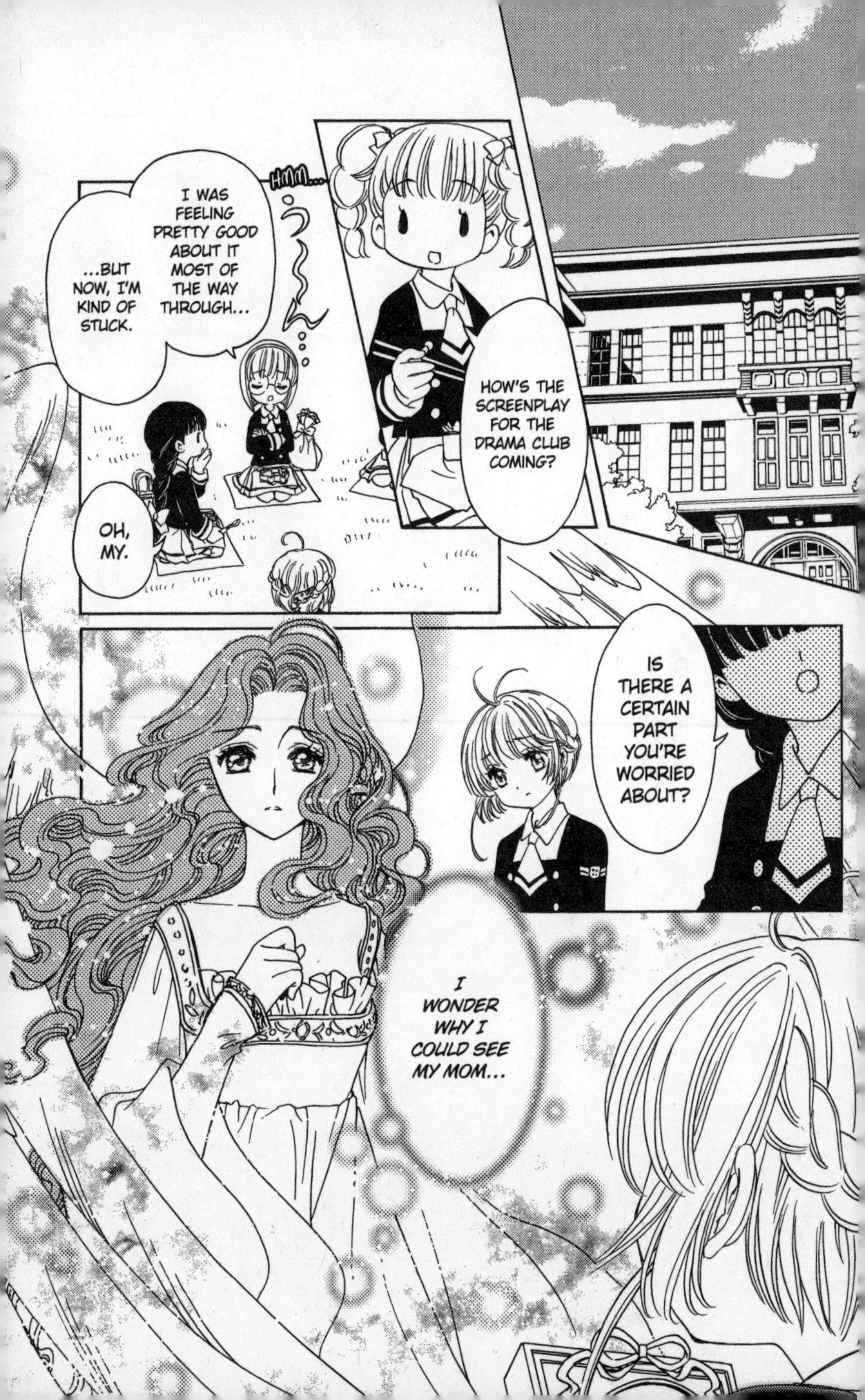
HOW'S THE SCREENPLAY FOR THE DRAMA CLUB COMING?
HMM...
I WAS FEELING PRETTY GOOD ABOUT IT MOST OF THE WAY THROUGH...
...BUT NOW, I'M KIND OF STUCK.
OH, MY.
IS THERE A CERTAIN PART YOU'RE WORRIED ABOUT?
I WONDER WHY I COULD SEE MY MOM...

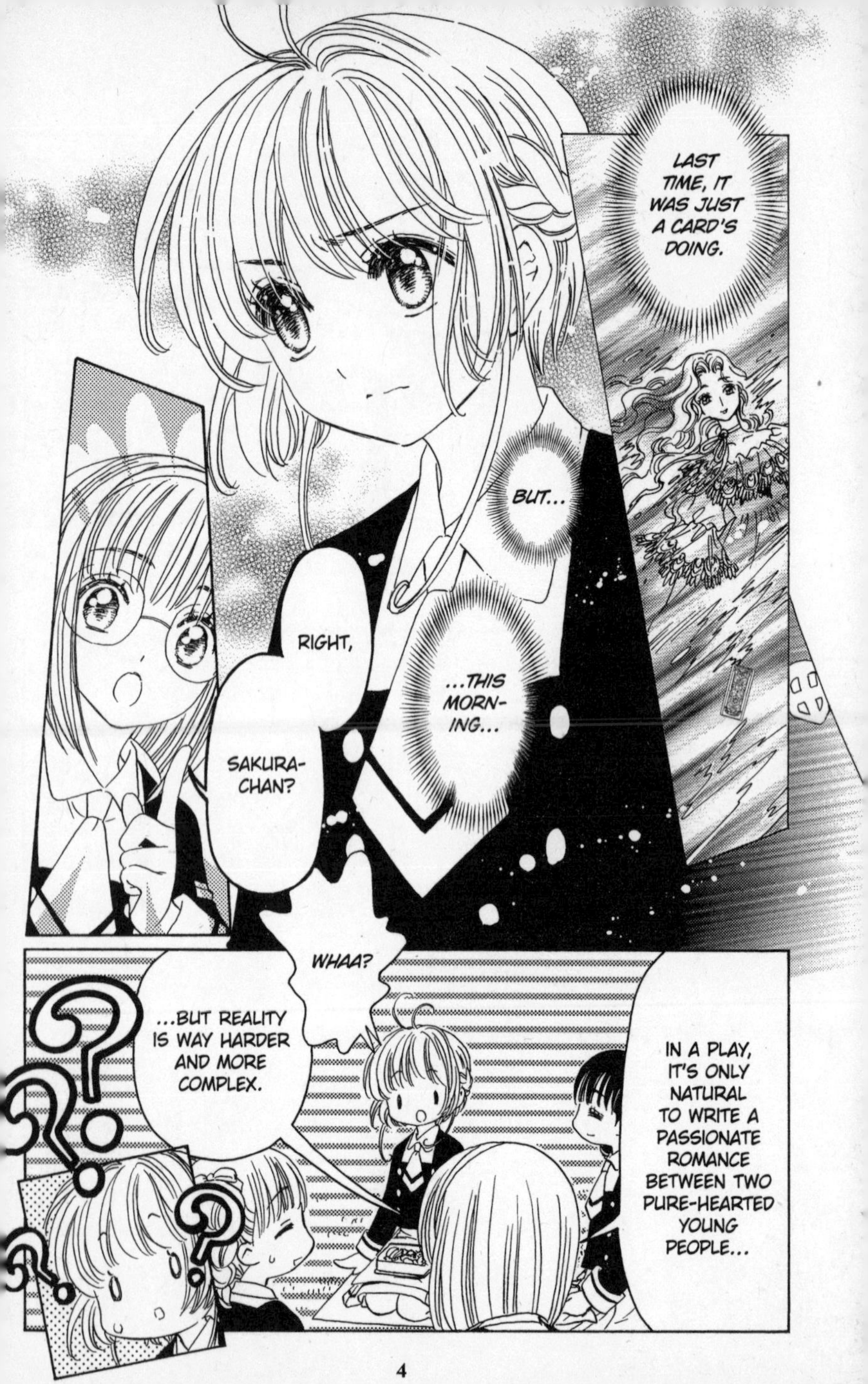
LAST TIME, IT WAS JUST A CARD'S DOING.
BUT...
...THIS MORNING...
RIGHT, SAKURA-CHAN?
IN A PLAY, IT'S ONLY NATURAL TO WRITE A PASSIONATE ROMANCE BETWEEN TWO PURE-HEARTED YOUNG PEOPLE...
...BUT REALITY IS WAY HARDER AND MORE COMPLEX.
WHAA?

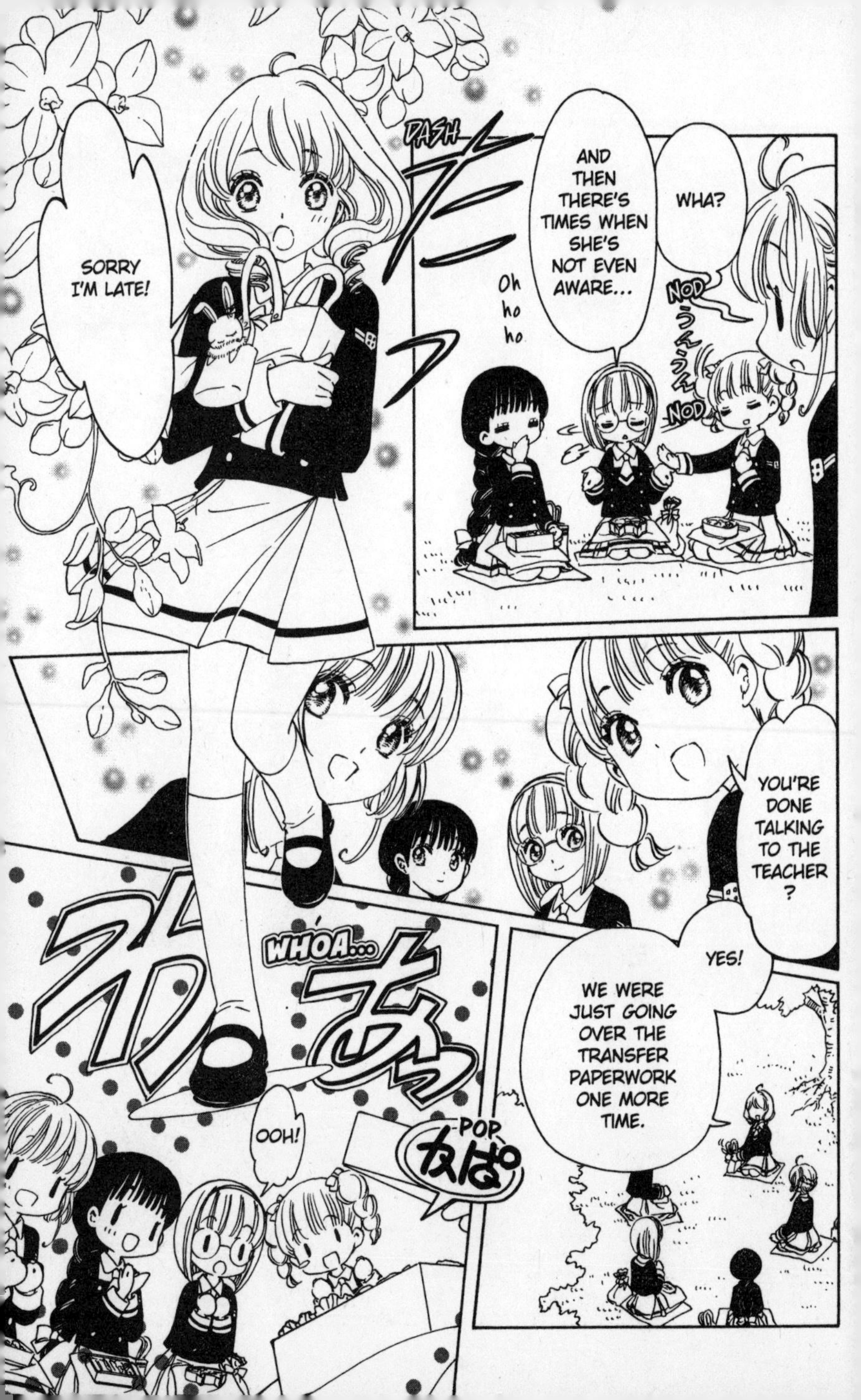
WHA?
AND THEN THERE'S TIMES WHEN SHE'S NOT EVEN AWARE...
Oh ho ho
NOD
NOD
DASH
SORRY I'M LATE!
YOU'RE DONE TALKING TO THE TEACHER?
YES!
WE WERE JUST GOING OVER THE TRANSFER PAPERWORK ONE MORE TIME.
WHOA...
POP
OOH!

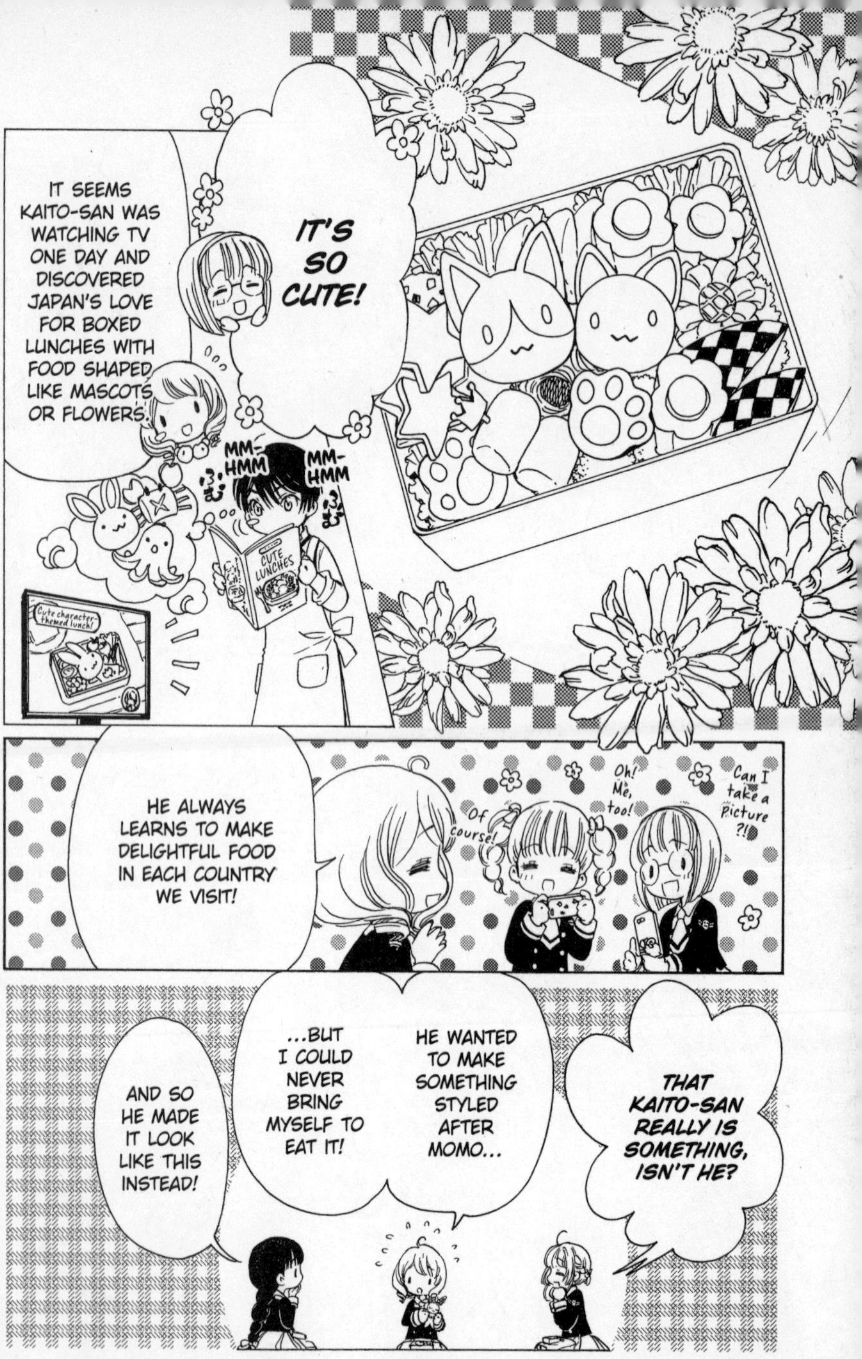
IT'S SO CUTE!
IT SEEMS KAITO-SAN WAS WATCHING TV ONE DAY AND DISCOVERED JAPAN'S LOVE FOR BOXED LUNCHES WITH FOOD SHAPED LIKE MASCOTS OR FLOWERS.
MM-HMM
MM-HMM
CUTE LUNCHES
Cute character-themed lunch!
Can I take a Picture?!
Oh! Me, too!
Of course!
HE ALWAYS LEARNS TO MAKE DELIGHTFUL FOOD IN EACH COUNTRY WE VISIT!
THAT KAITO-SAN REALLY IS SOMETHING, ISN'T HE?
HE WANTED TO MAKE SOMETHING STYLED AFTER MOMO...
...BUT I COULD NEVER BRING MYSELF TO EAT IT!
AND SO HE MADE IT LOOK LIKE THIS INSTEAD!

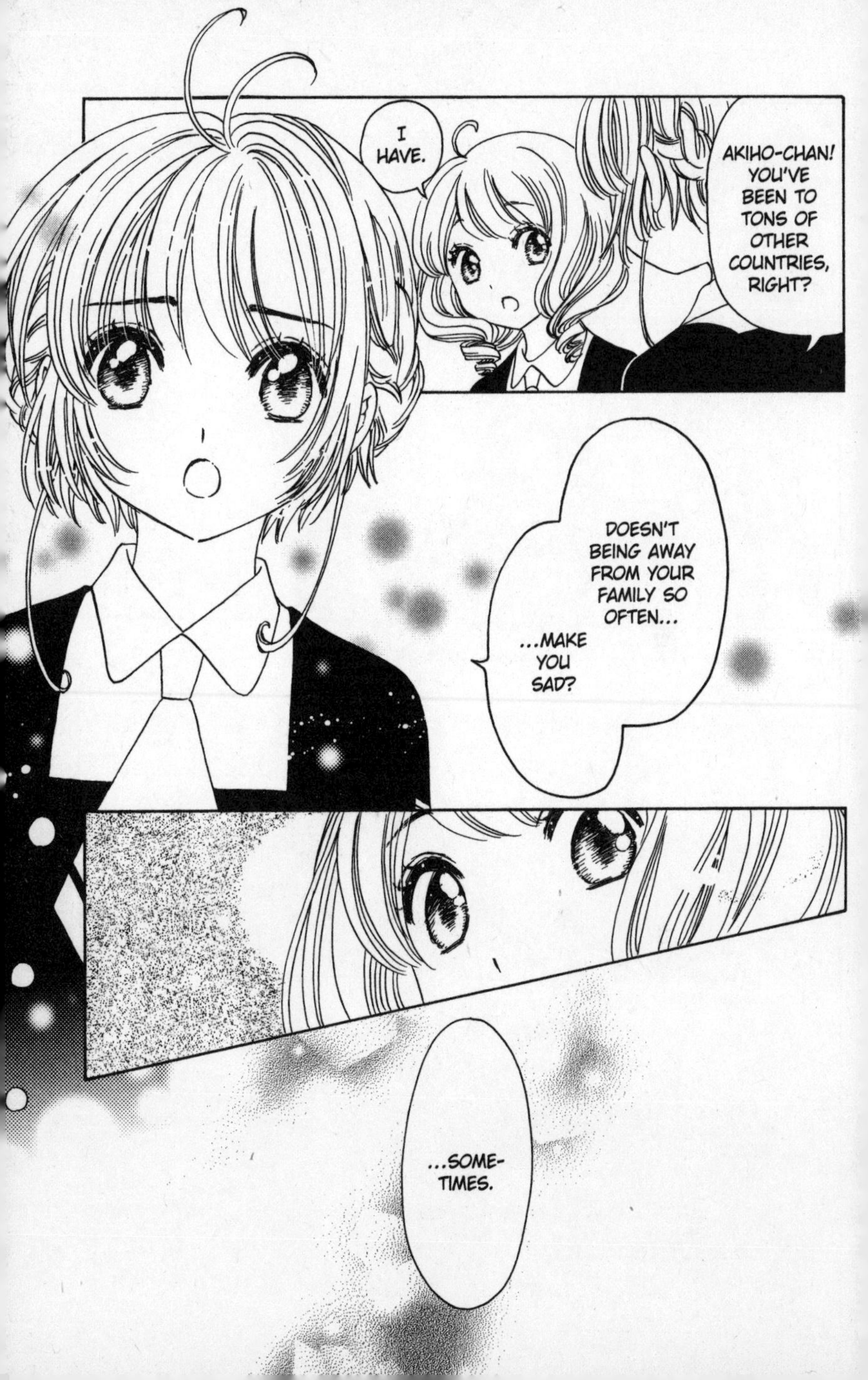
AKIHO-CHAN! YOU'VE BEEN TO TONS OF OTHER COUNTRIES, RIGHT?
I HAVE.
DOESN'T BEING AWAY FROM YOUR FAMILY SO OFTEN...
...MAKE YOU SAD?
...SOME-TIMES.

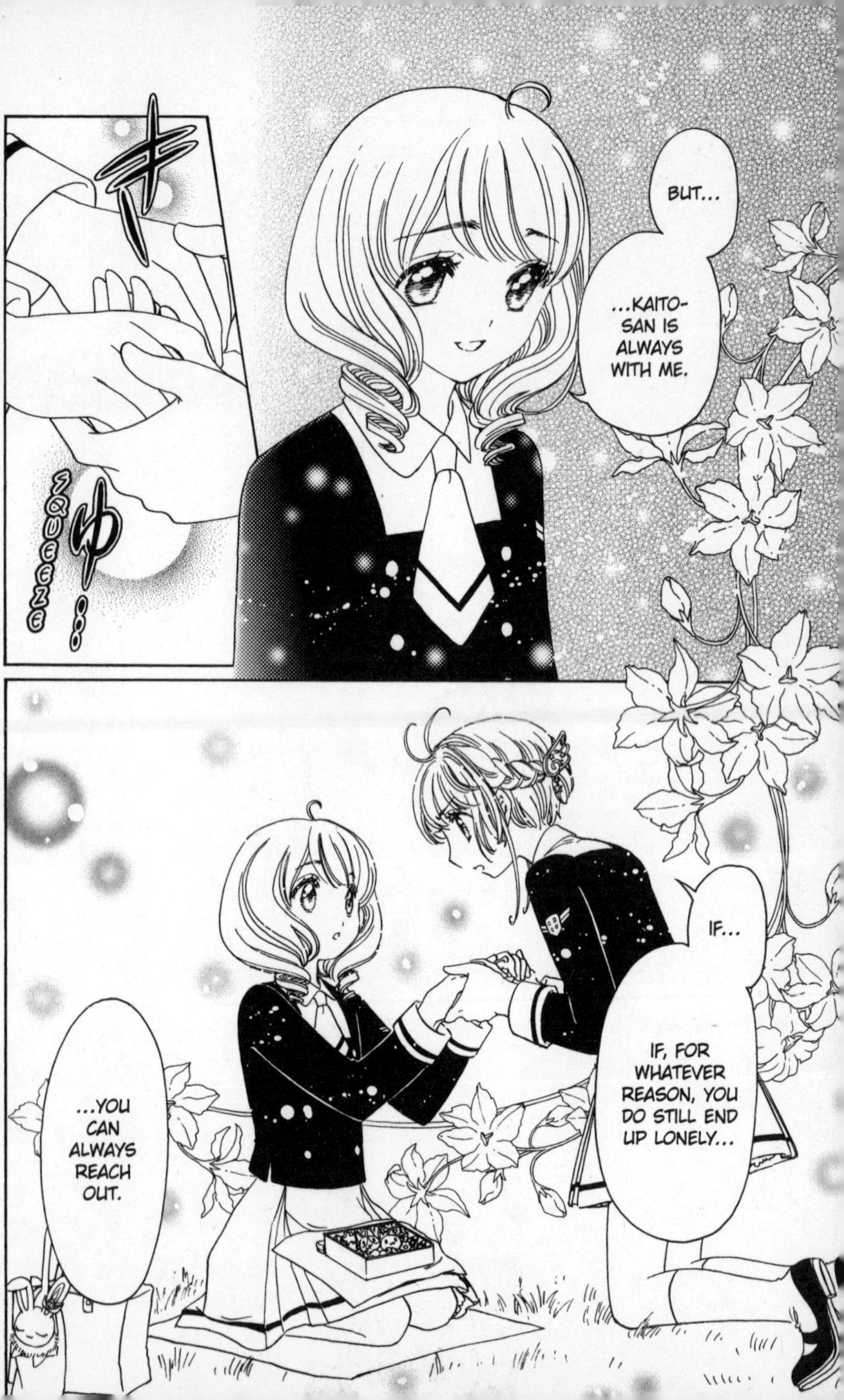
BUT...
...KAITO-SAN IS ALWAYS WITH ME.
SQUEEZE
IF...
IF, FOR WHATEVER REASON, YOU DO STILL END UP LONELY...
...YOU CAN ALWAYS REACH OUT.

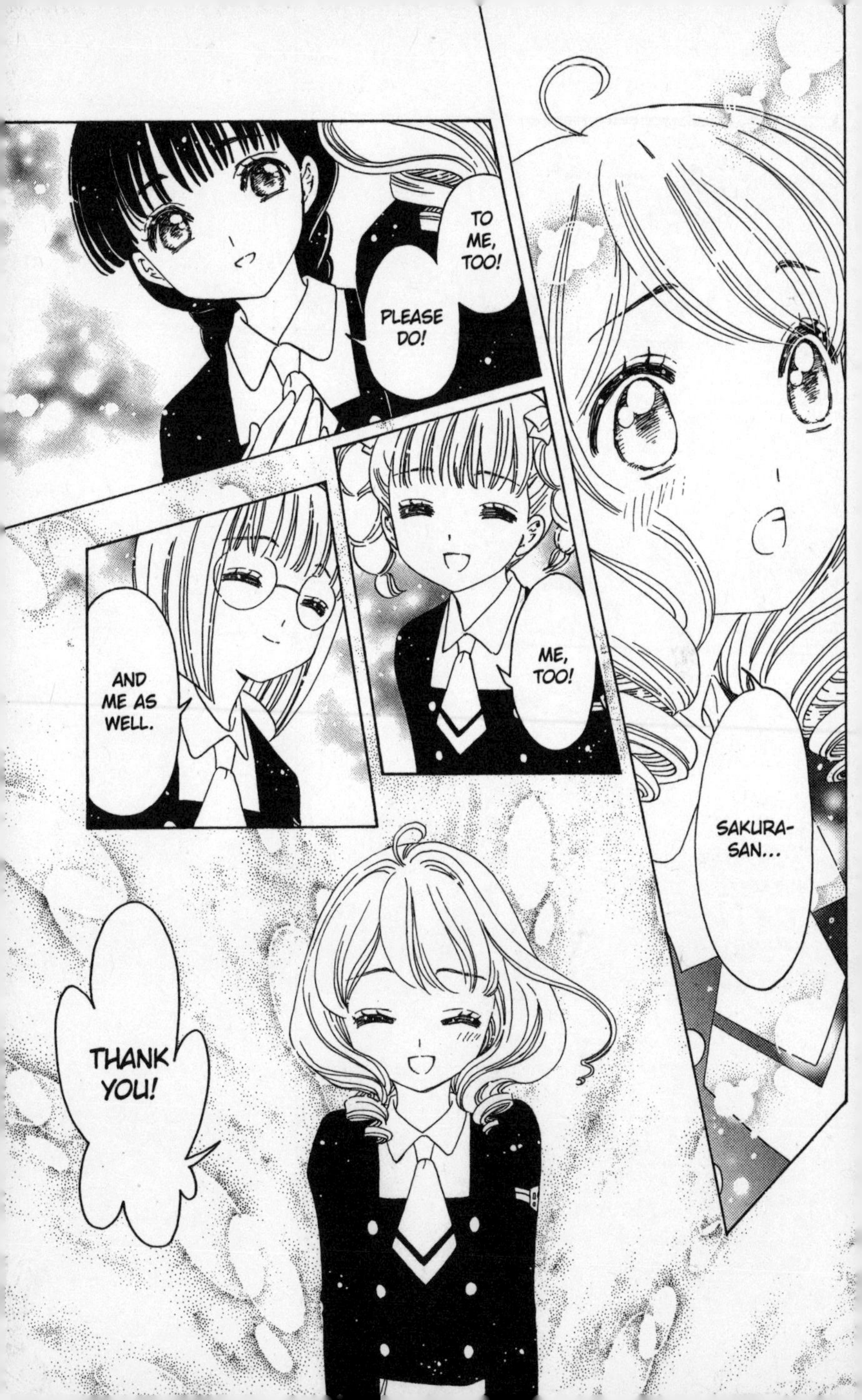
SAKURA-SAN...
TO ME, TOO!
PLEASE DO!
ME, TOO!
AND ME AS WELL.
THANK YOU!

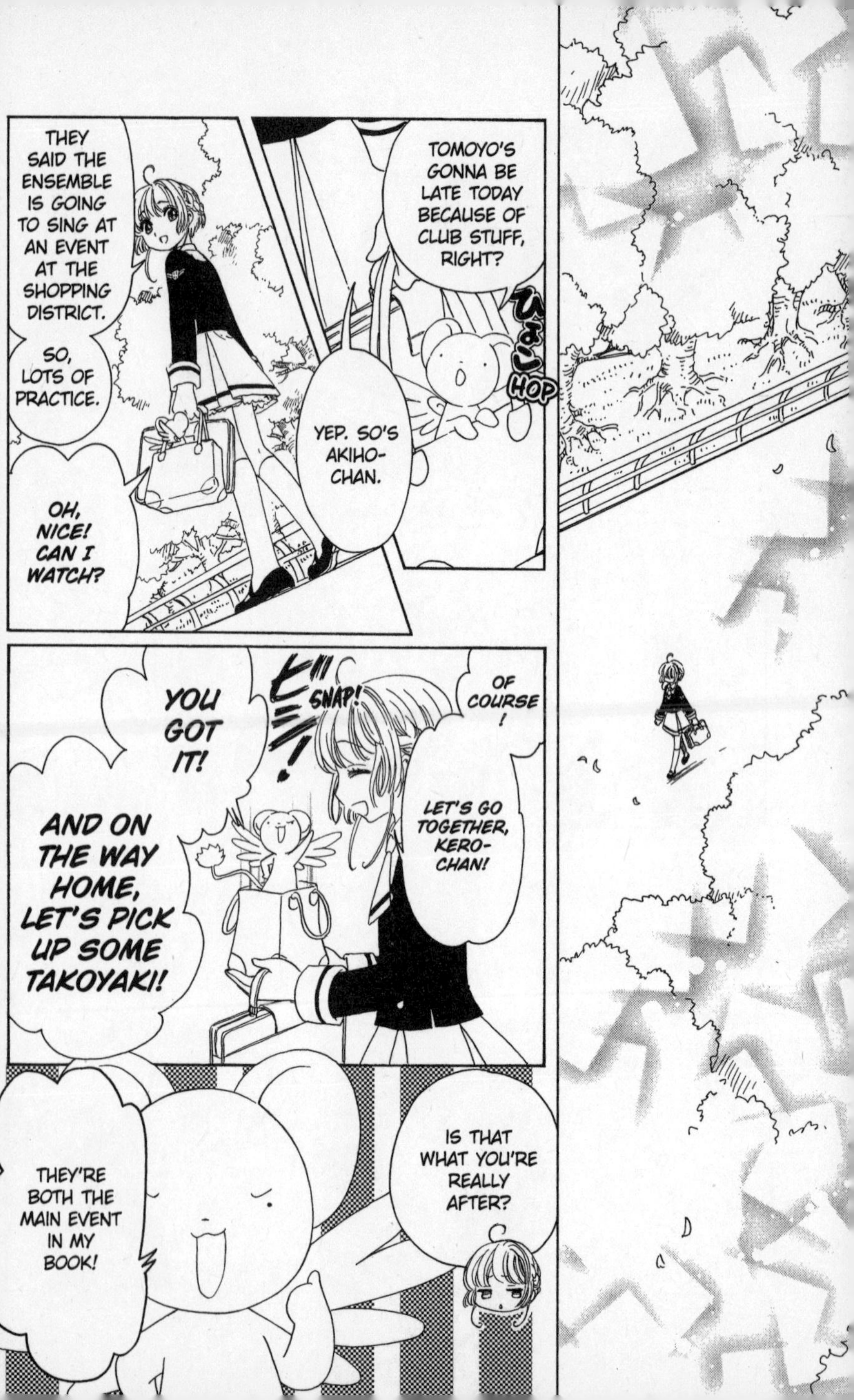
TOMOYO'S GONNA BE LATE TODAY BECAUSE OF CLUB STUFF, RIGHT?
HOP
YEP. SO'S AKIHO-CHAN.
THEY SAID THE ENSEMBLE IS GOING TO SING AT AN EVENT AT THE SHOPPING DISTRICT.
SO, LOTS OF PRACTICE.
OH, NICE! CAN I WATCH?
OF COURSE!
LET'S GO TOGETHER, KERO-CHAN!
SNAP!
YOU GOT IT!
AND ON THE WAY HOME, LET'S PICK UP SOME TAKOYAKI!
IS THAT WHAT YOU'RE REALLY AFTER?
THEY'RE BOTH THE MAIN EVENT IN MY BOOK!

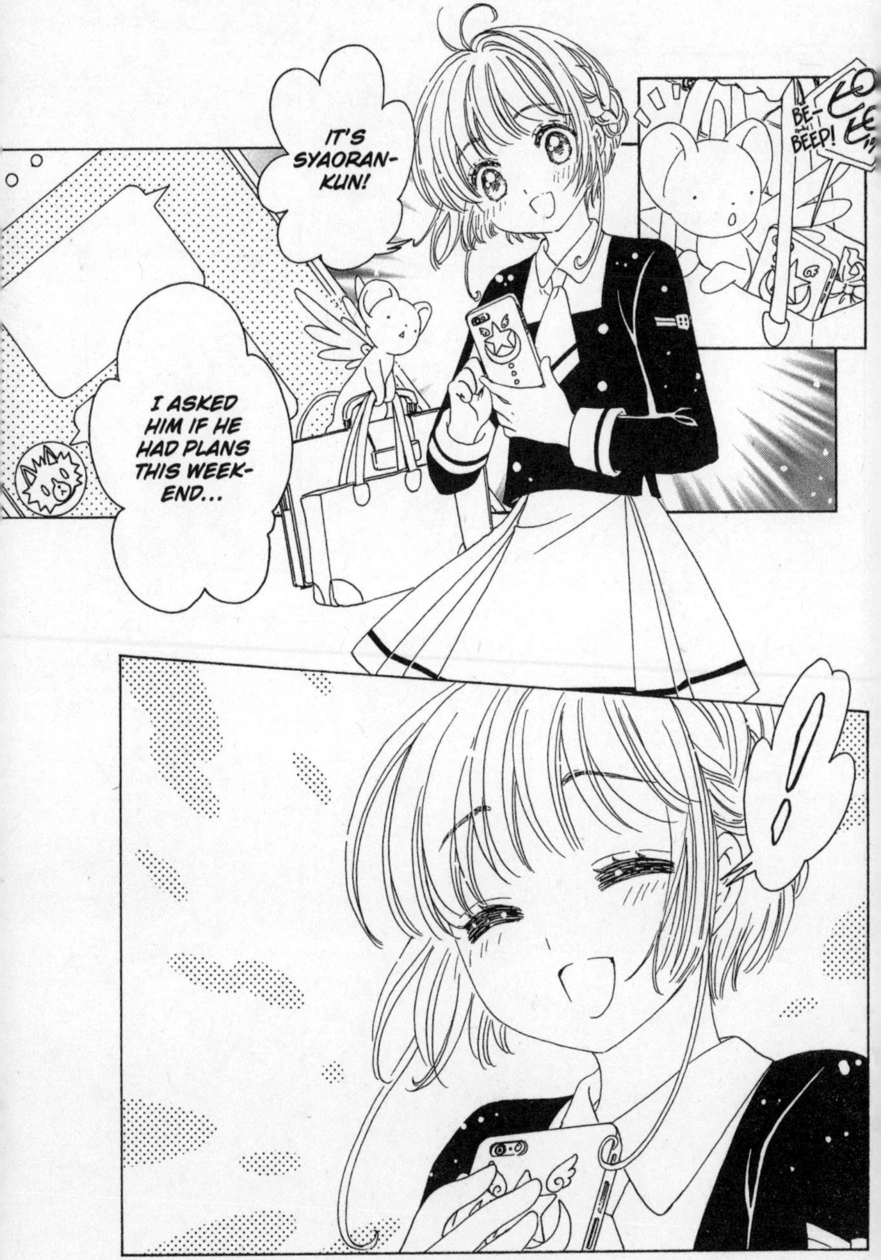
BE-BEEP!
IT'S SYAORAN-KUN!
I ASKED HIM IF HE HAD PLANS THIS WEEK-END...
!

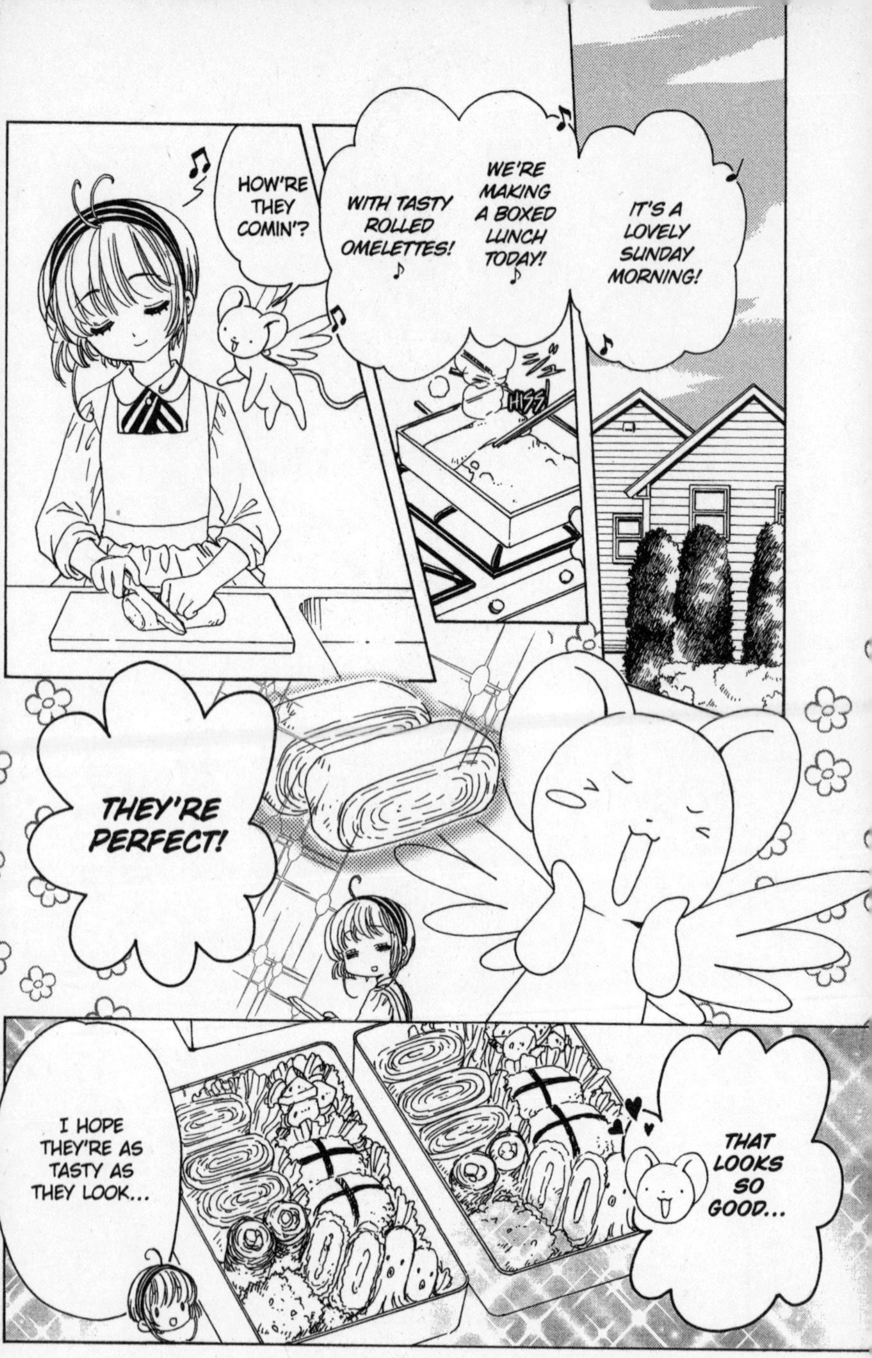
IT'S A LOVELY SUNDAY MORNING!
WE'RE MAKING A BOXED LUNCH TODAY! ♪
WITH TASTY ROLLED OMELETTES! ♪
HISS
HOW'RE THEY COMIN'?
THEY'RE PERFECT!
THAT LOOKS SO GOOD...
I HOPE THEY'RE AS TASTY AS THEY LOOK...

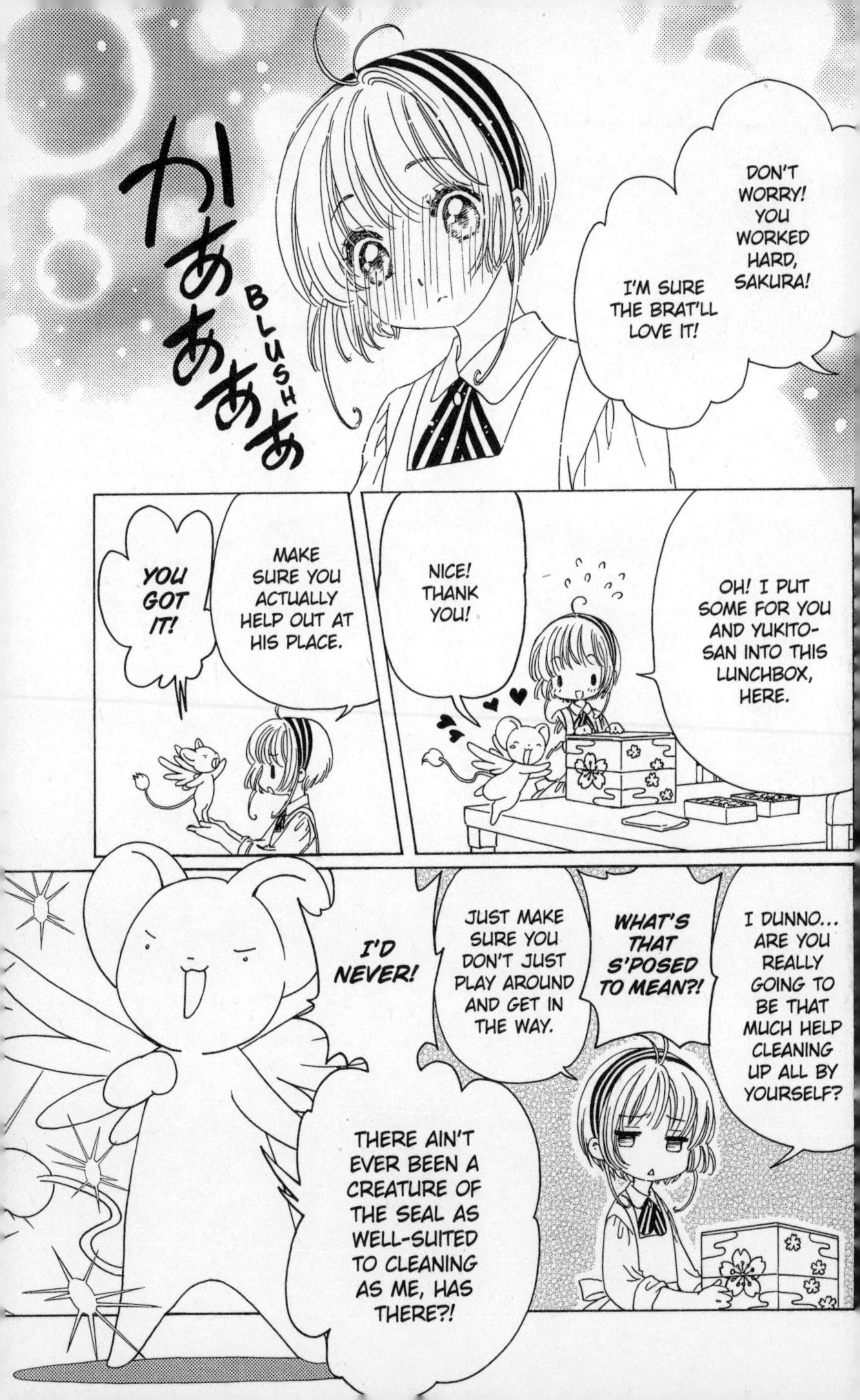

DON'T WORRY! YOU WORKED HARD, SAKURA!
I'M SURE THE BRAT'LL LOVE IT!
かあああ
BLUSH
OH! I PUT SOME FOR YOU AND YUKITO-SAN INTO THIS LUNCHBOX, HERE.
NICE! THANK YOU!
MAKE SURE YOU ACTUALLY HELP OUT AT HIS PLACE.
YOU GOT IT!
I DUNNO... ARE YOU REALLY GOING TO BE THAT MUCH HELP CLEANING UP ALL BY YOURSELF?
WHAT'S THAT S'POSED TO MEAN?!
JUST MAKE SURE YOU DON'T JUST PLAY AROUND AND GET IN THE WAY.
I'D NEVER!
THERE AIN'T EVER BEEN A CREATURE OF THE SEAL AS WELL-SUITED TO CLEANING AS ME, HAS THERE?!

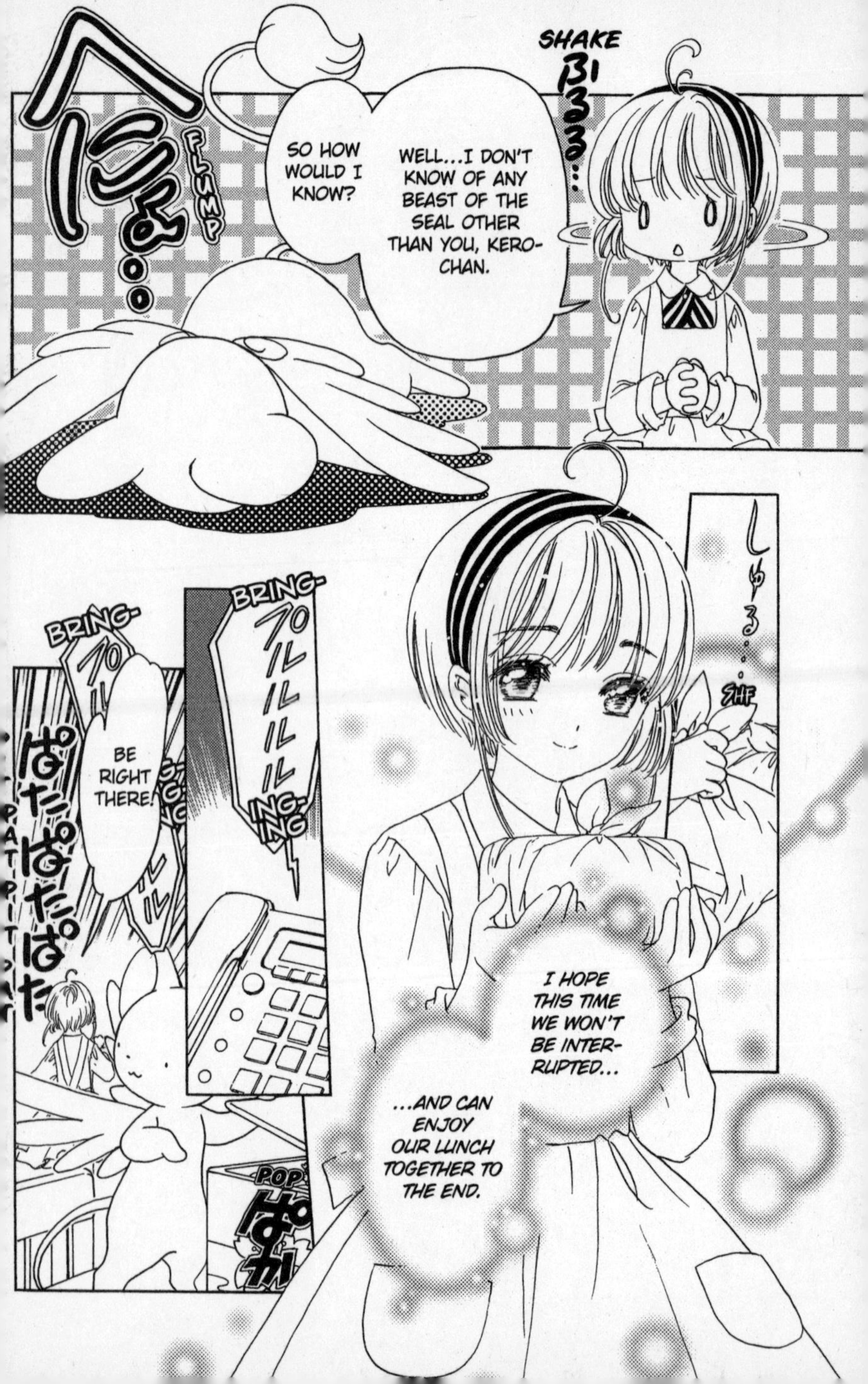
SHAKE
ふるる…
WELL...I DON'T KNOW OF ANY BEAST OF THE SEAL OTHER THAN YOU, KERO-CHAN.
SO HOW WOULD I KNOW?
FLUMP
へにょ…
しゅる…
SHF
I HOPE THIS TIME WE WON'T BE INTER-RUPTED...
...AND CAN ENJOY OUR LUNCH TOGETHER TO THE END.
BRING-
プルルルル
ING-ING
BRING-
BE RIGHT THERE!
ぱたぱたぱた
POP

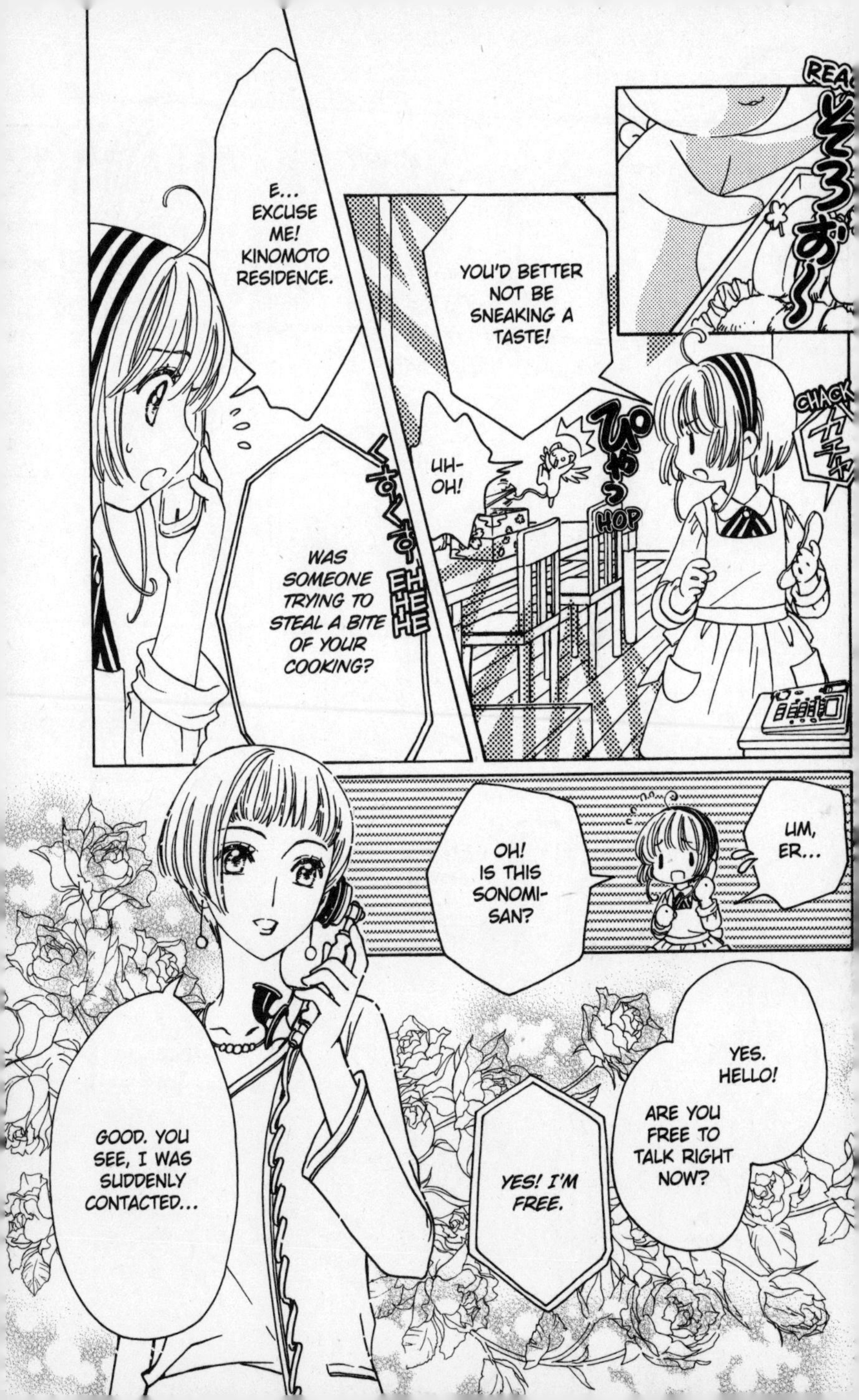
REA
そろぉ〜
CHACK
カチャ
YOU'D BETTER NOT BE SNEAKING A TASTE!
ぴょっ
HOP
UH-OH!
E... EXCUSE ME! KINOMOTO RESIDENCE.
WAS SOMEONE TRYING TO STEAL A BITE OF YOUR COOKING?
EHHEHE
UM, ER...
OH! IS THIS SONOMI-SAN?
YES. HELLO!
ARE YOU FREE TO TALK RIGHT NOW?
YES! I'M FREE.
GOOD. YOU SEE, I WAS SUDDENLY CONTACTED...

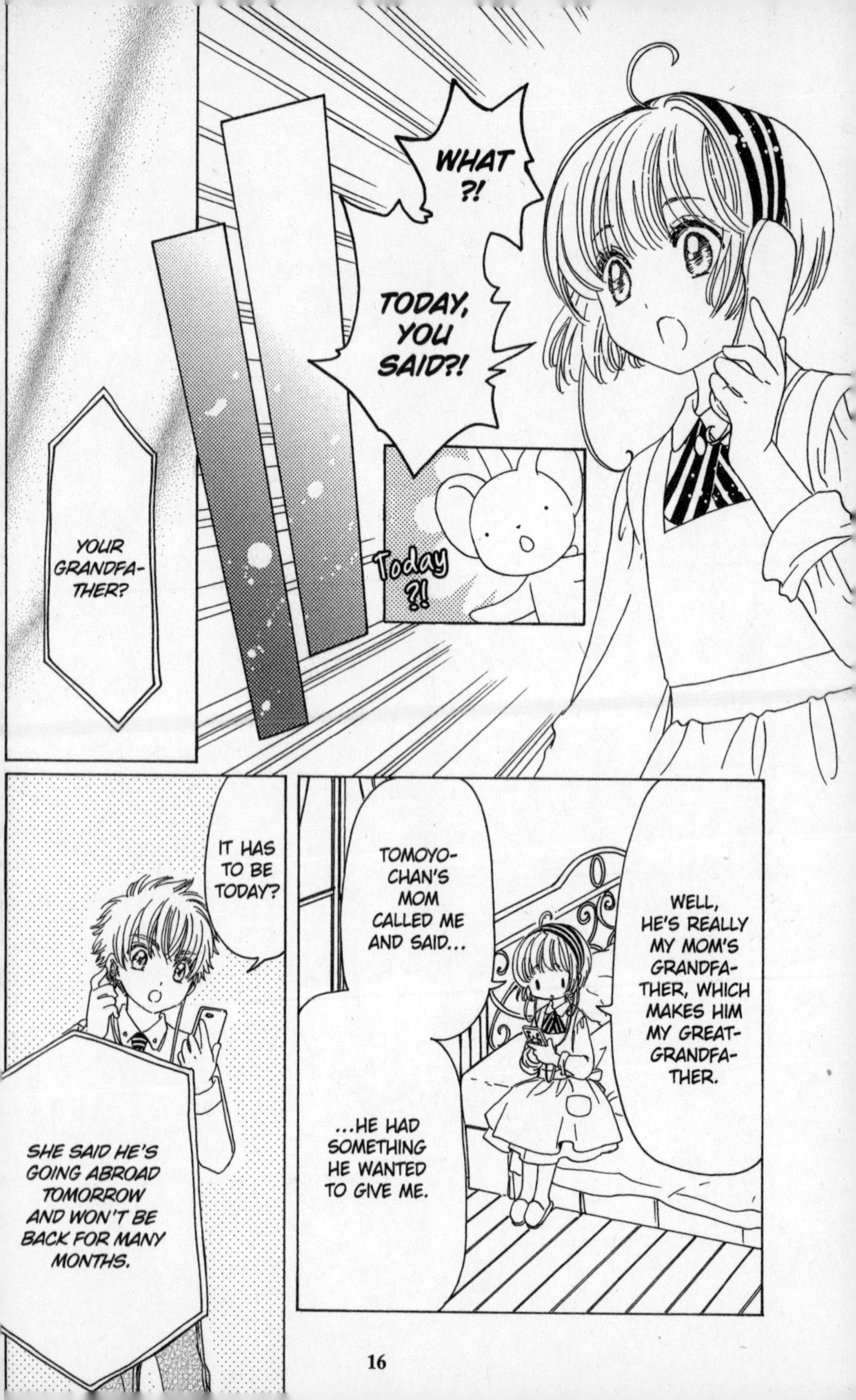
WHAT ?!
TODAY, YOU SAID?!
Today ?!
YOUR GRANDFA-THER?
WELL, HE'S REALLY MY MOM'S GRANDFA-THER, WHICH MAKES HIM MY GREAT-GRANDFA-THER.
TOMOYO-CHAN'S MOM CALLED ME AND SAID...
...HE HAD SOMETHING HE WANTED TO GIVE ME.
IT HAS TO BE TODAY?
SHE SAID HE'S GOING ABROAD TOMORROW AND WON'T BE BACK FOR MANY MONTHS.

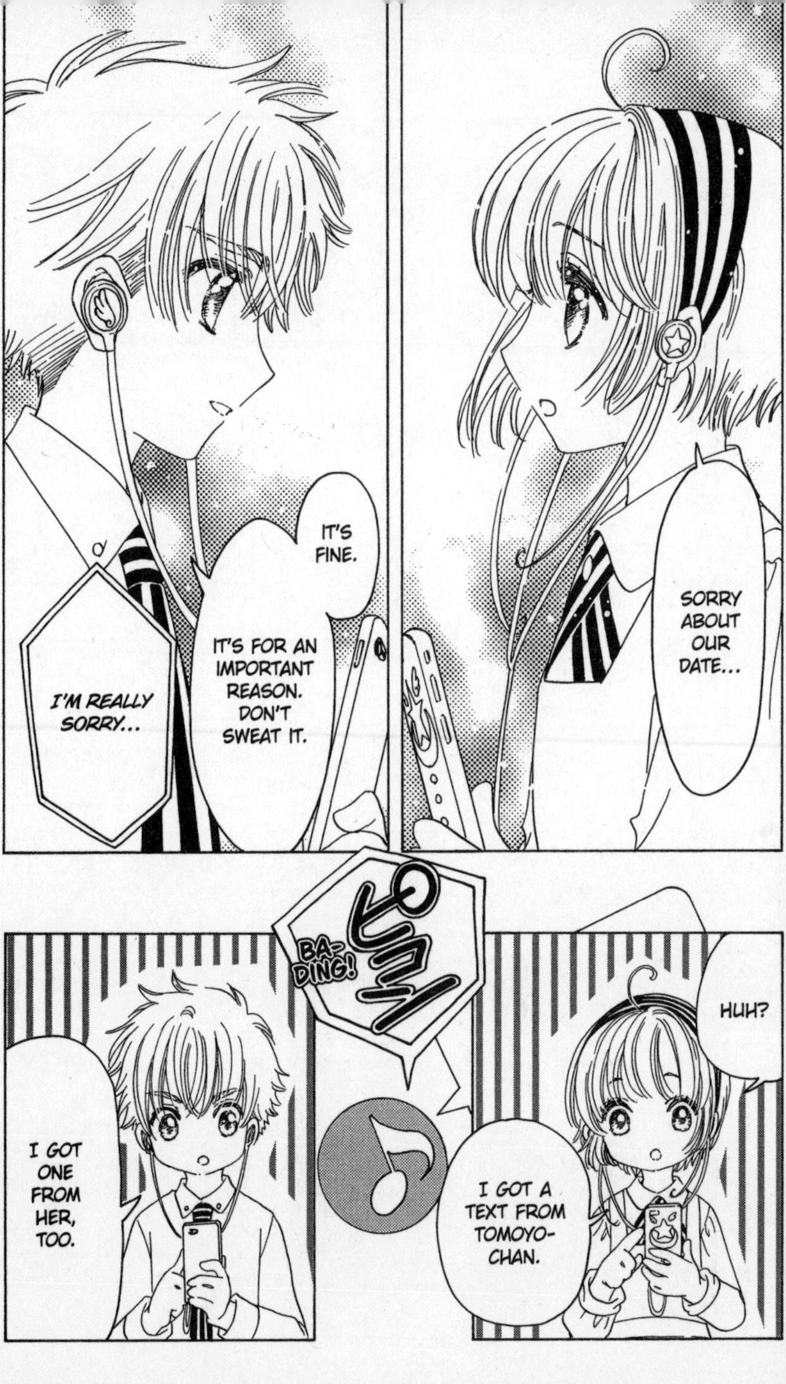
SORRY ABOUT OUR DATE...
IT'S FINE.
IT'S FOR AN IMPORTANT REASON. DON'T SWEAT IT.
I'M REALLY SORRY...
BA-DING!
HUH?
I GOT A TEXT FROM TOMOYO-CHAN.
I GOT ONE FROM HER, TOO.

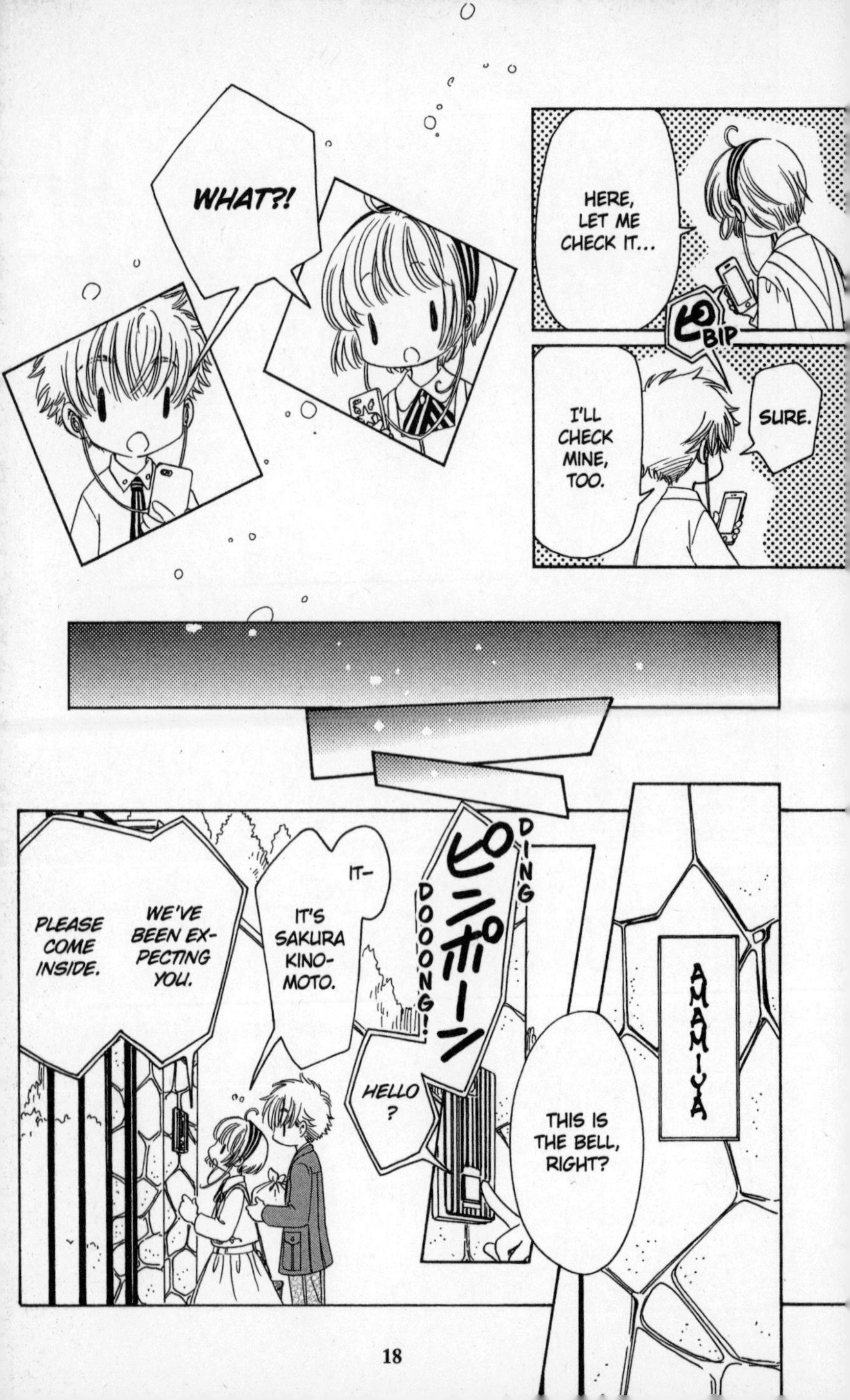
HERE, LET ME CHECK IT...
ピ BIP
SURE.
I'LL CHECK MINE, TOO.
WHAT?!
AMAMIYA
THIS IS THE BELL, RIGHT?
ピンポーン DING DOOOONG!
HELLO?
IT–
IT'S SAKURA KINO-MOTO.
WE'VE BEEN EX-PECTING YOU.
PLEASE COME INSIDE.

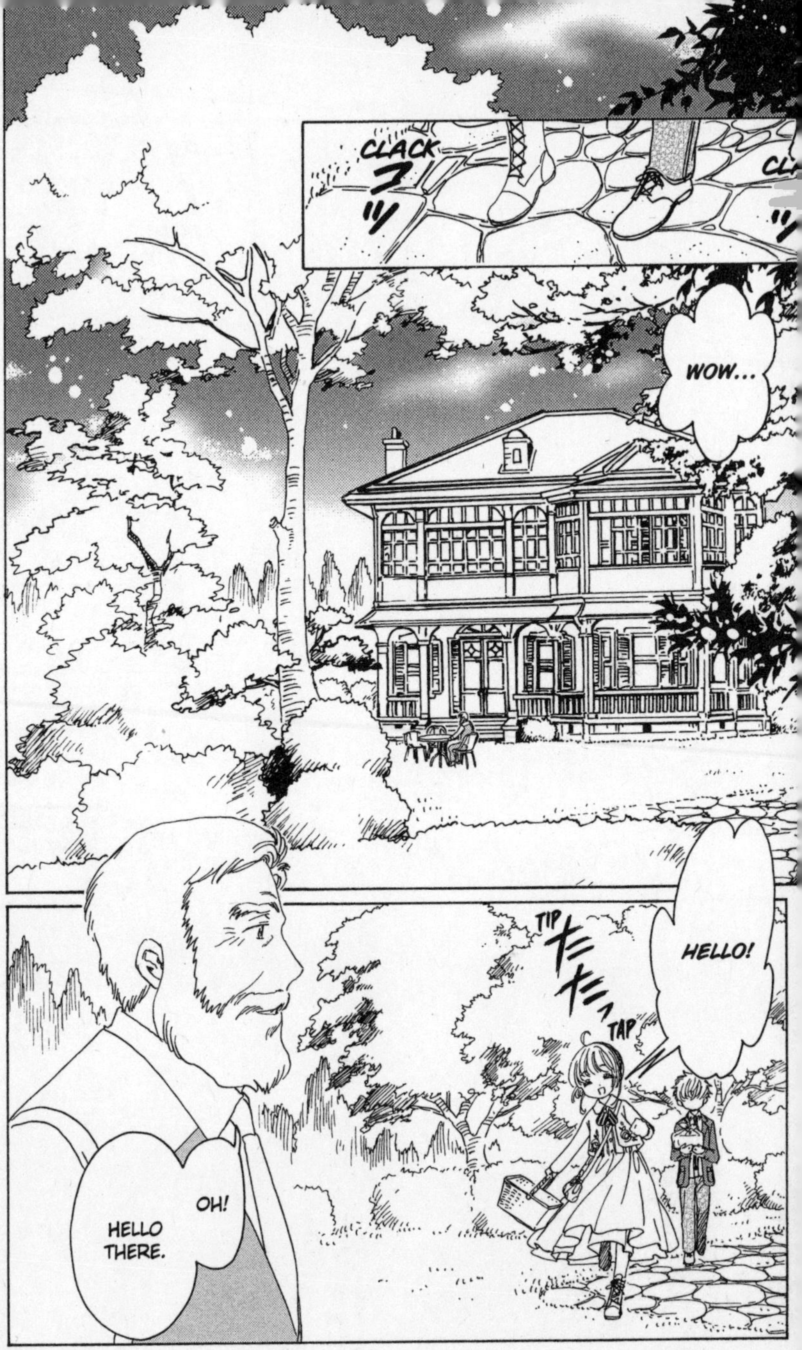
CLACK
コツ
WOW...
HELLO!
TIP
TAP
OH!
HELLO THERE.

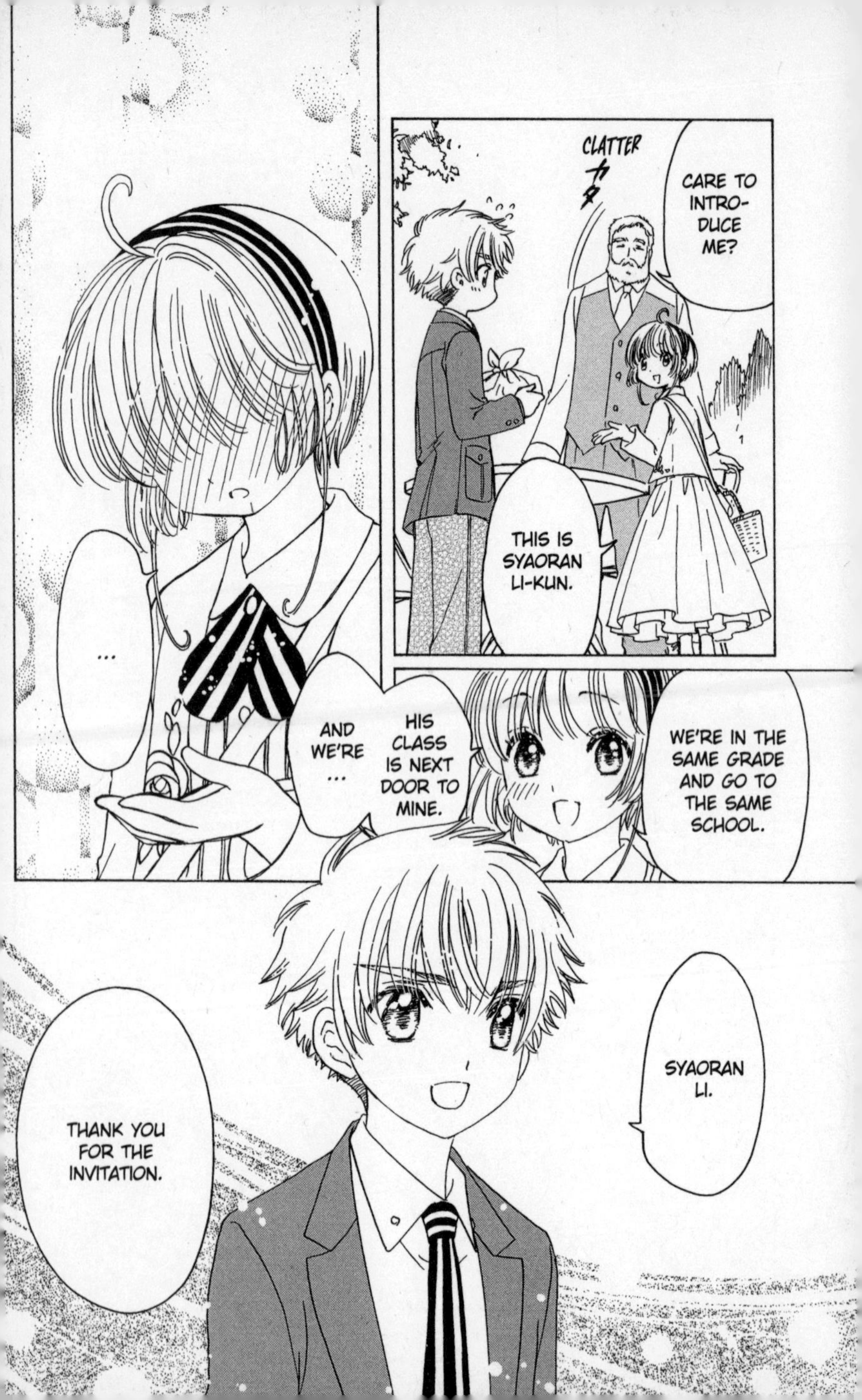
CARE TO INTRODUCE ME?
CLATTER
カタ
THIS IS SYAORAN LI-KUN.
WE'RE IN THE SAME GRADE AND GO TO THE SAME SCHOOL.
HIS CLASS IS NEXT DOOR TO MINE.
AND WE'RE ...
...
SYAORAN LI.
THANK YOU FOR THE INVITATION.

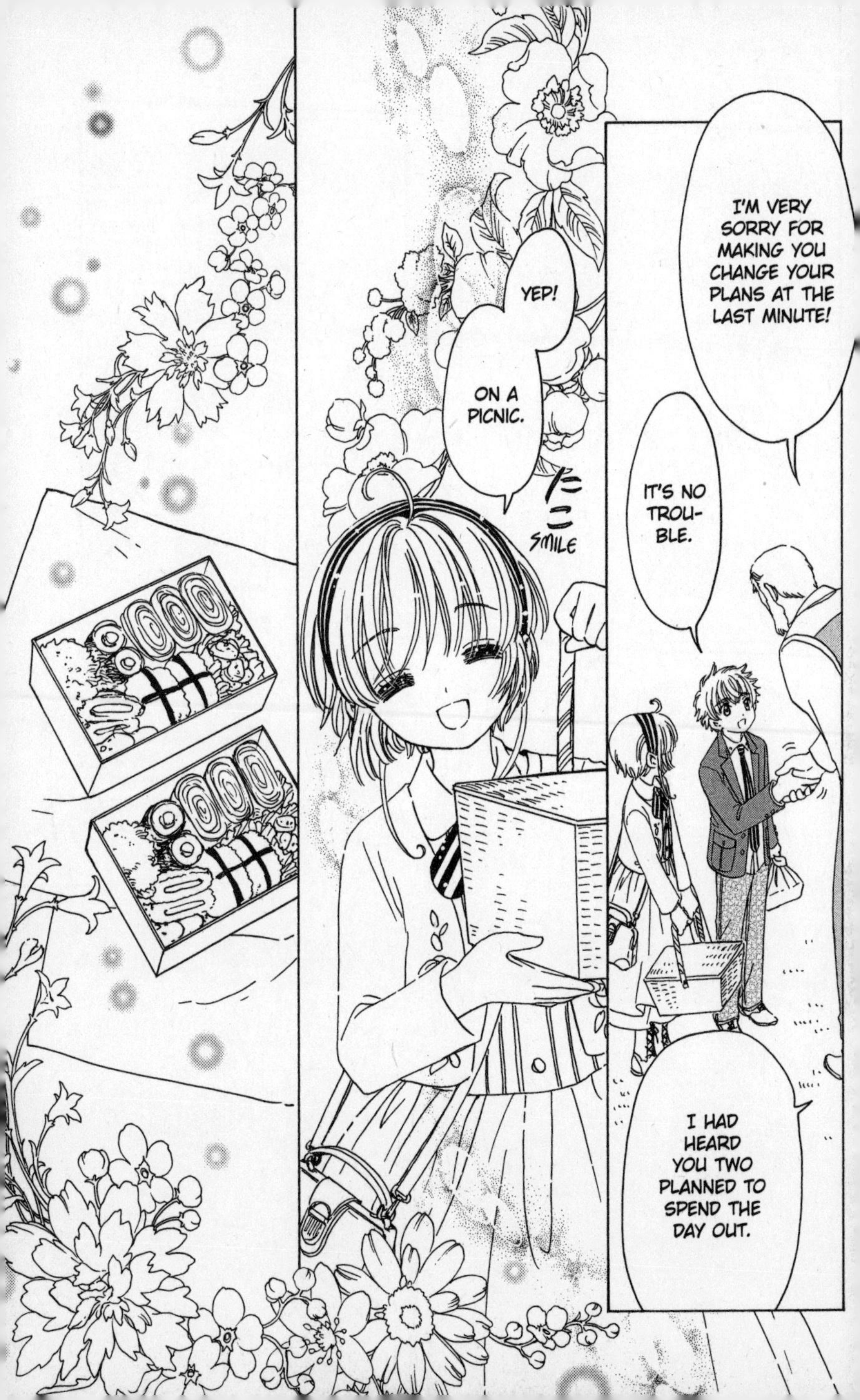
I'M VERY SORRY FOR MAKING YOU CHANGE YOUR PLANS AT THE LAST MINUTE!
IT'S NO TROUBLE.
I HAD HEARD YOU TWO PLANNED TO SPEND THE DAY OUT.
YEP!
ON A PICNIC.
SMILE

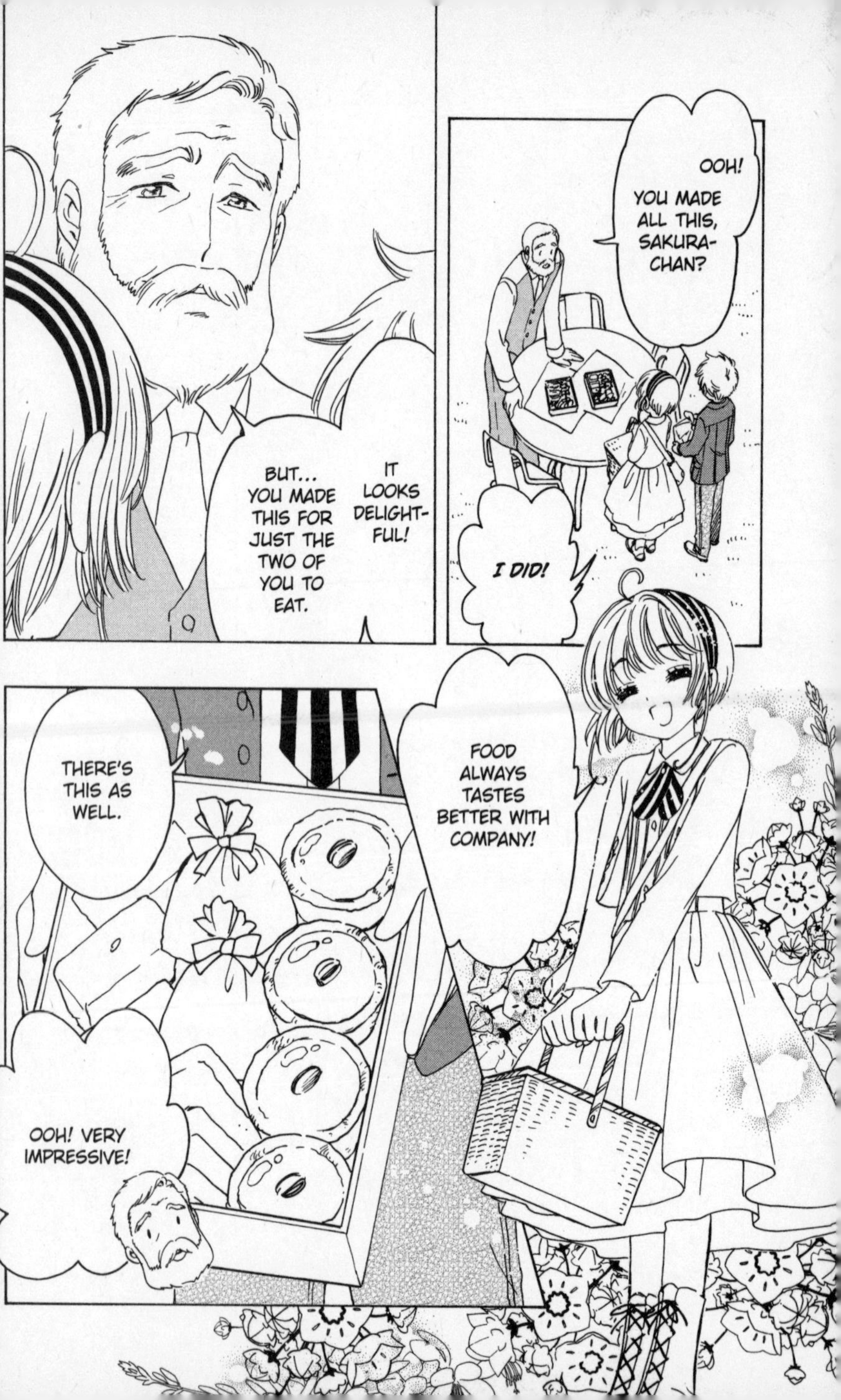
OOH! YOU MADE ALL THIS, SAKURA-CHAN?
I DID!
IT LOOKS DELIGHTFUL!
BUT... YOU MADE THIS FOR JUST THE TWO OF YOU TO EAT.
FOOD ALWAYS TASTES BETTER WITH COMPANY!
THERE'S THIS AS WELL.
OOH! VERY IMPRESSIVE!

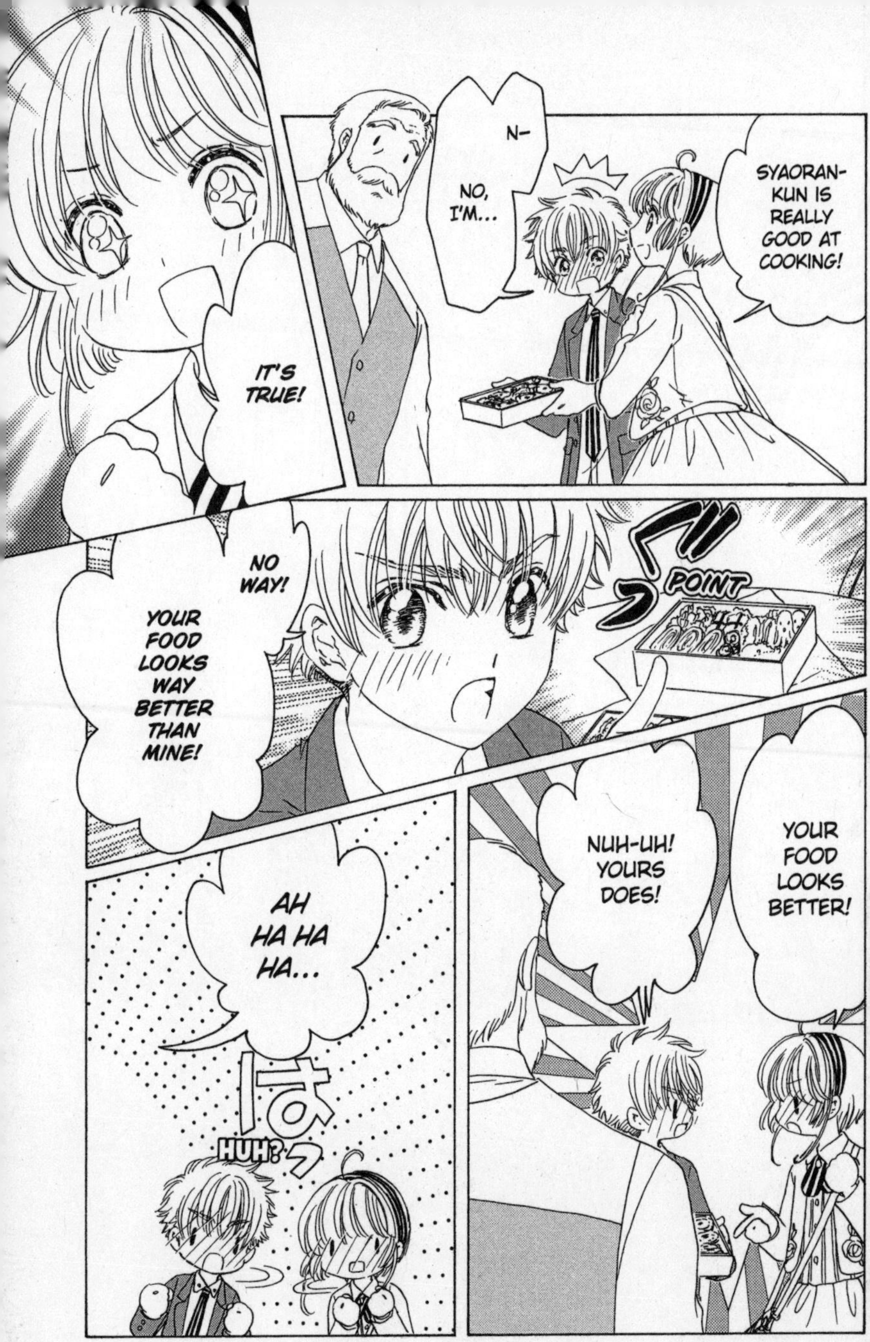
SYAORAN-KUN IS REALLY GOOD AT COOKING!
N-
NO, I'M...
IT'S TRUE!
POINT
NO WAY!
YOUR FOOD LOOKS WAY BETTER THAN MINE!
YOUR FOOD LOOKS BETTER!
NUH-UH! YOURS DOES!
AH HA HA HA...
はっ
HUH?

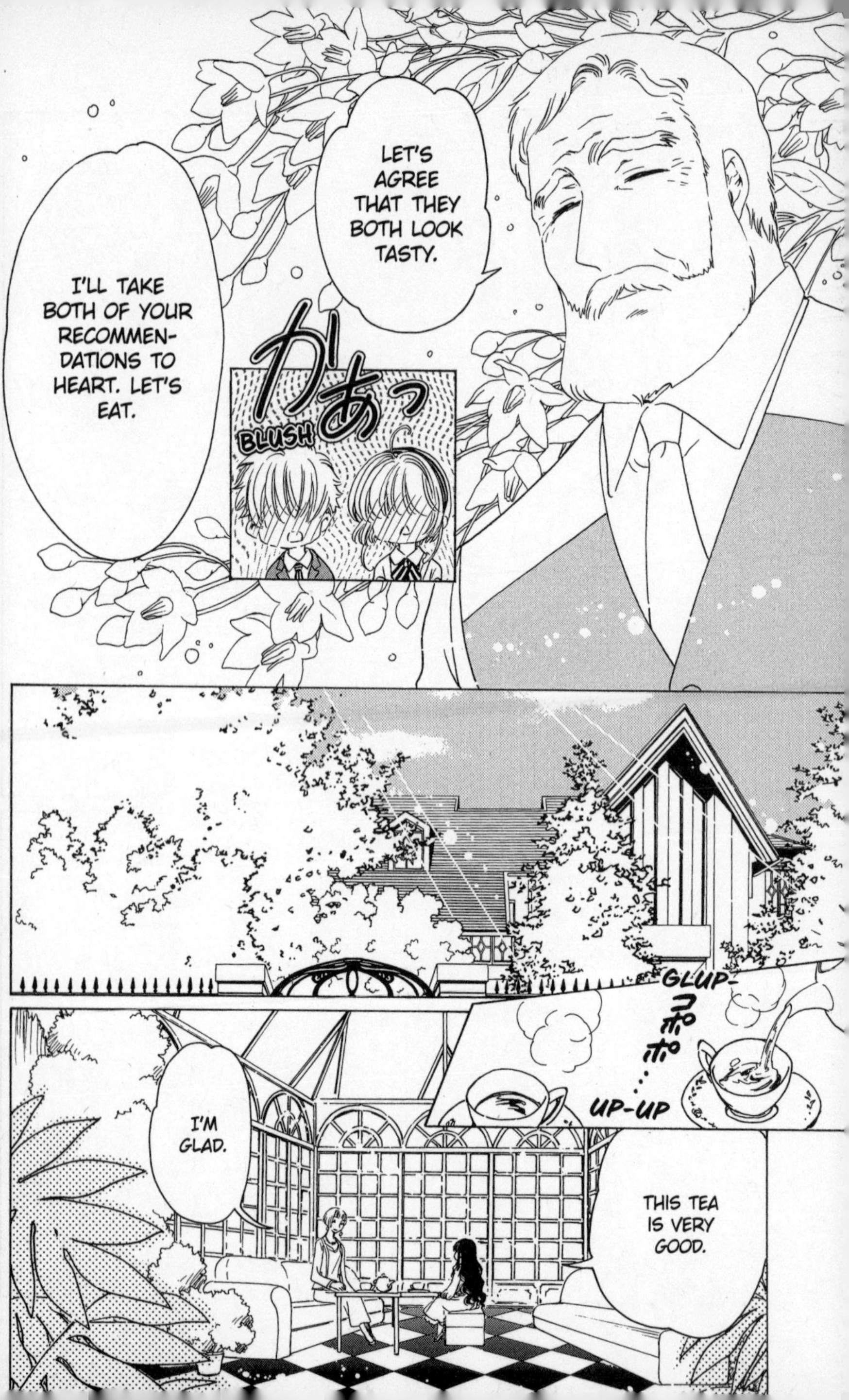
LET'S AGREE THAT THEY BOTH LOOK TASTY.
かあっ
BLUSH
I'LL TAKE BOTH OF YOUR RECOMMEN-DATIONS TO HEART. LET'S EAT.
コポポ…
GLUP-UP-UP
THIS TEA IS VERY GOOD.
I'M GLAD.

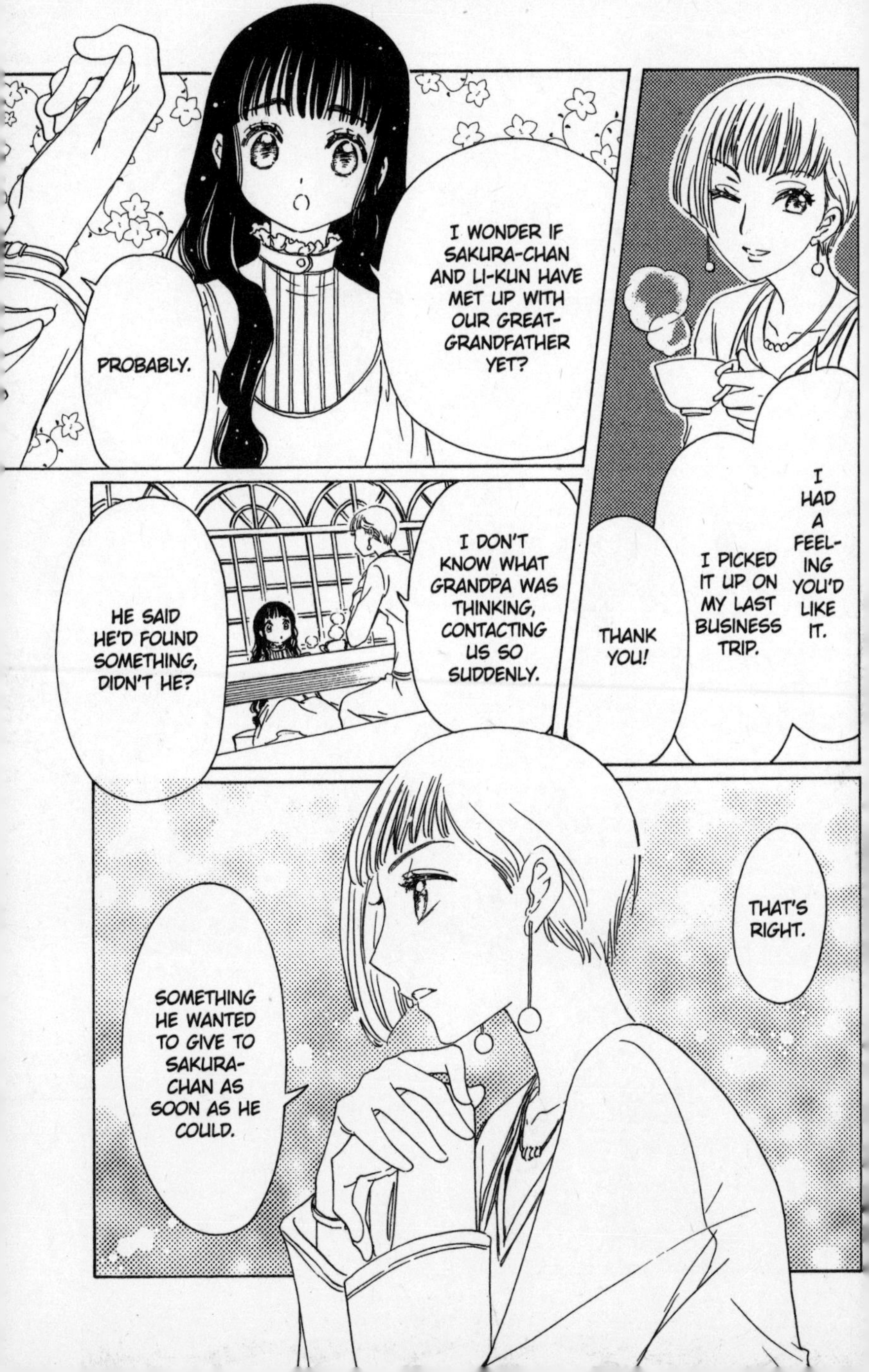

I HAD A FEELING YOU'D LIKE IT.
I PICKED IT UP ON MY LAST BUSINESS TRIP.
THANK YOU!
I WONDER IF SAKURA-CHAN AND LI-KUN HAVE MET UP WITH OUR GREAT-GRANDFATHER YET?
PROBABLY.
I DON'T KNOW WHAT GRANDPA WAS THINKING, CONTACTING US SO SUDDENLY.
HE SAID HE'D FOUND SOMETHING, DIDN'T HE?
THAT'S RIGHT.
SOMETHING HE WANTED TO GIVE TO SAKURA-CHAN AS SOON AS HE COULD.

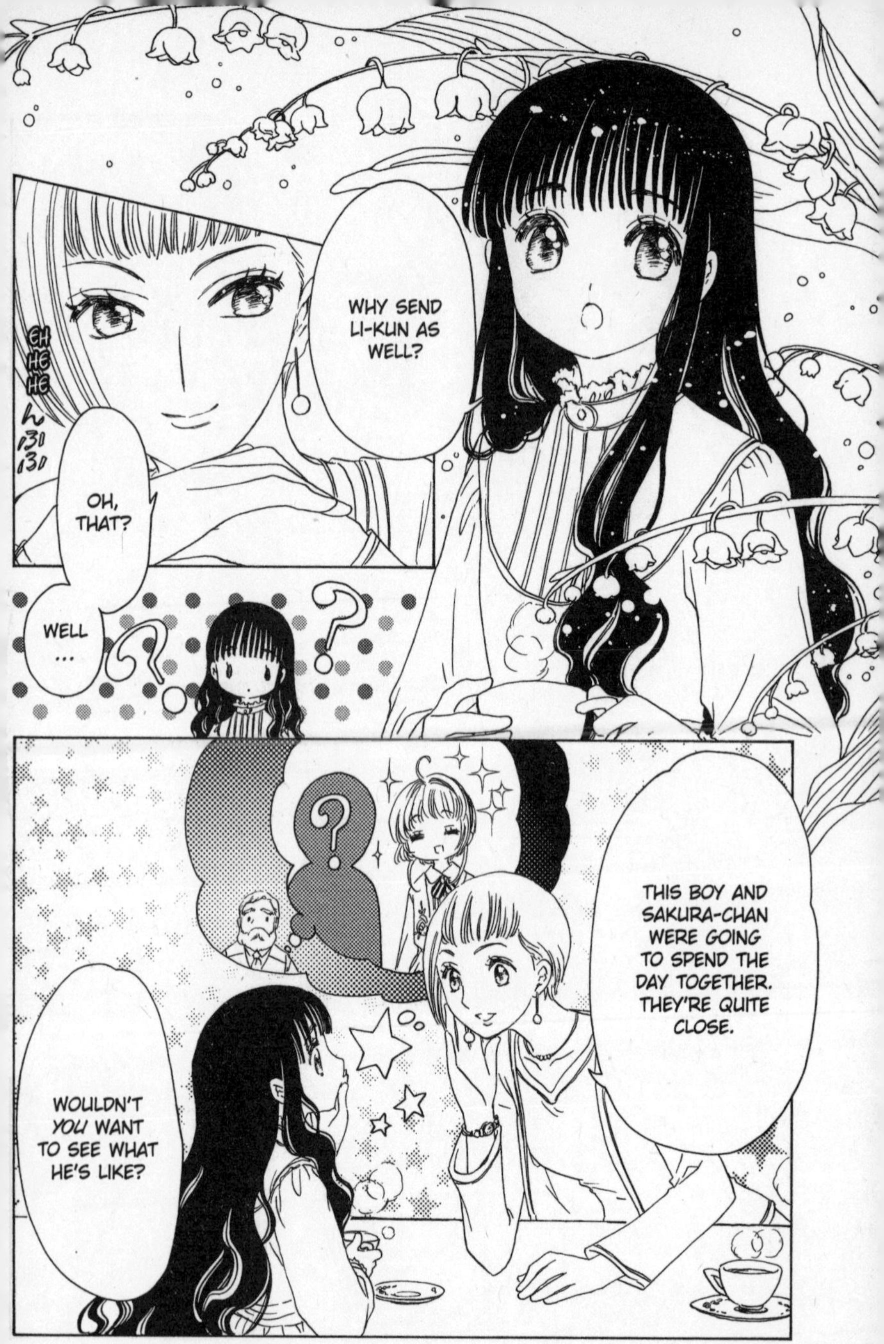
WHY SEND LI-KUN AS WELL?
EH HE HE
OH, THAT?
WELL ...
THIS BOY AND SAKURA-CHAN WERE GOING TO SPEND THE DAY TOGETHER. THEY'RE QUITE CLOSE.
WOULDN'T *YOU* WANT TO SEE WHAT HE'S LIKE?

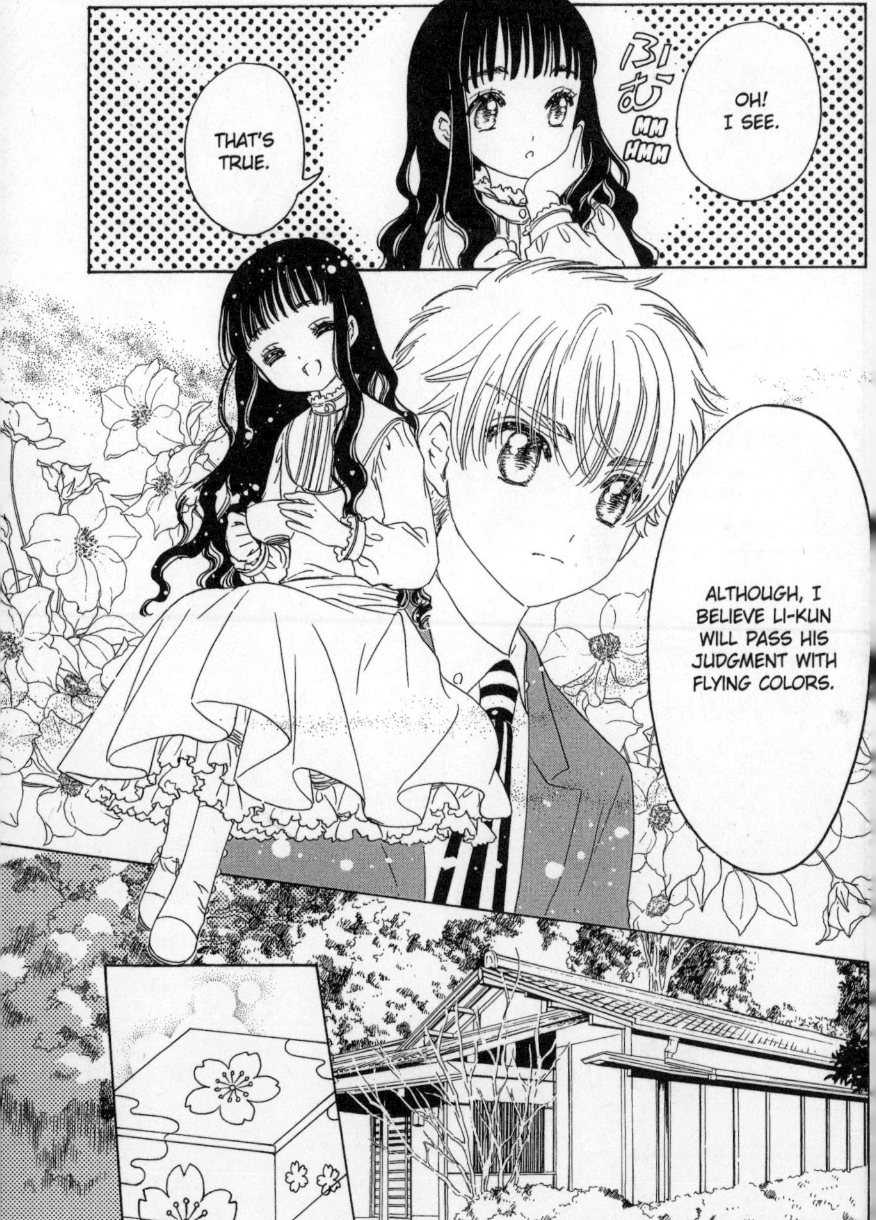
OH! I SEE.
ふむー
MM HMM
THAT'S TRUE.
ALTHOUGH, I BELIEVE LI-KUN WILL PASS HIS JUDGMENT WITH FLYING COLORS.

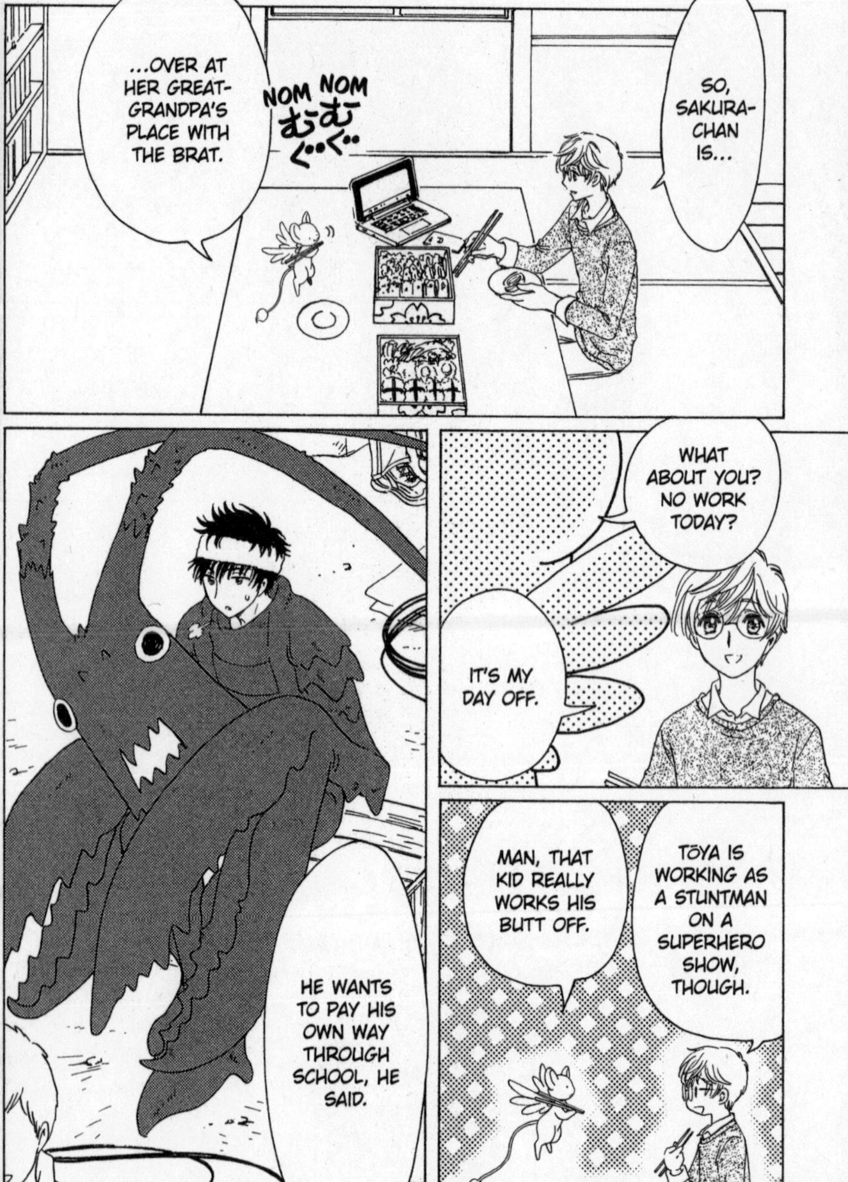
SO, SAKURA-CHAN IS...
NOM NOM
むぐむぐ
...OVER AT HER GREAT-GRANDPA'S PLACE WITH THE BRAT.
WHAT ABOUT YOU? NO WORK TODAY?
IT'S MY DAY OFF.
TŌYA IS WORKING AS A STUNTMAN ON A SUPERHERO SHOW, THOUGH.
MAN, THAT KID REALLY WORKS HIS BUTT OFF.
HE WANTS TO PAY HIS OWN WAY THROUGH SCHOOL, HE SAID.

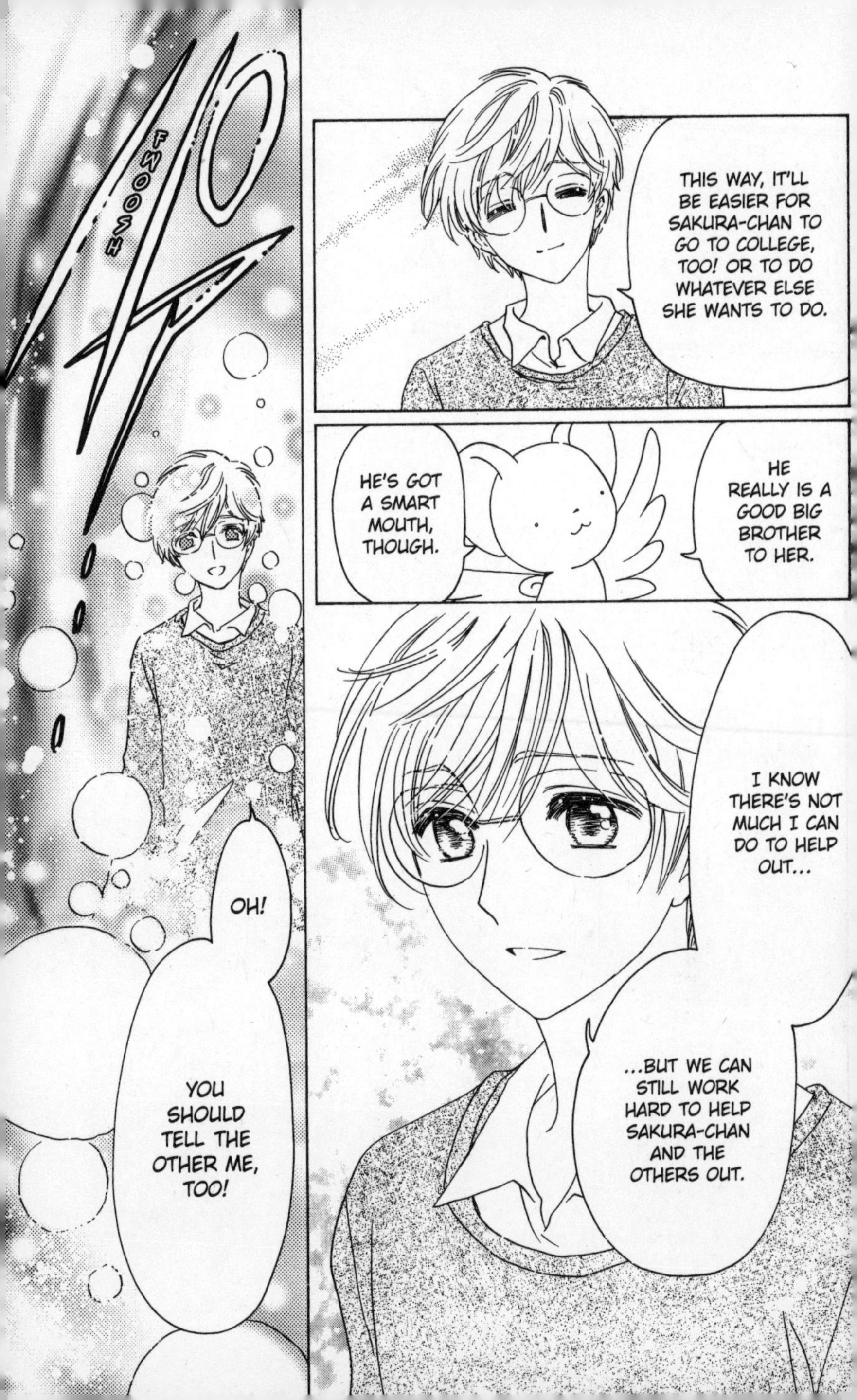
THIS WAY, IT'LL BE EASIER FOR SAKURA-CHAN TO GO TO COLLEGE, TOO! OR TO DO WHATEVER ELSE SHE WANTS TO DO.
HE REALLY IS A GOOD BIG BROTHER TO HER.
HE'S GOT A SMART MOUTH, THOUGH.
I KNOW THERE'S NOT MUCH I CAN DO TO HELP OUT...
...BUT WE CAN STILL WORK HARD TO HELP SAKURA-CHAN AND THE OTHERS OUT.
FWOOSH
OH!
YOU SHOULD TELL THE OTHER ME, TOO!

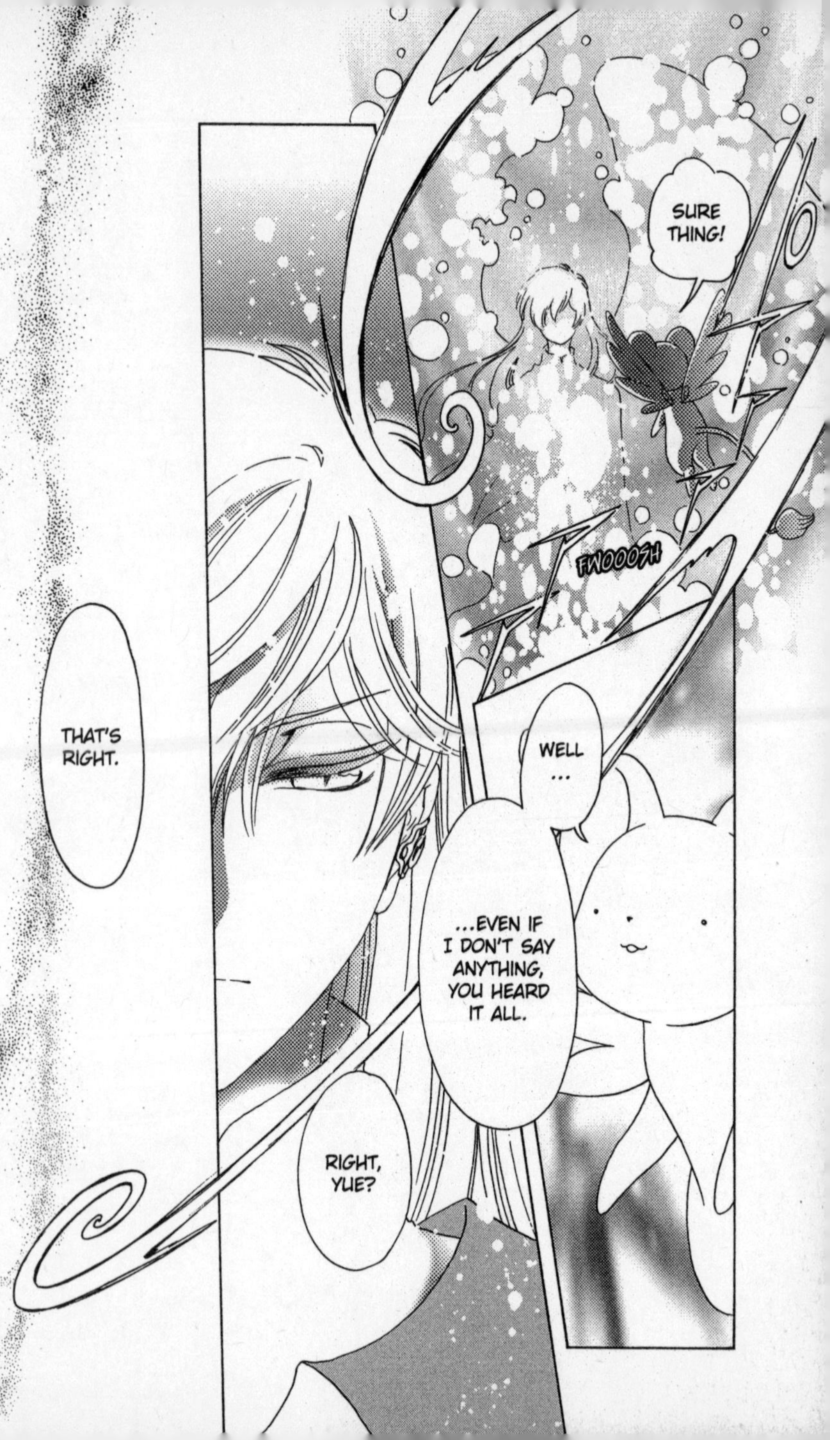
SURE THING!
FWOOOSH
WELL ...
...EVEN IF I DON'T SAY ANYTHING, YOU HEARD IT ALL.
RIGHT, YUE?
THAT'S RIGHT.

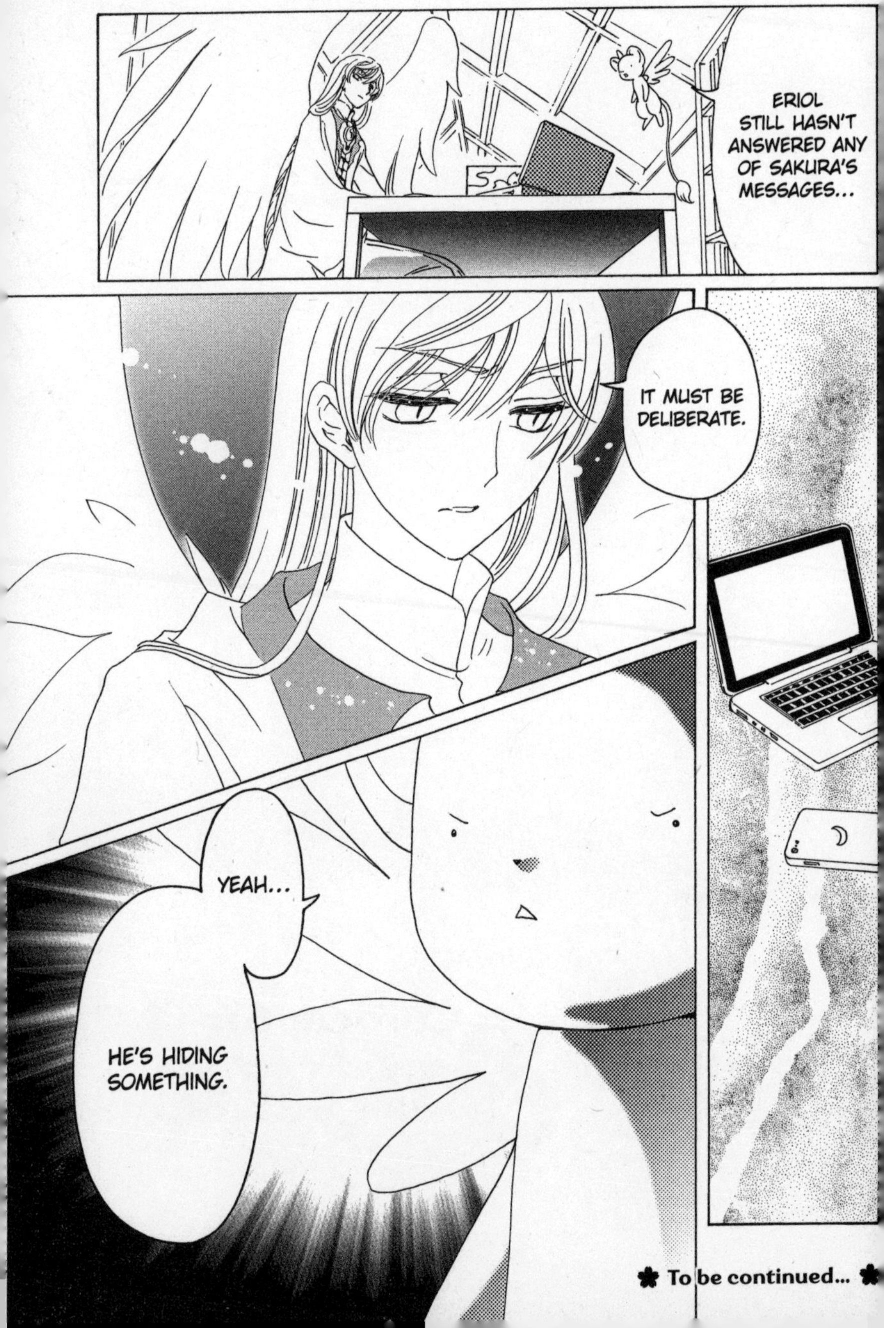
ERIOL STILL HASN'T ANSWERED ANY OF SAKURA'S MESSAGES...
IT MUST BE DELIBERATE.
YEAH...
HE'S HIDING SOMETHING.
To be continued...

Cardcaptor Sakura

CLEAR CARD

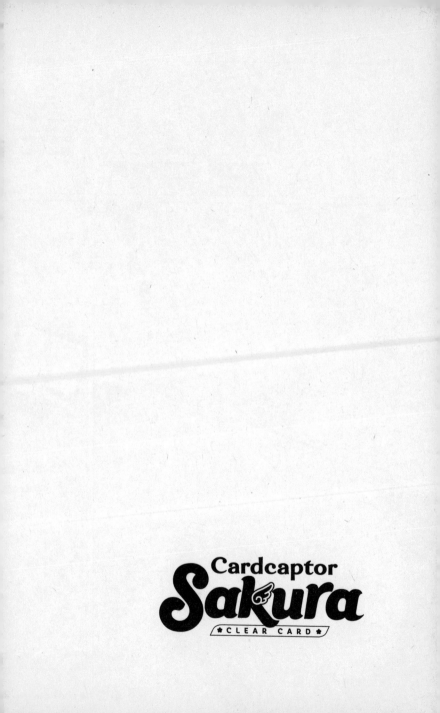

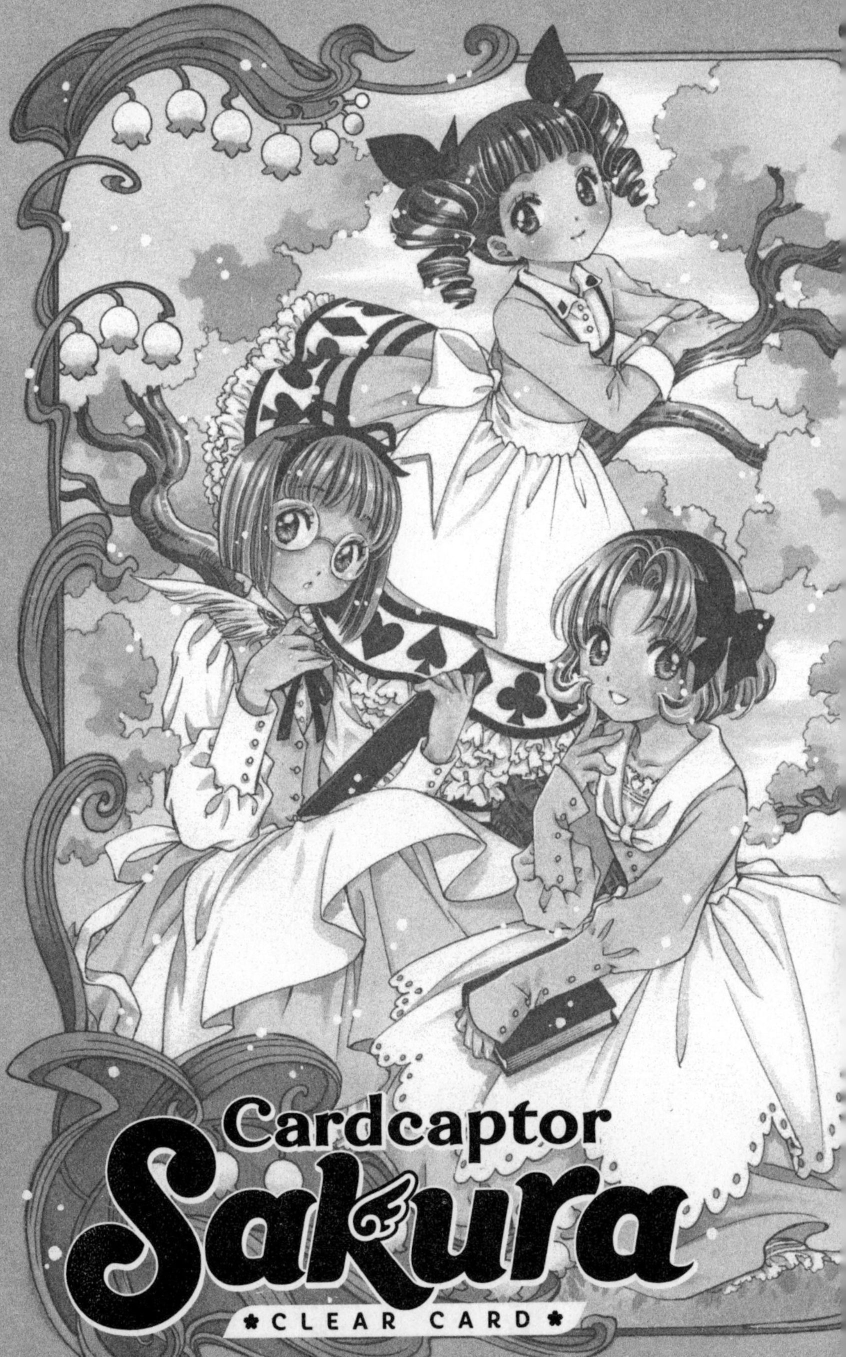
Cardcaptor
Sakura
CLEAR CARD

Cardcaptor Sakura
CLEAR CARD

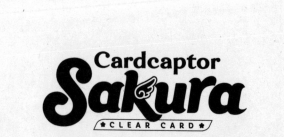

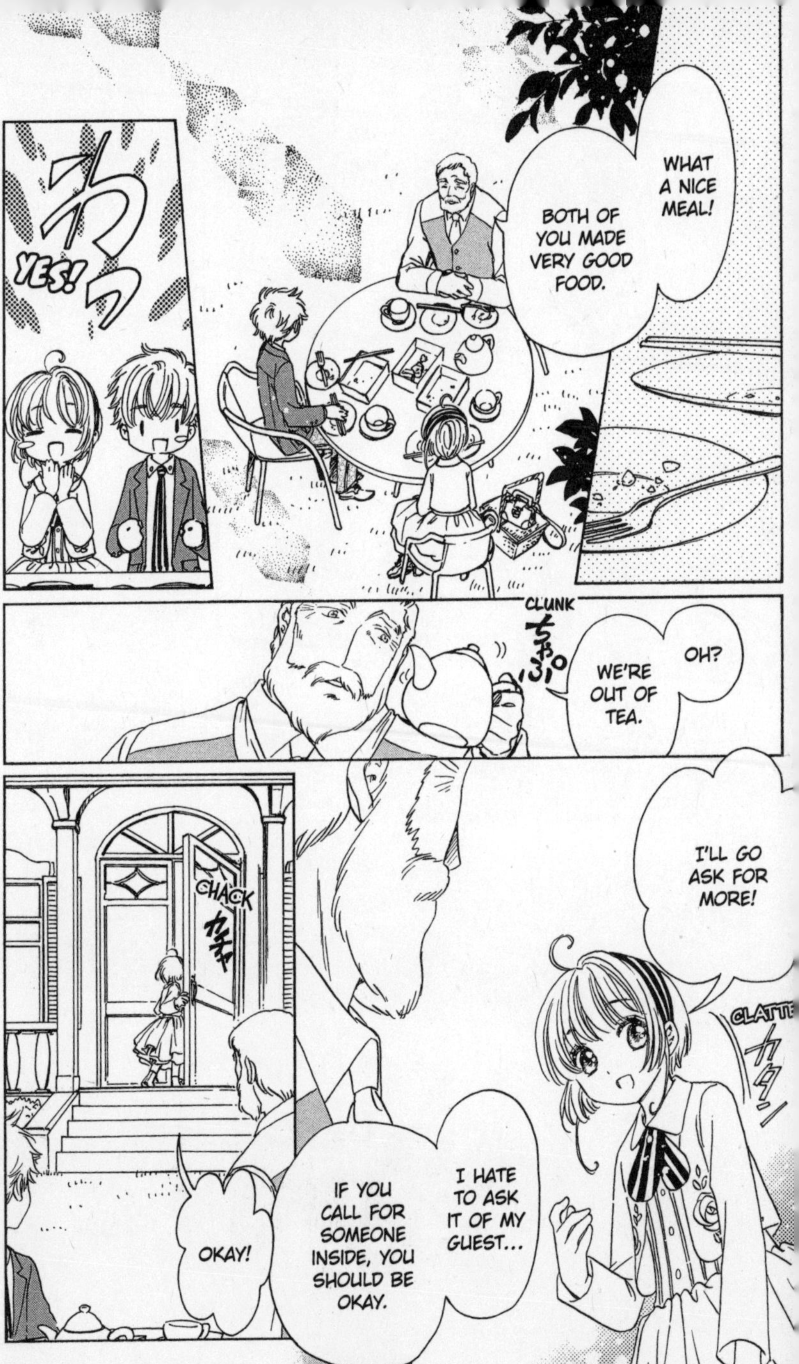
WHAT A NICE MEAL!
BOTH OF YOU MADE VERY GOOD FOOD.
YES!
OH?
WE'RE OUT OF TEA.
CLUNK
I'LL GO ASK FOR MORE!
CLATTE
I HATE TO ASK IT OF MY GUEST...
IF YOU CALL FOR SOMEONE INSIDE, YOU SHOULD BE OKAY.
OKAY!
CHACK
....

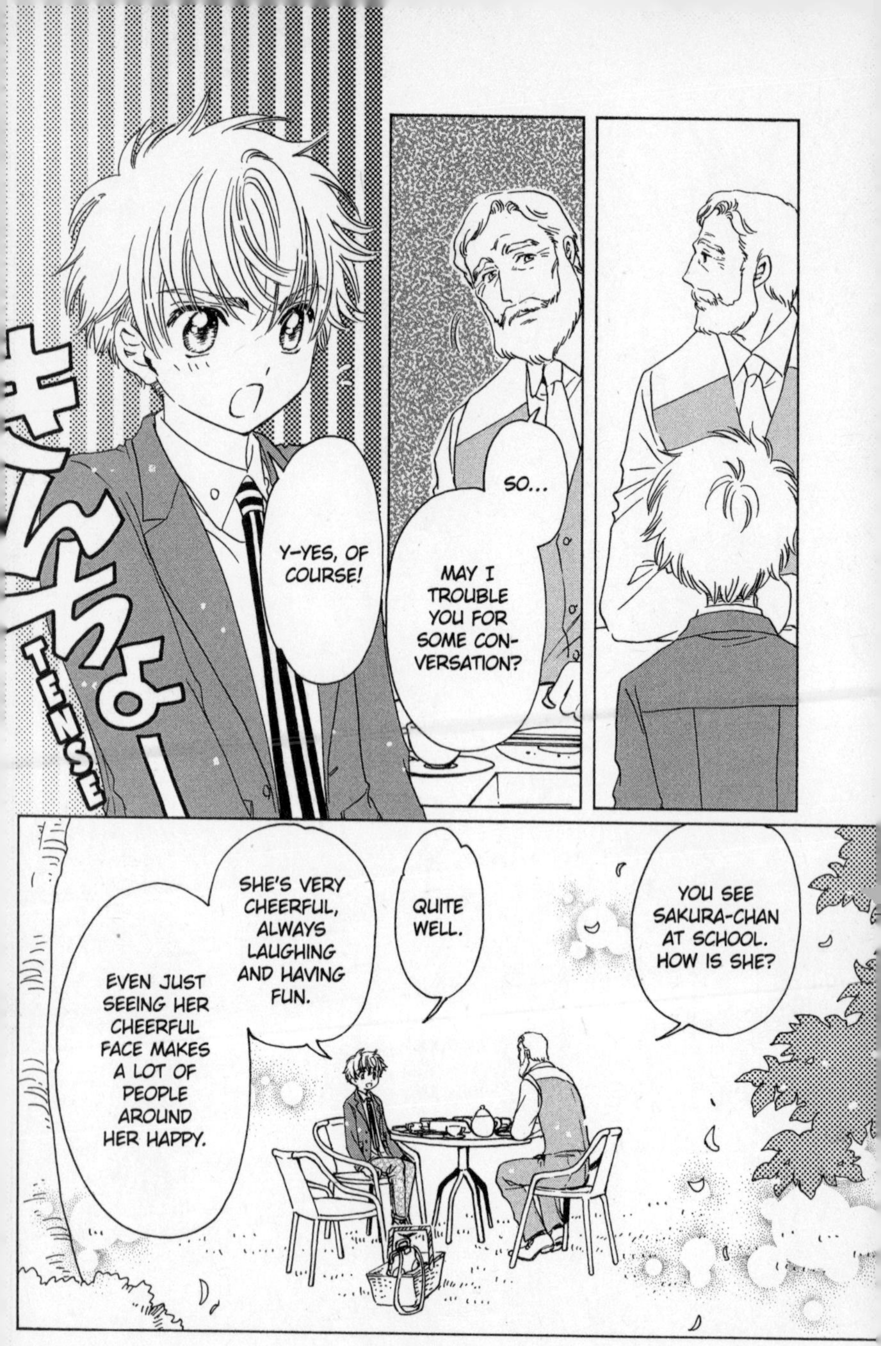
SO...
MAY I TROUBLE YOU FOR SOME CONVERSATION?
Y-YES, OF COURSE!
TENSE
YOU SEE SAKURA-CHAN AT SCHOOL. HOW IS SHE?
QUITE WELL.
SHE'S VERY CHEERFUL, ALWAYS LAUGHING AND HAVING FUN.
EVEN JUST SEEING HER CHEERFUL FACE MAKES A LOT OF PEOPLE AROUND HER HAPPY.

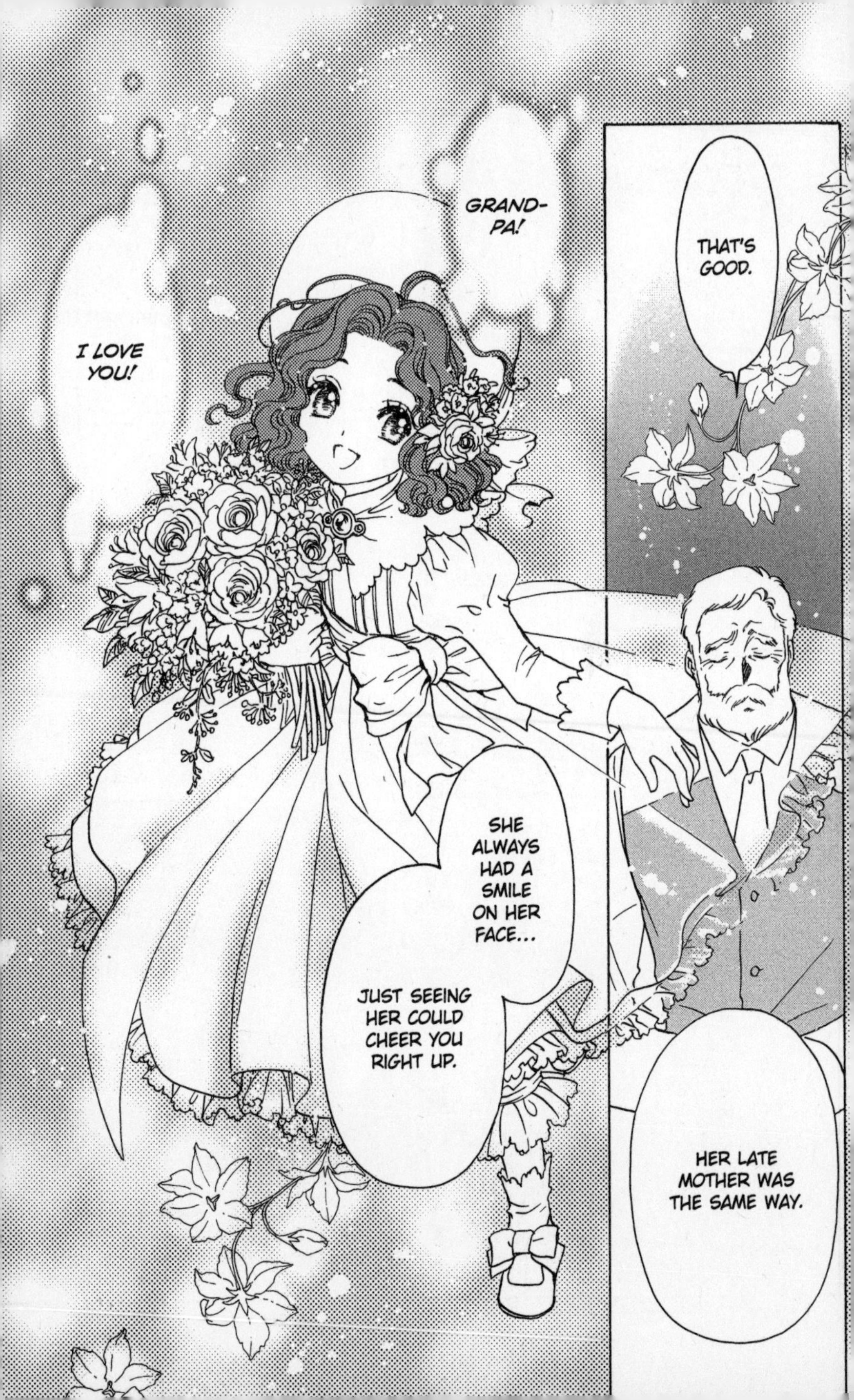
THAT'S GOOD.
HER LATE MOTHER WAS THE SAME WAY.
GRAND-PA!
I LOVE YOU!
SHE ALWAYS HAD A SMILE ON HER FACE...
JUST SEEING HER COULD CHEER YOU RIGHT UP.

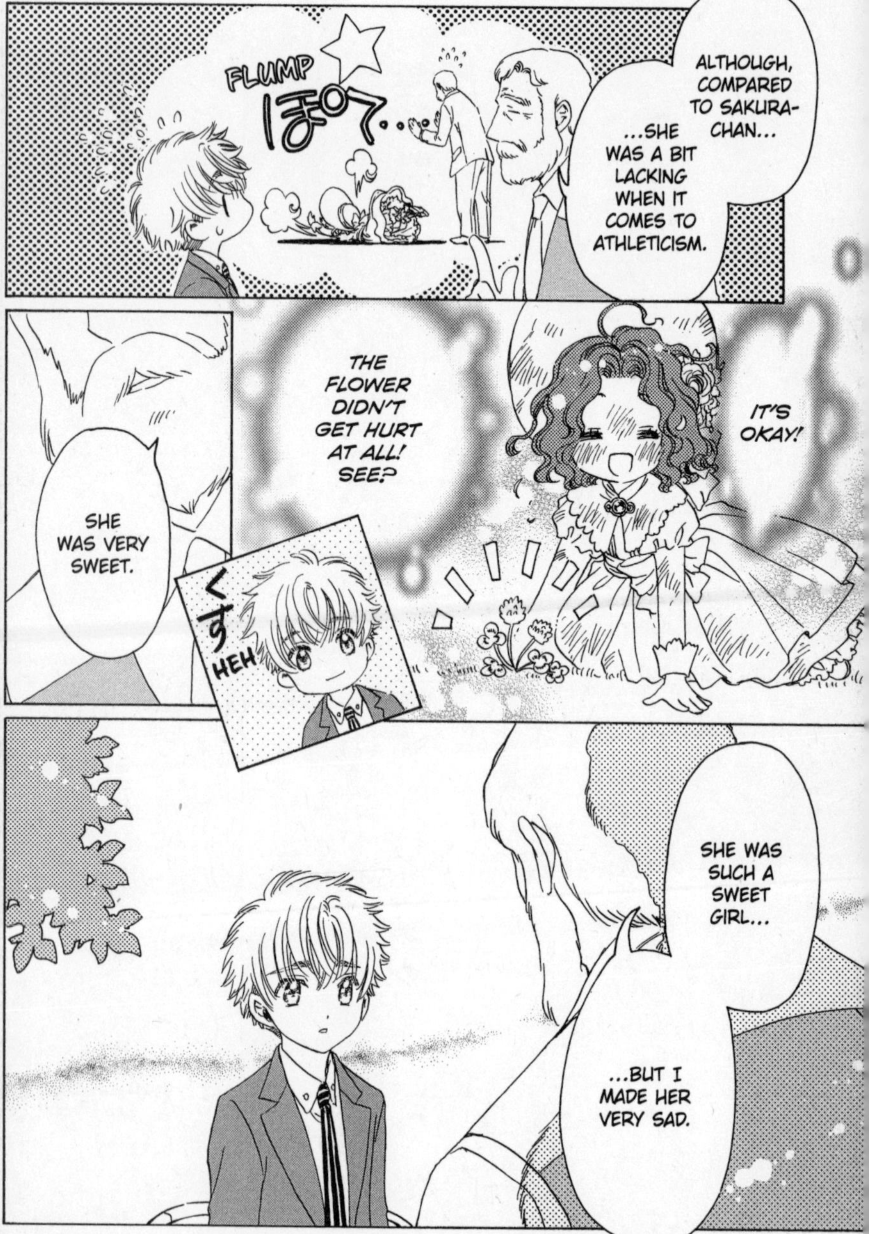
ALTHOUGH, COMPARED TO SAKURA-CHAN...
...SHE WAS A BIT LACKING WHEN IT COMES TO ATHLETICISM.
FLUMP
ぽて...
IT'S OKAY!
THE FLOWER DIDN'T GET HURT AT ALL! SEE?
くす
HEH
SHE WAS VERY SWEET.
SHE WAS SUCH A SWEET GIRL...
...BUT I MADE HER VERY SAD.

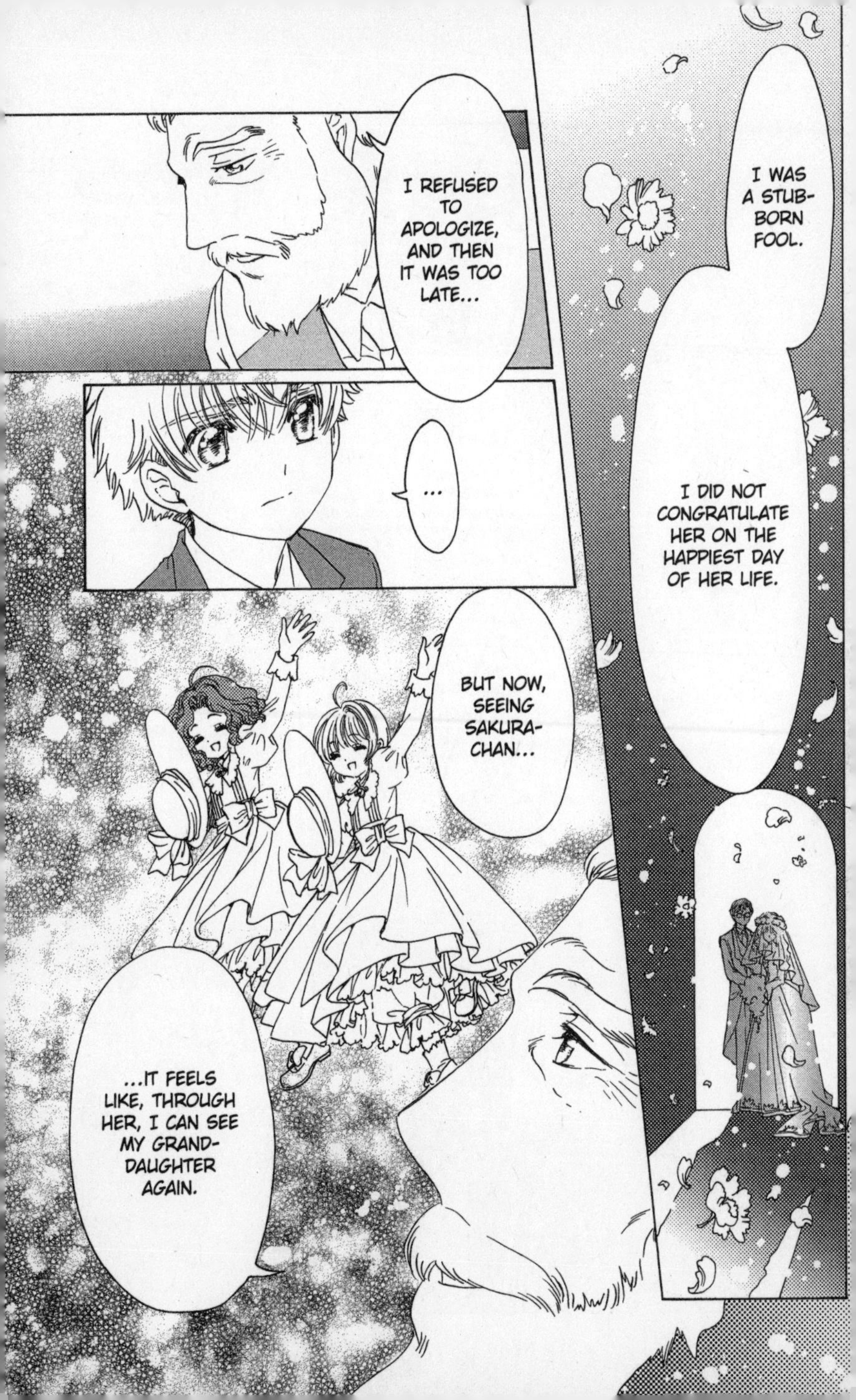
I WAS A STUBBORN FOOL.
I DID NOT CONGRATULATE HER ON THE HAPPIEST DAY OF HER LIFE.
I REFUSED TO APOLOGIZE, AND THEN IT WAS TOO LATE...
...
BUT NOW, SEEING SAKURA-CHAN...
...IT FEELS LIKE, THROUGH HER, I CAN SEE MY GRANDDAUGHTER AGAIN.

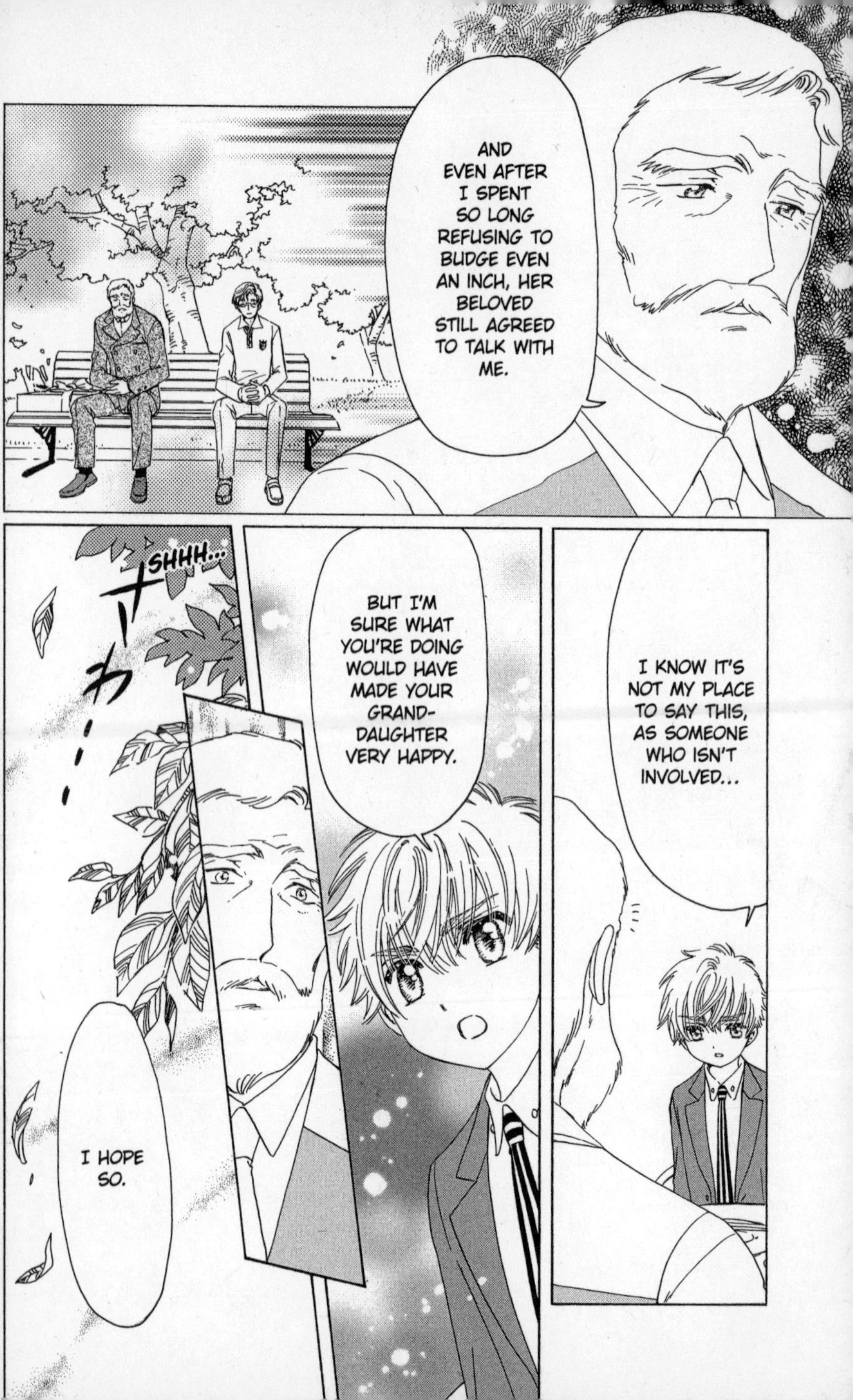
AND EVEN AFTER I SPENT SO LONG REFUSING TO BUDGE EVEN AN INCH, HER BELOVED STILL AGREED TO TALK WITH ME.
I KNOW IT'S NOT MY PLACE TO SAY THIS, AS SOMEONE WHO ISN'T INVOLVED...
BUT I'M SURE WHAT YOU'RE DOING WOULD HAVE MADE YOUR GRAND-DAUGHTER VERY HAPPY.
SHHH...
I HOPE SO.

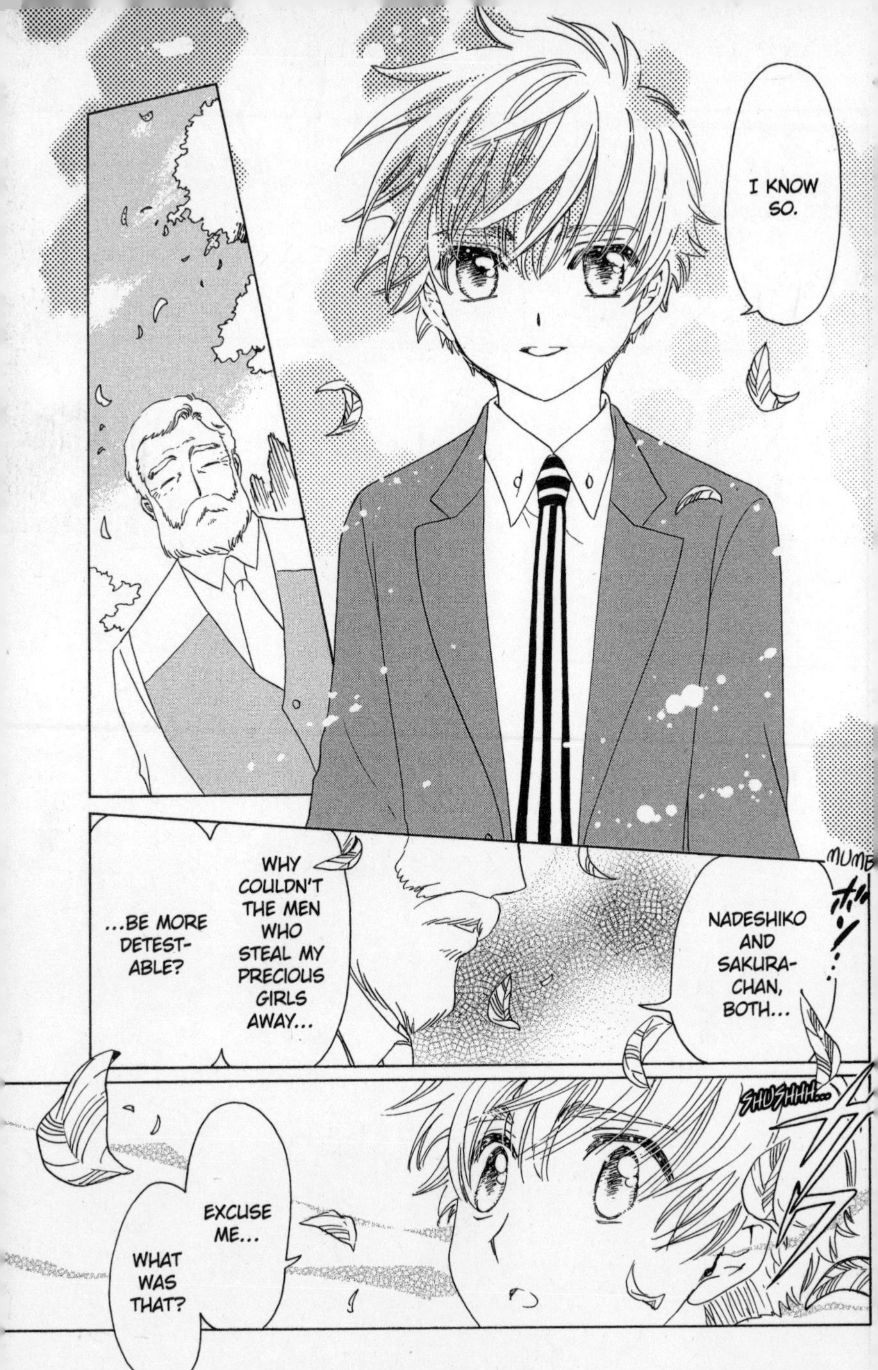
I KNOW SO.
MUMB
NADESHIKO AND SAKURA-CHAN, BOTH...
WHY COULDN'T THE MEN WHO STEAL MY PRECIOUS GIRLS AWAY...
...BE MORE DETEST-ABLE?
SHUSHHH...
EXCUSE ME...
WHAT WAS THAT?

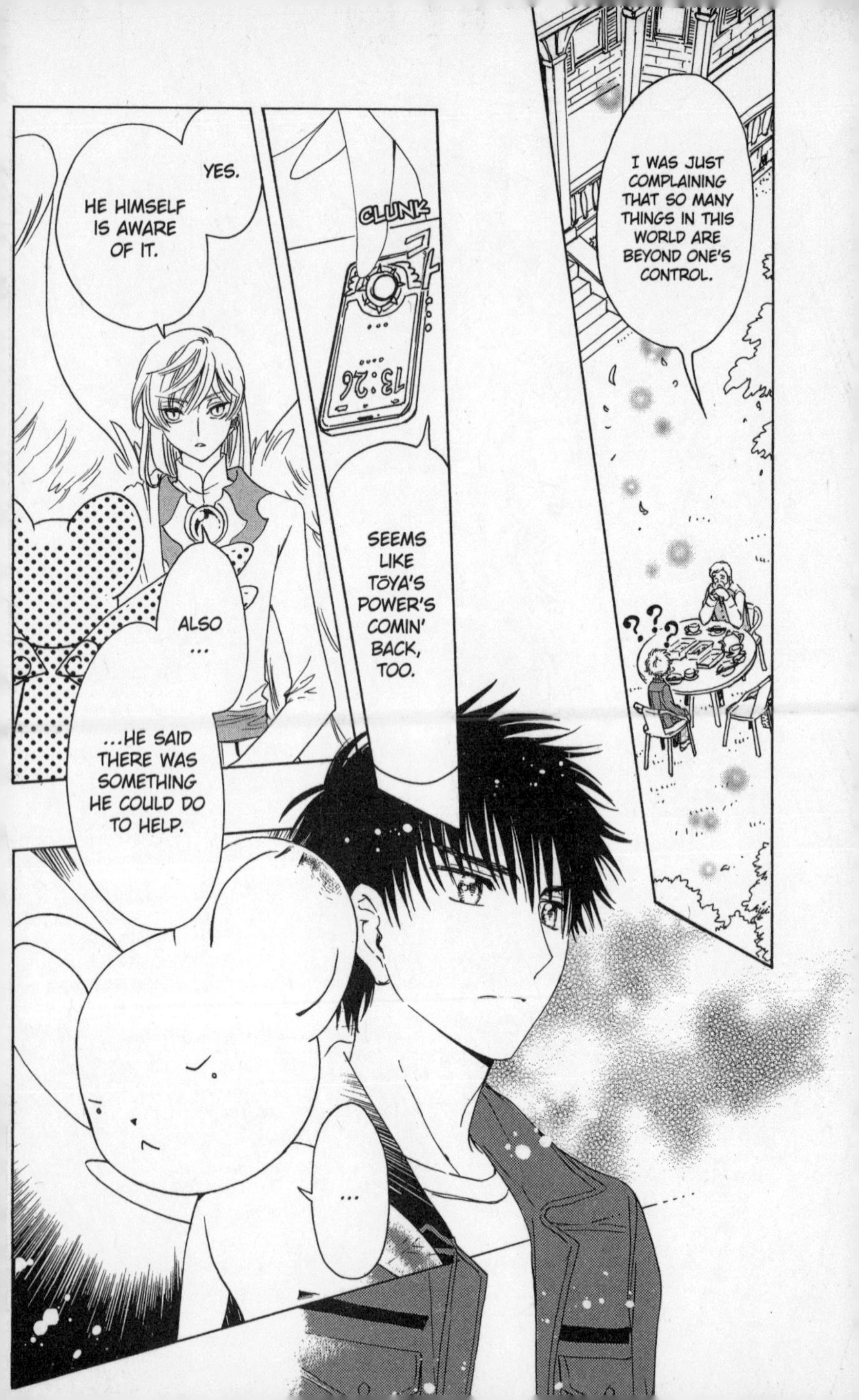
I WAS JUST COMPLAINING THAT SO MANY THINGS IN THIS WORLD ARE BEYOND ONE'S CONTROL.
CLUNK
13:26
SEEMS LIKE TŌYA'S POWER'S COMIN' BACK, TOO.
YES.
HE HIMSELF IS AWARE OF IT.
ALSO ...
...HE SAID THERE WAS SOMETHING HE COULD DO TO HELP.
...

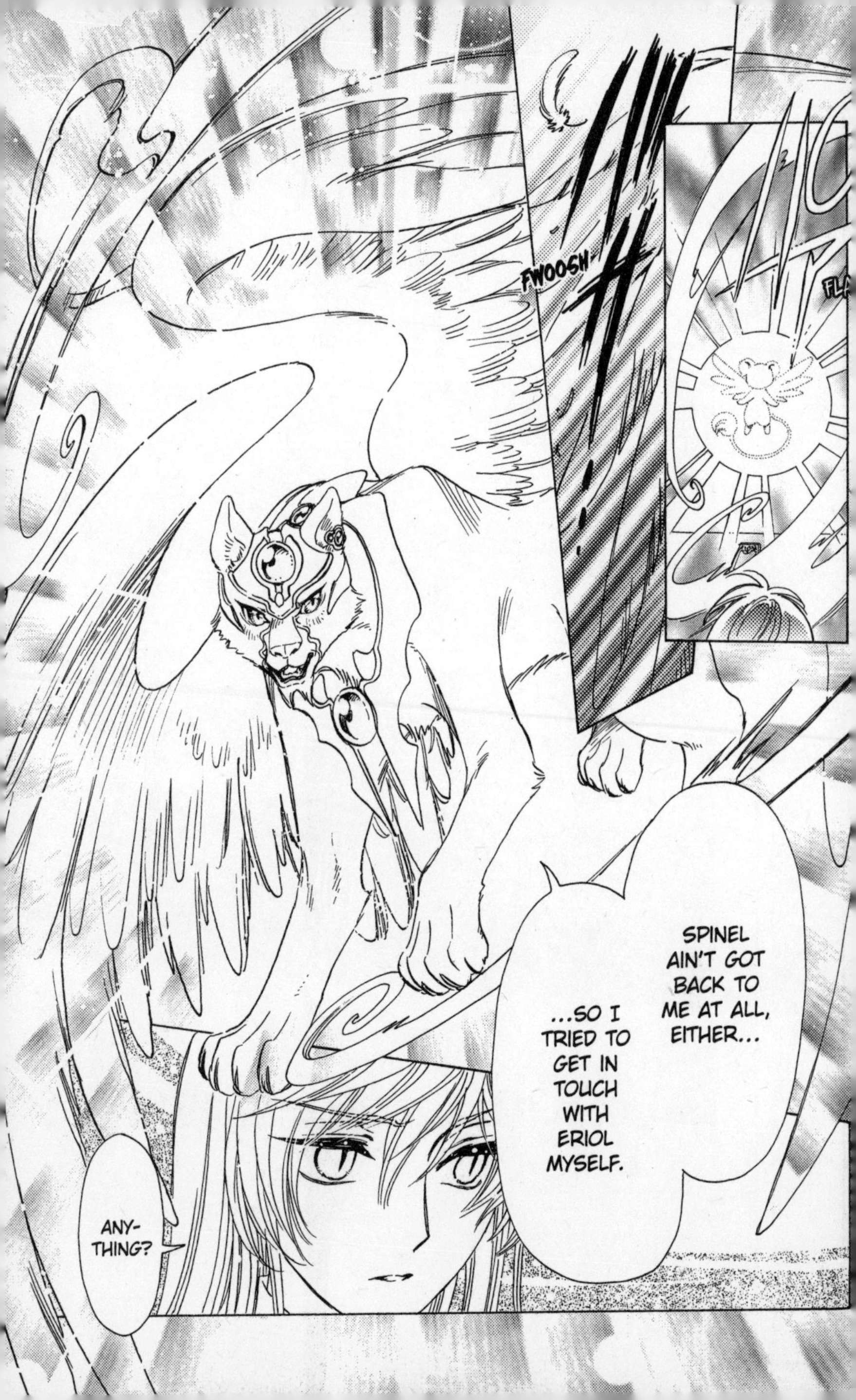
FWOOSH
SPINEL AIN'T GOT BACK TO ME AT ALL, EITHER...
...SO I TRIED TO GET IN TOUCH WITH ERIOL MYSELF.
ANY-THING?

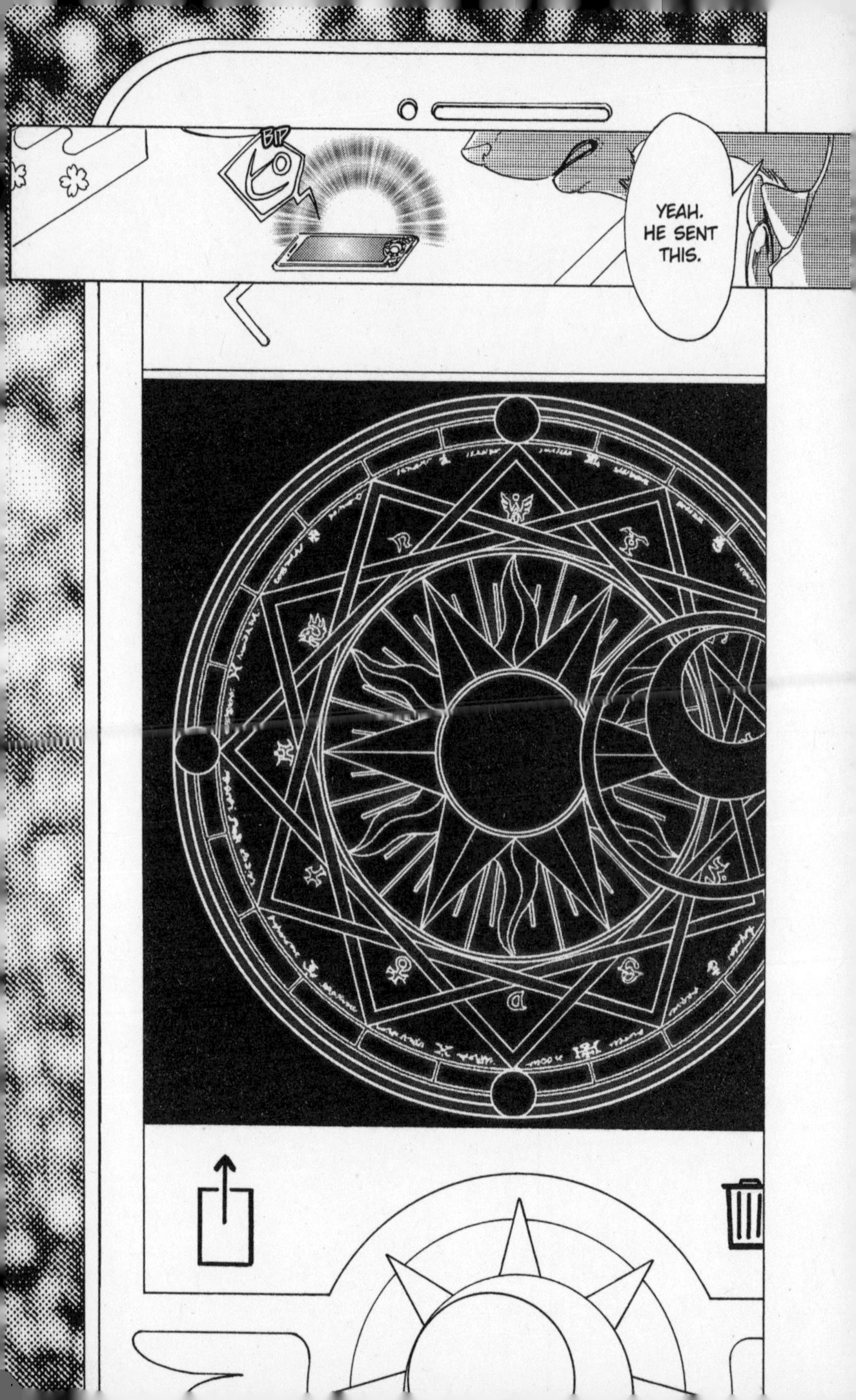
YEAH. HE SENT THIS.
BIP

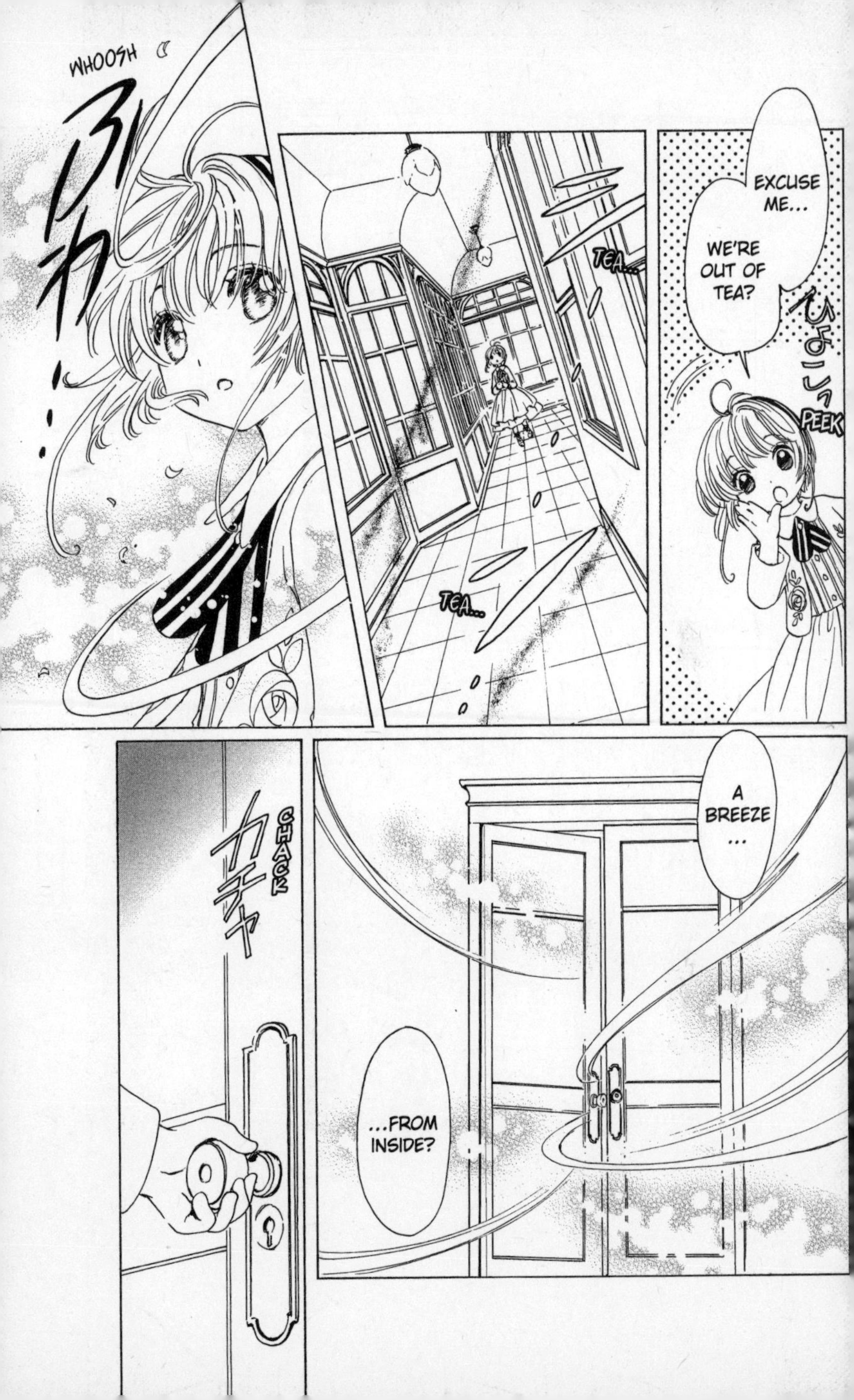
EXCUSE ME...
WE'RE OUT OF TEA?
ひょこっ
PEEK
TEA...
TEA...
WHOOSH
ふわ
A BREEZE ...
...FROM INSIDE?
CHACK
カチャ

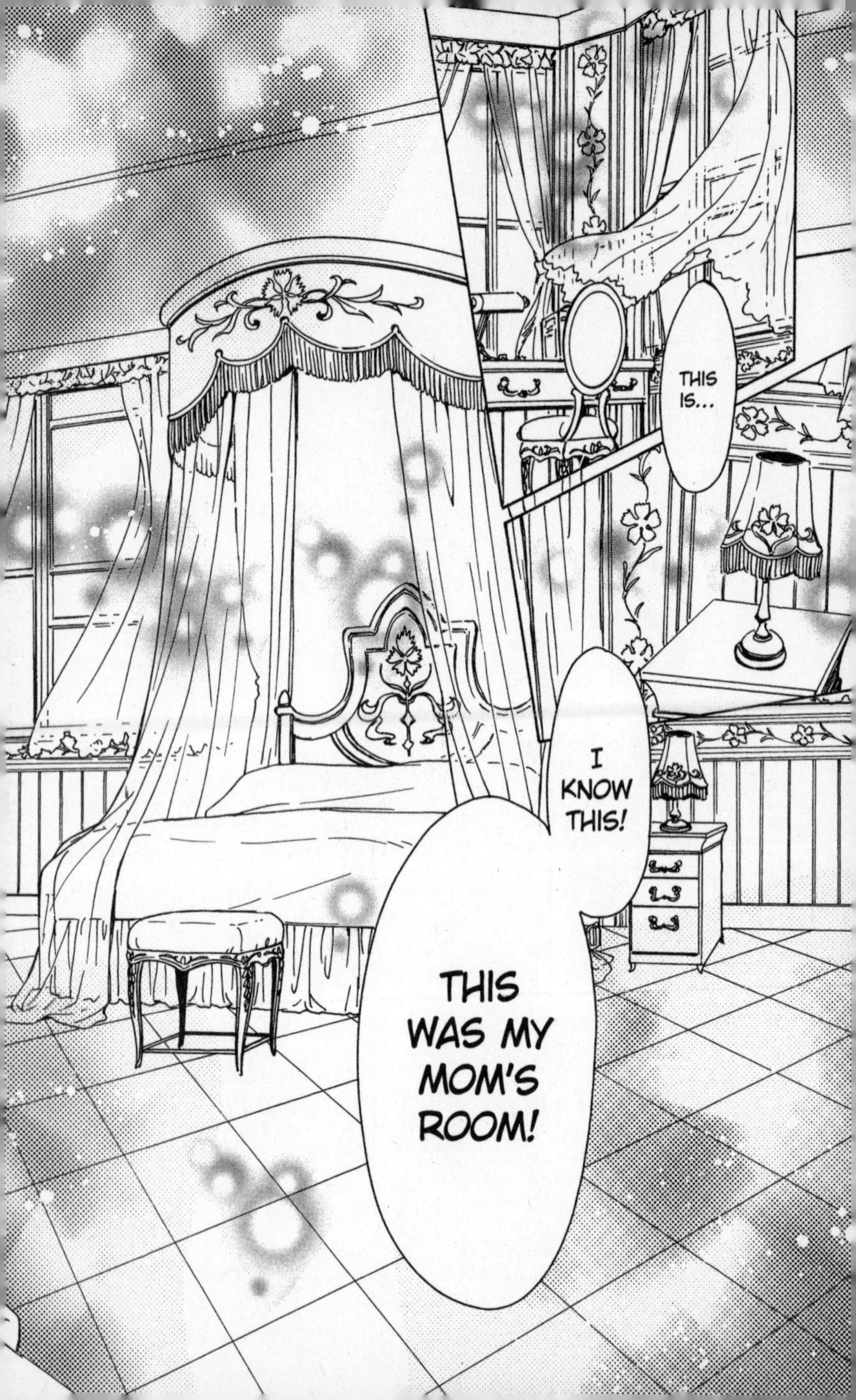
THIS IS...
I KNOW THIS!
THIS WAS MY MOM'S ROOM!

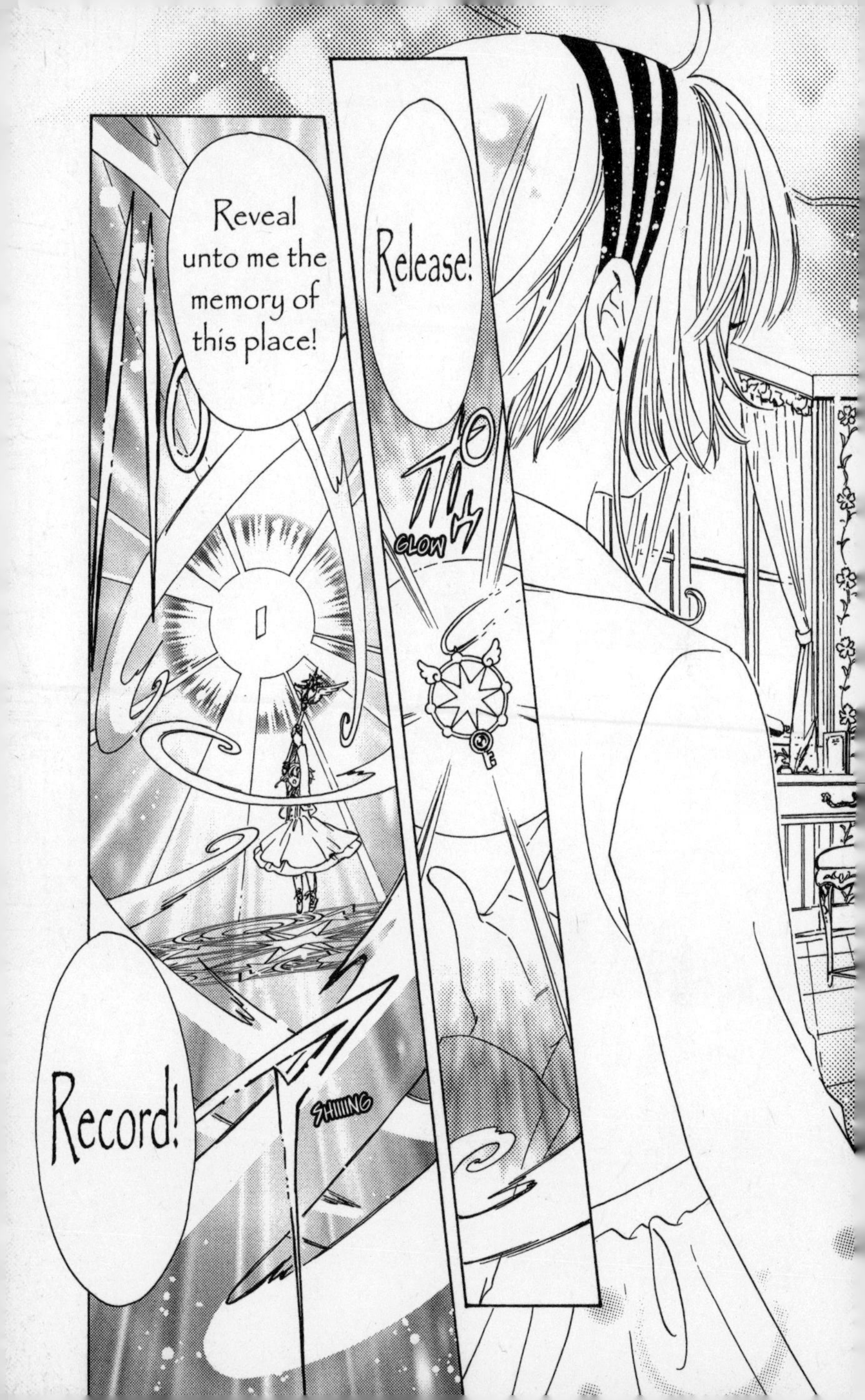

Release!
GLOW
Reveal unto me the memory of this place!
SHIIIING
Record!

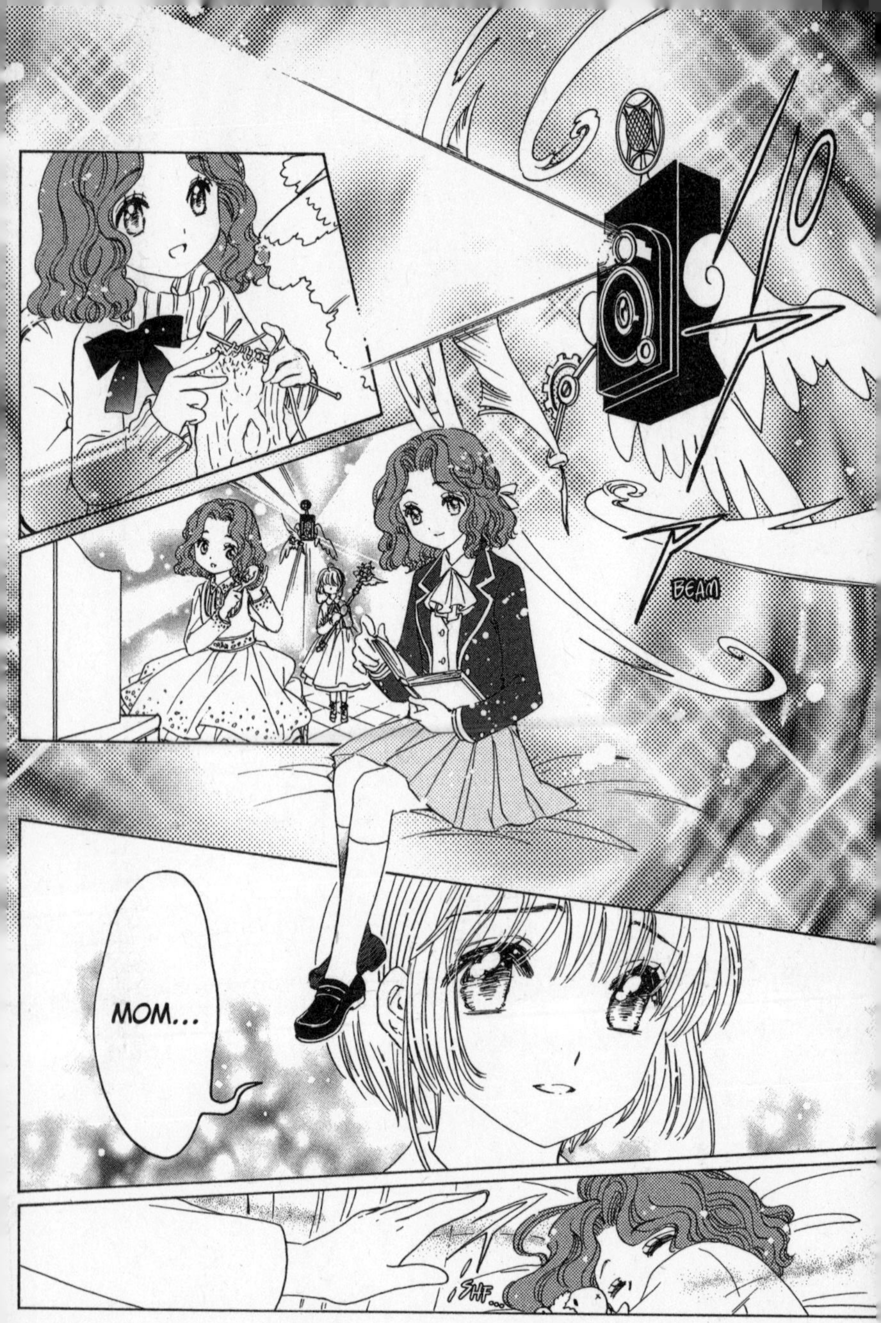
BEAM
MOM...
SHF...

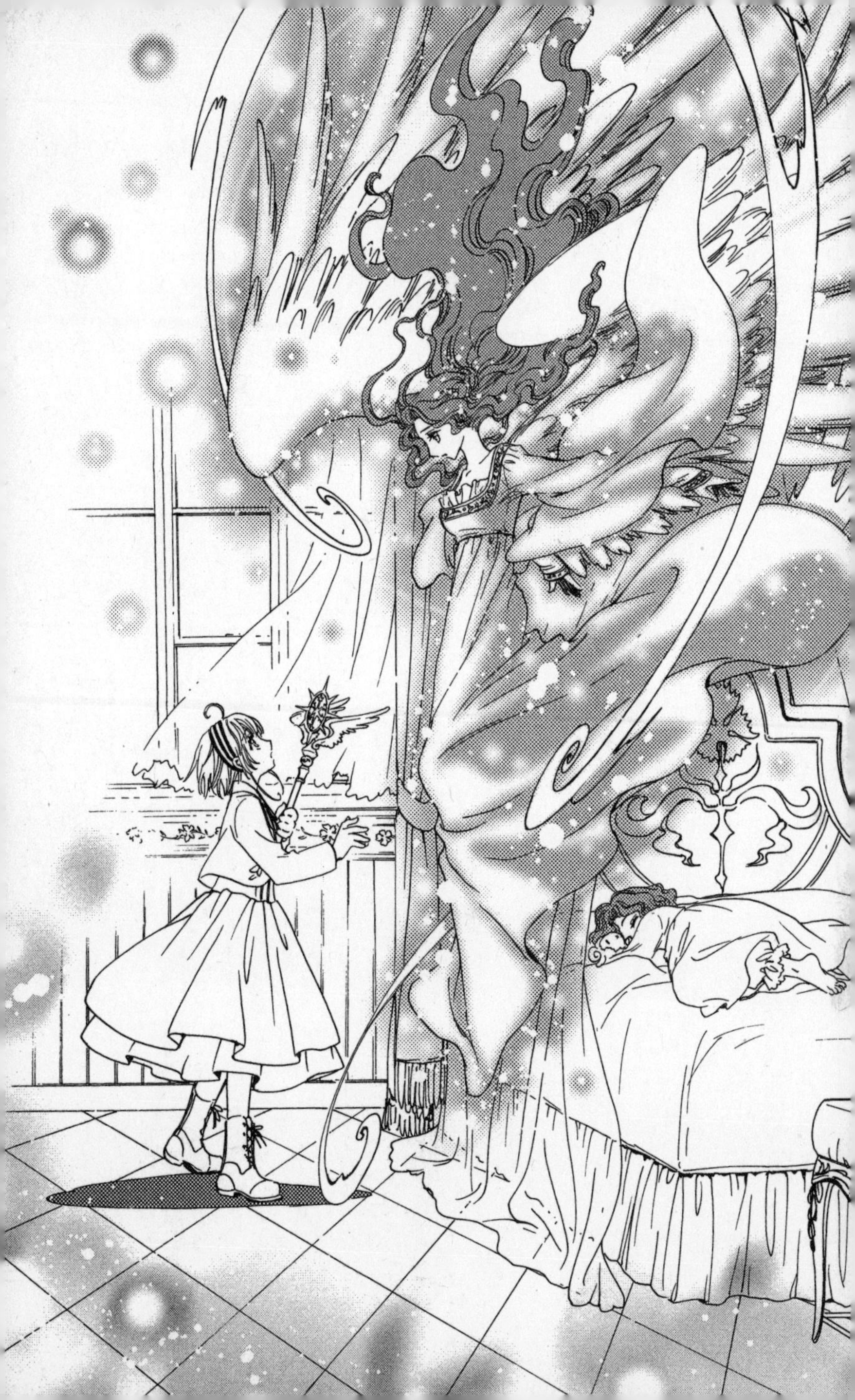

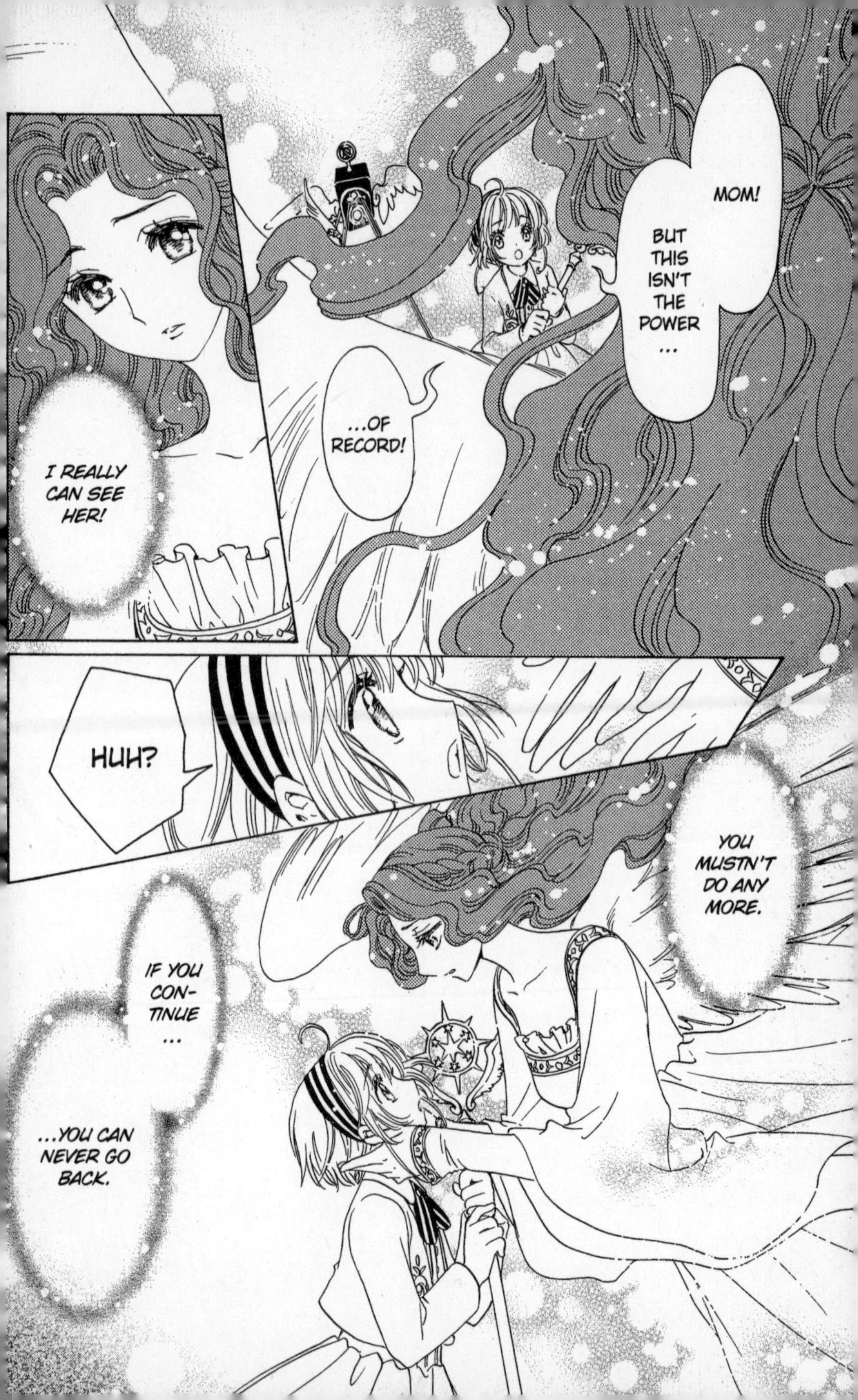
MOM!
BUT THIS ISN'T THE POWER...
...OF RECORD!
I REALLY CAN SEE HER!
HUH?
YOU MUSTN'T DO ANY MORE.
IF YOU CON-TINUE...
...YOU CAN NEVER GO BACK.

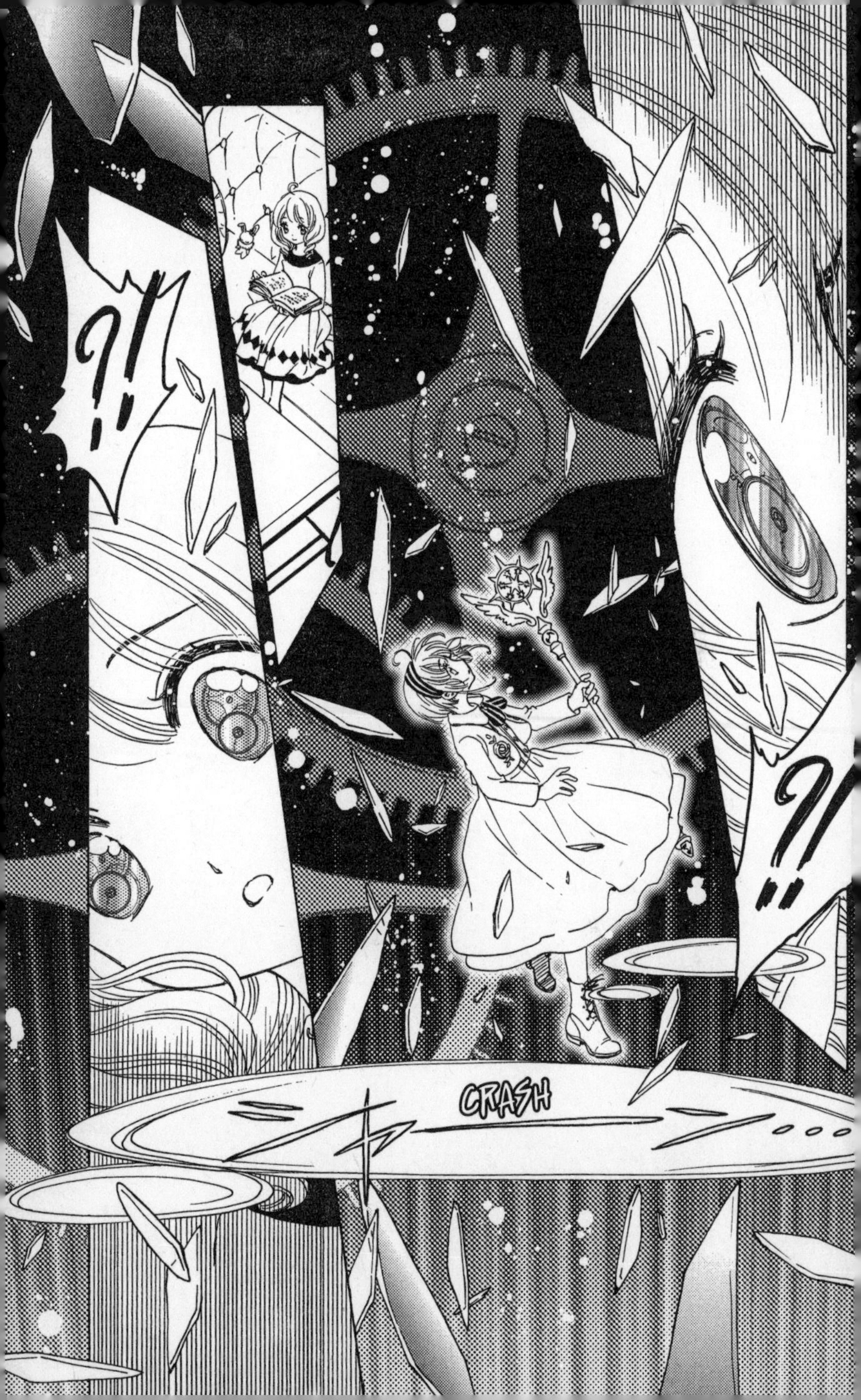
?!!
?!!
CRASH

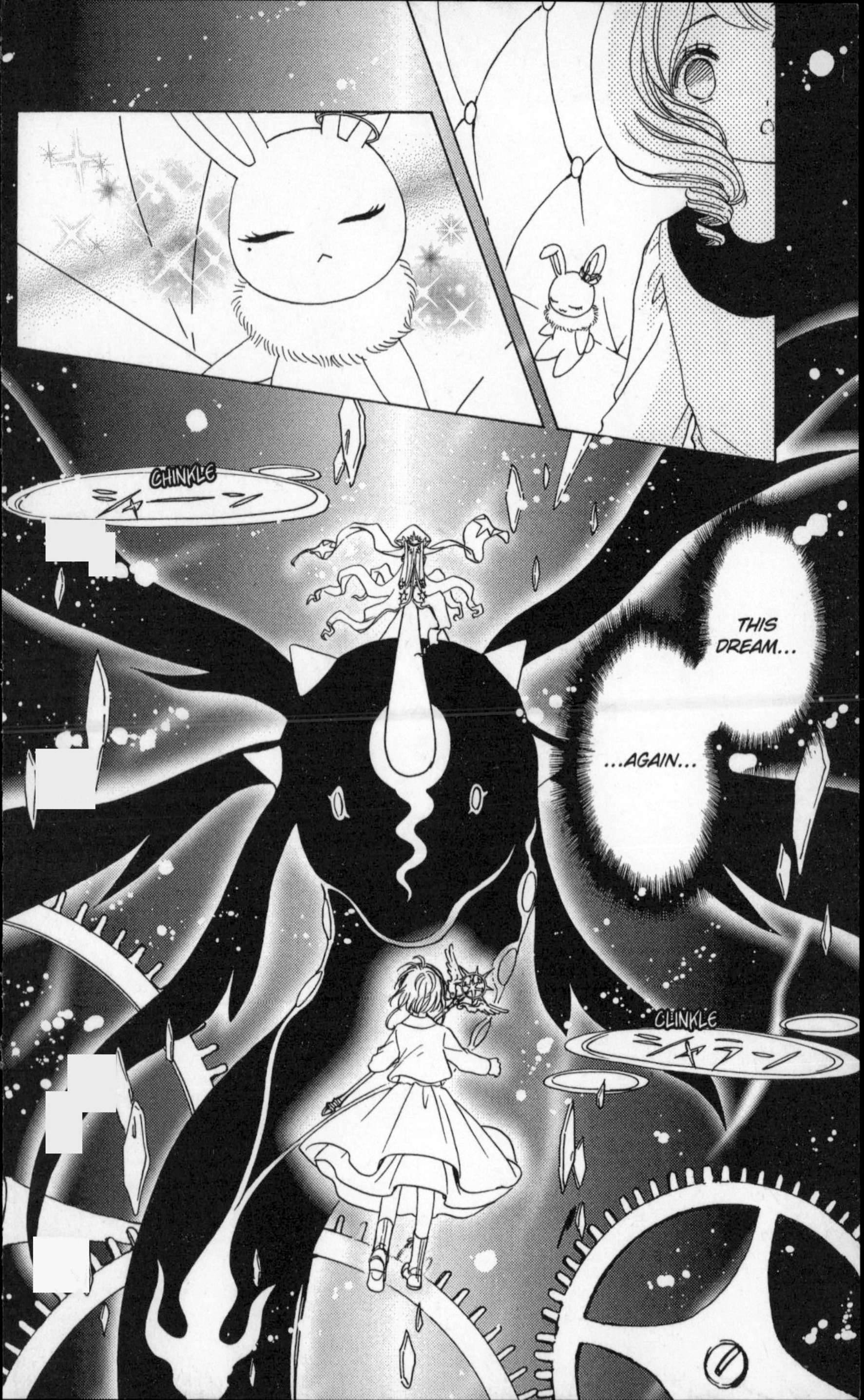
CHINKLE
シャーーン
THIS DREAM...
...AGAIN...
CLINKLE
シャラーン

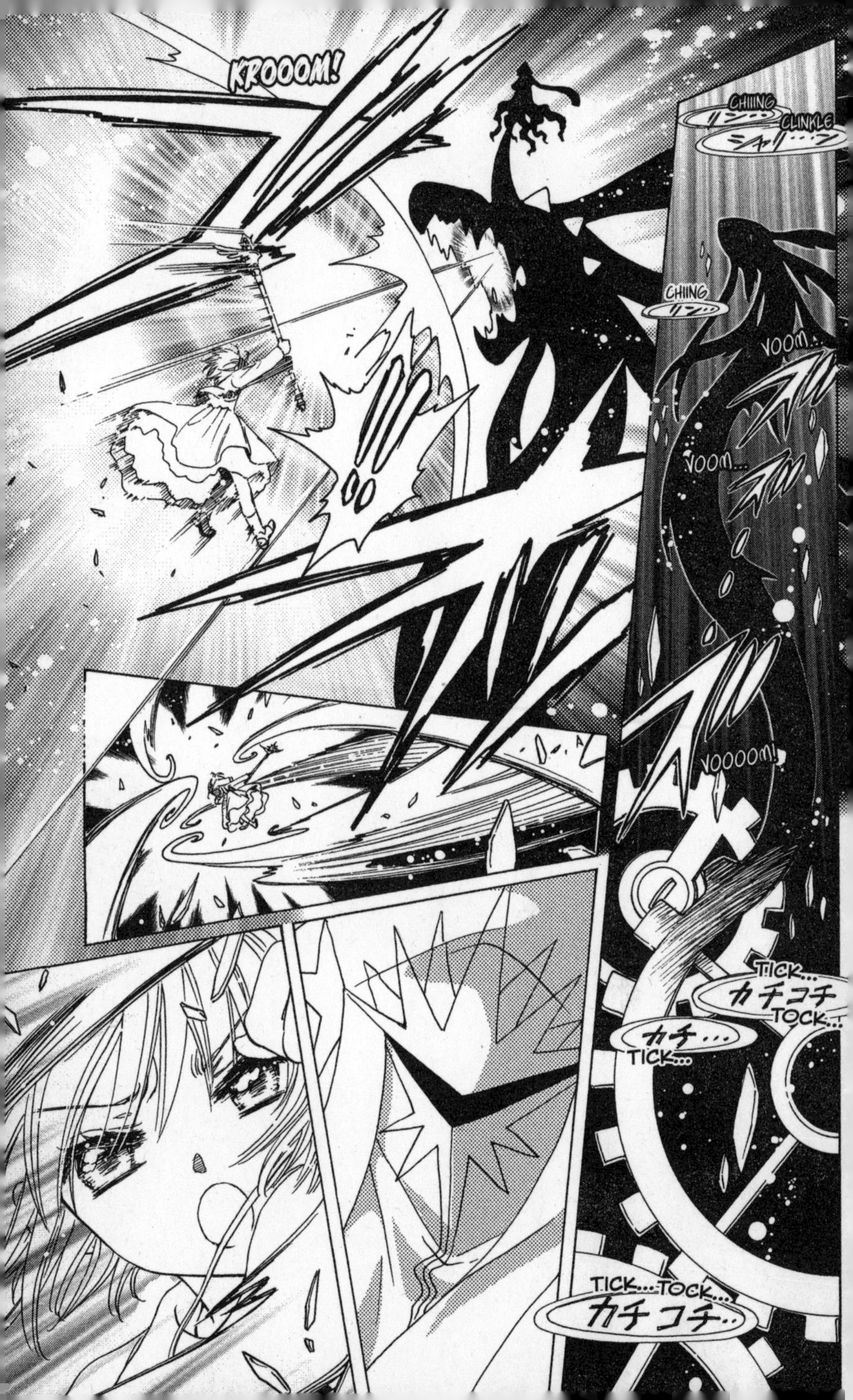
CHIING
リン…
CLINKLE
シャリ…ッ
KROOOM!
CHIING
リンッ
VOOM...
VOOM...
VOOOOM!
TICK...
カチコチ
TOCK...
カチ…
TICK...
TICK... TOCK...
カチコチ…

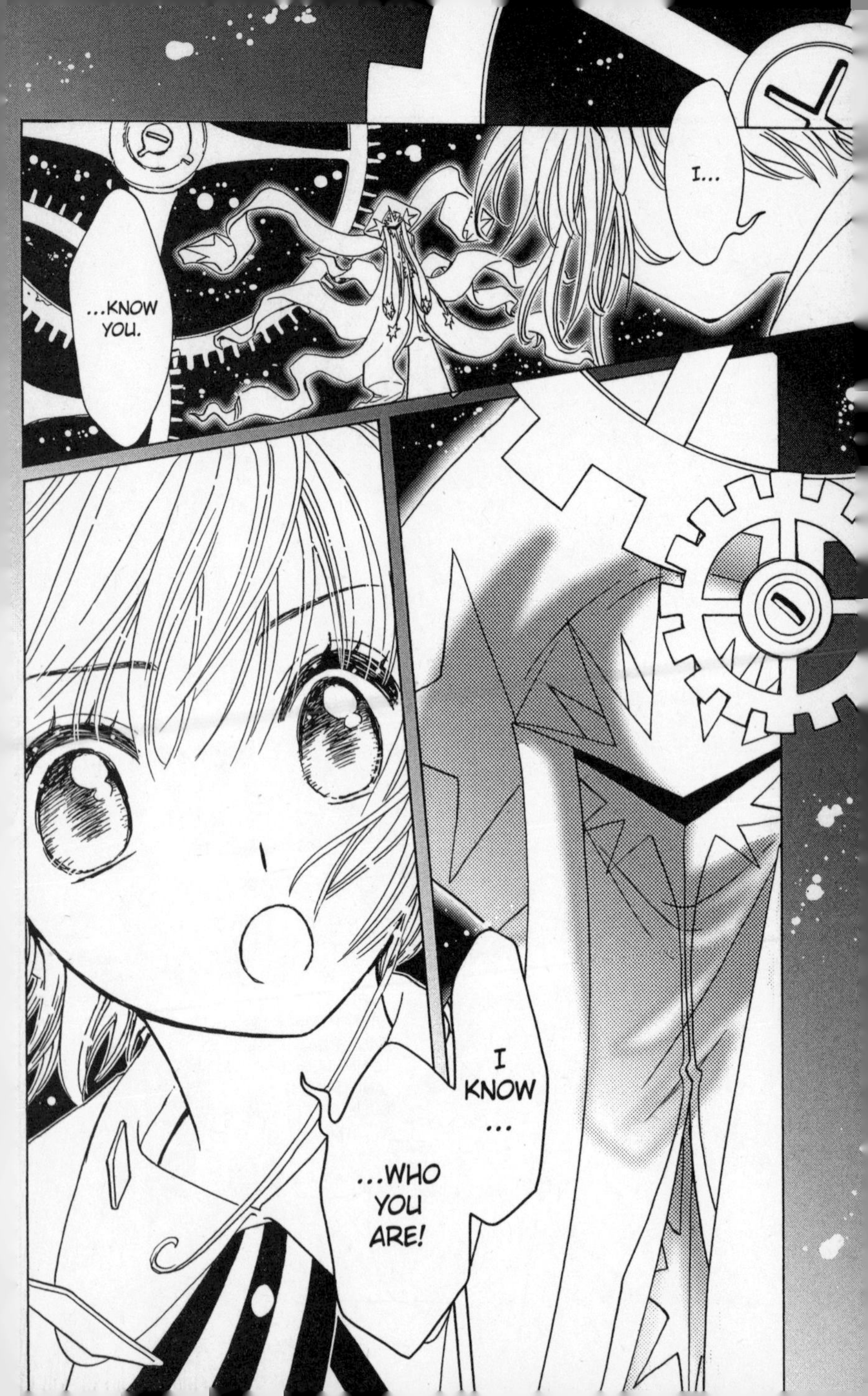
I...
...KNOW YOU.
I KNOW ...
...WHO YOU ARE!

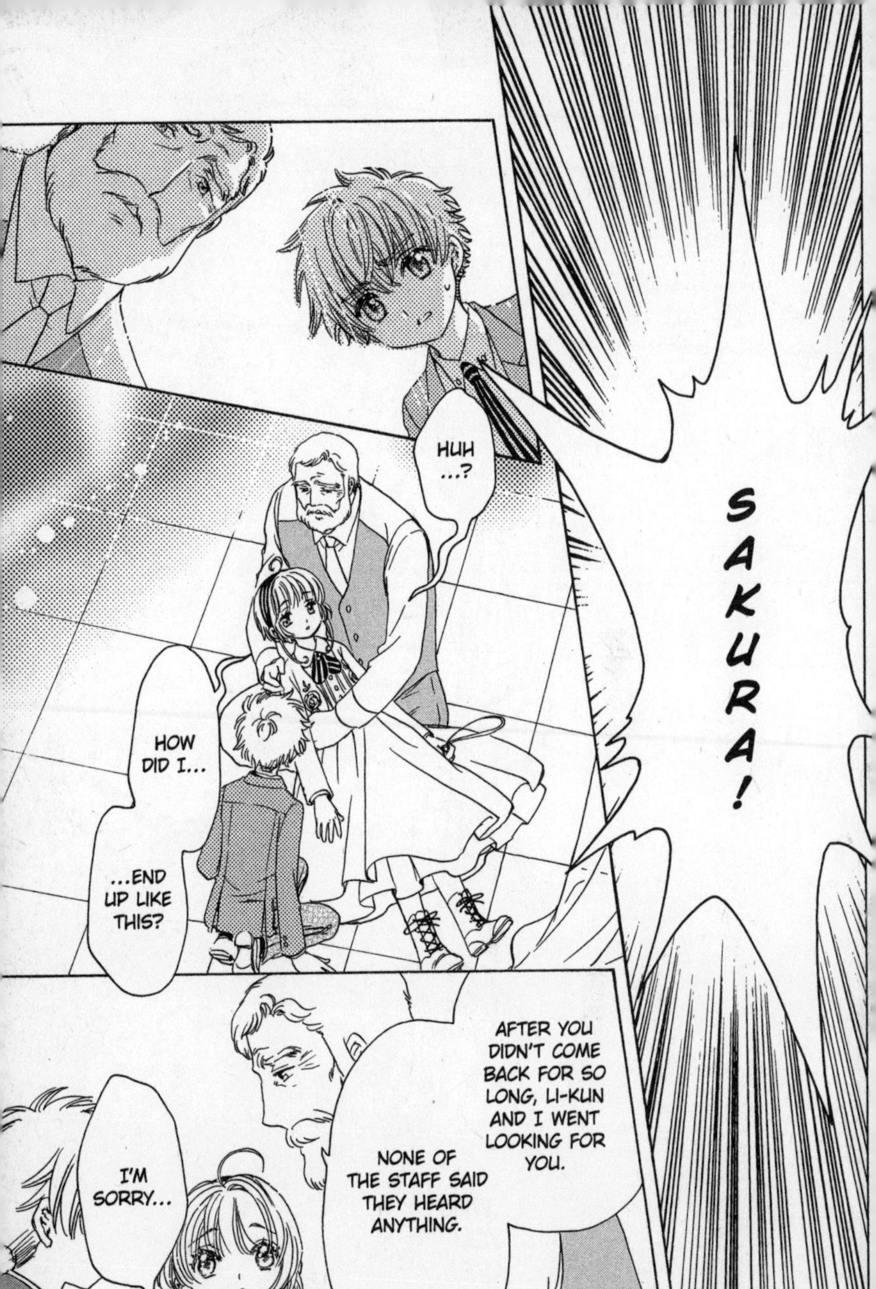
SAKURA!
HUH ...?
HOW DID I...
...END UP LIKE THIS?
AFTER YOU DIDN'T COME BACK FOR SO LONG, LI-KUN AND I WENT LOOKING FOR YOU.
NONE OF THE STAFF SAID THEY HEARD ANYTHING.
I'M SORRY...

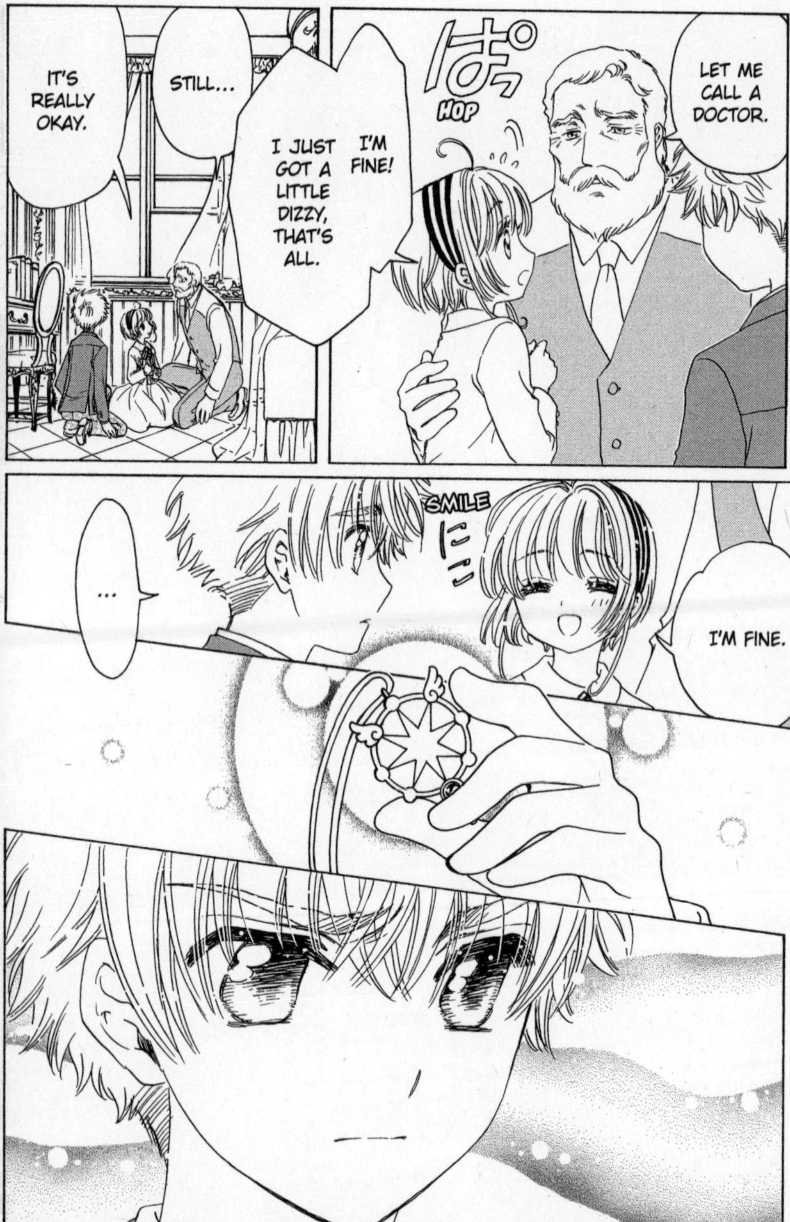
LET ME CALL A DOCTOR.
ぱっ
HOP
I'M FINE!
I JUST GOT A LITTLE DIZZY, THAT'S ALL.
STILL...
IT'S REALLY OKAY.
I'M FINE.
SMILE
にこ
...

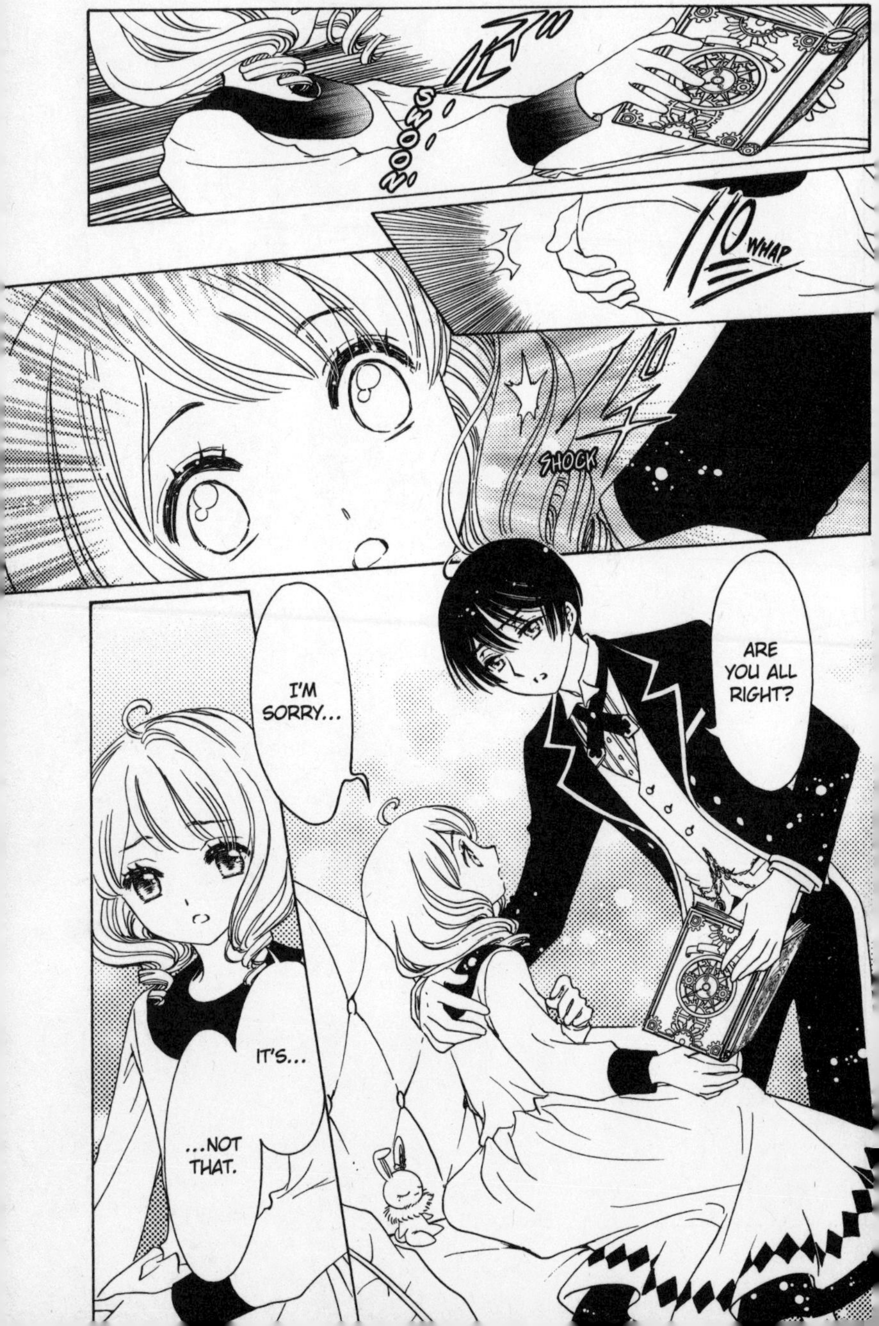
ZOOMS
WHAP
SHOCK
ARE YOU ALL RIGHT?
I'M SORRY...
IT'S...
...NOT THAT.

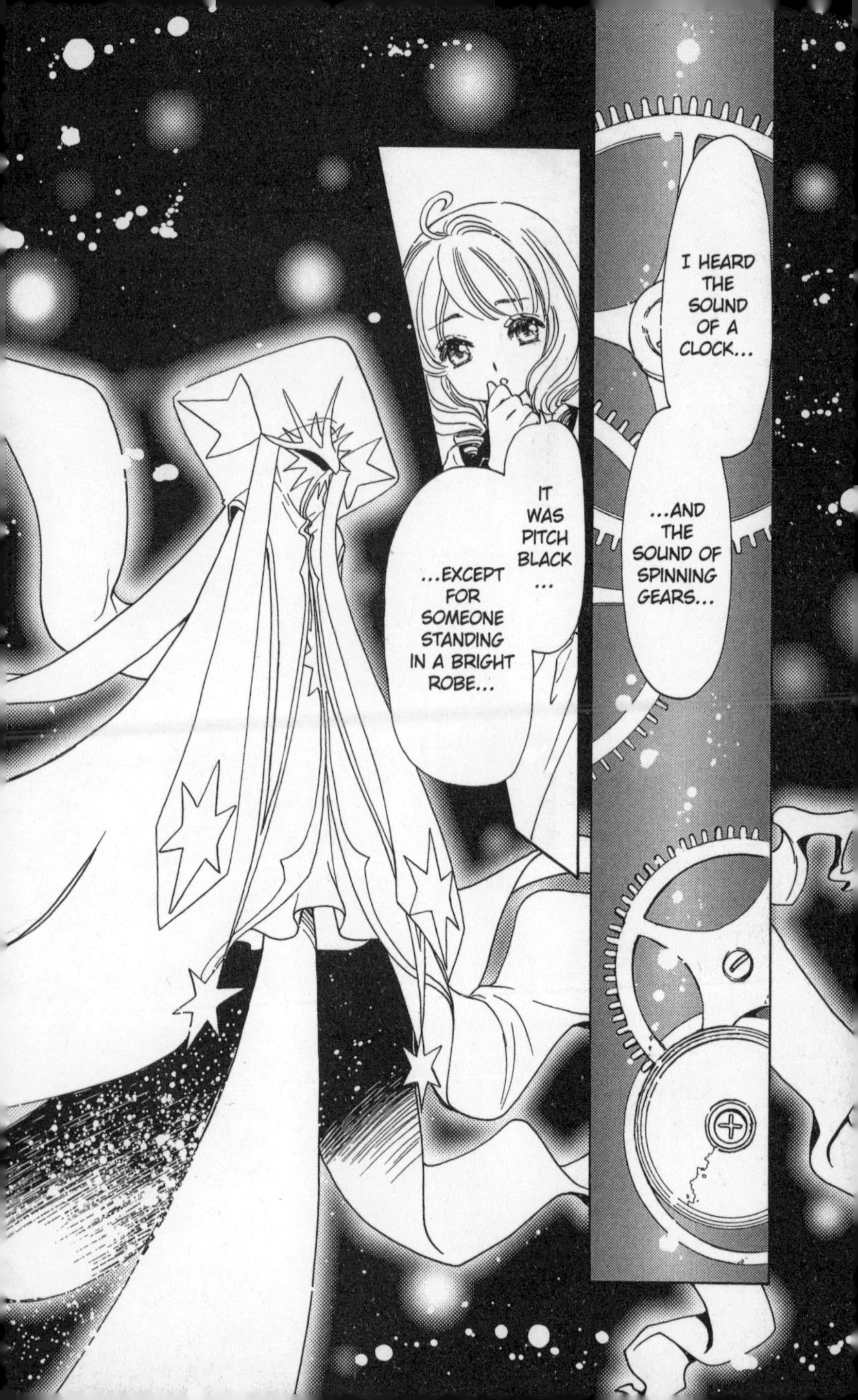
I HEARD THE SOUND OF A CLOCK...
...AND THE SOUND OF SPINNING GEARS...
IT WAS PITCH BLACK...
...EXCEPT FOR SOMEONE STANDING IN A BRIGHT ROBE...

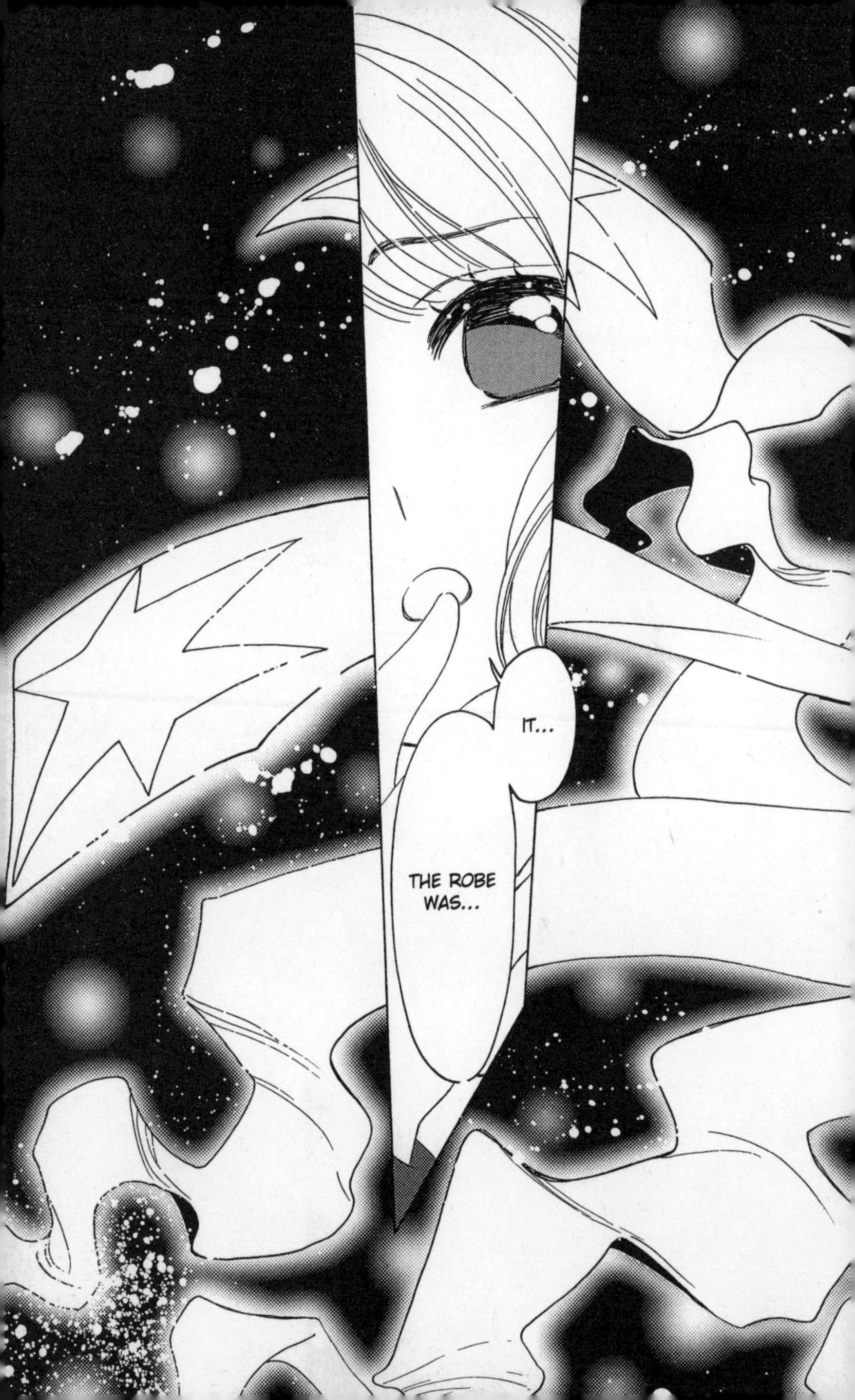
IT...
THE ROBE WAS...

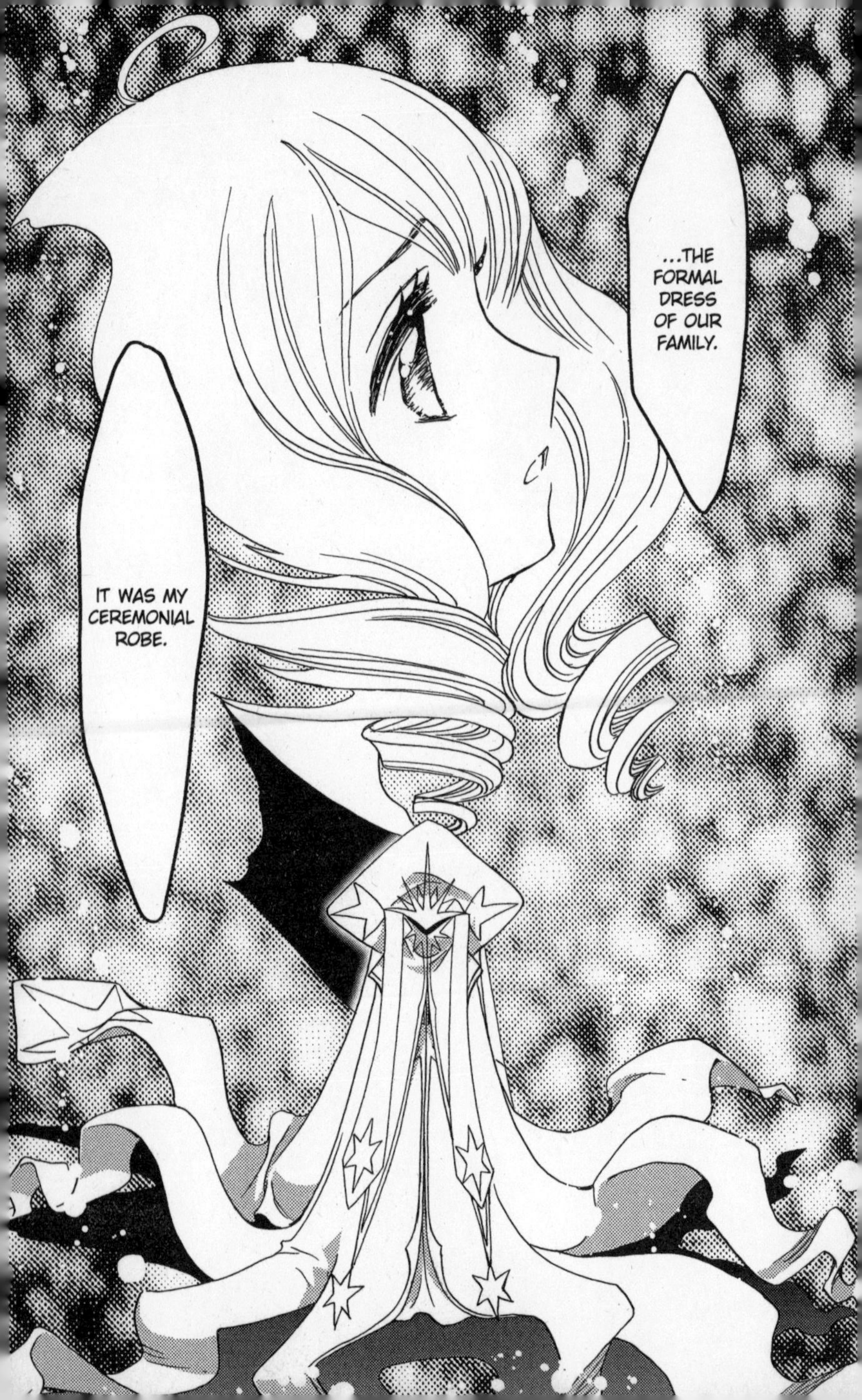
...THE FORMAL DRESS OF OUR FAMILY.
IT WAS MY CEREMONIAL ROBE.

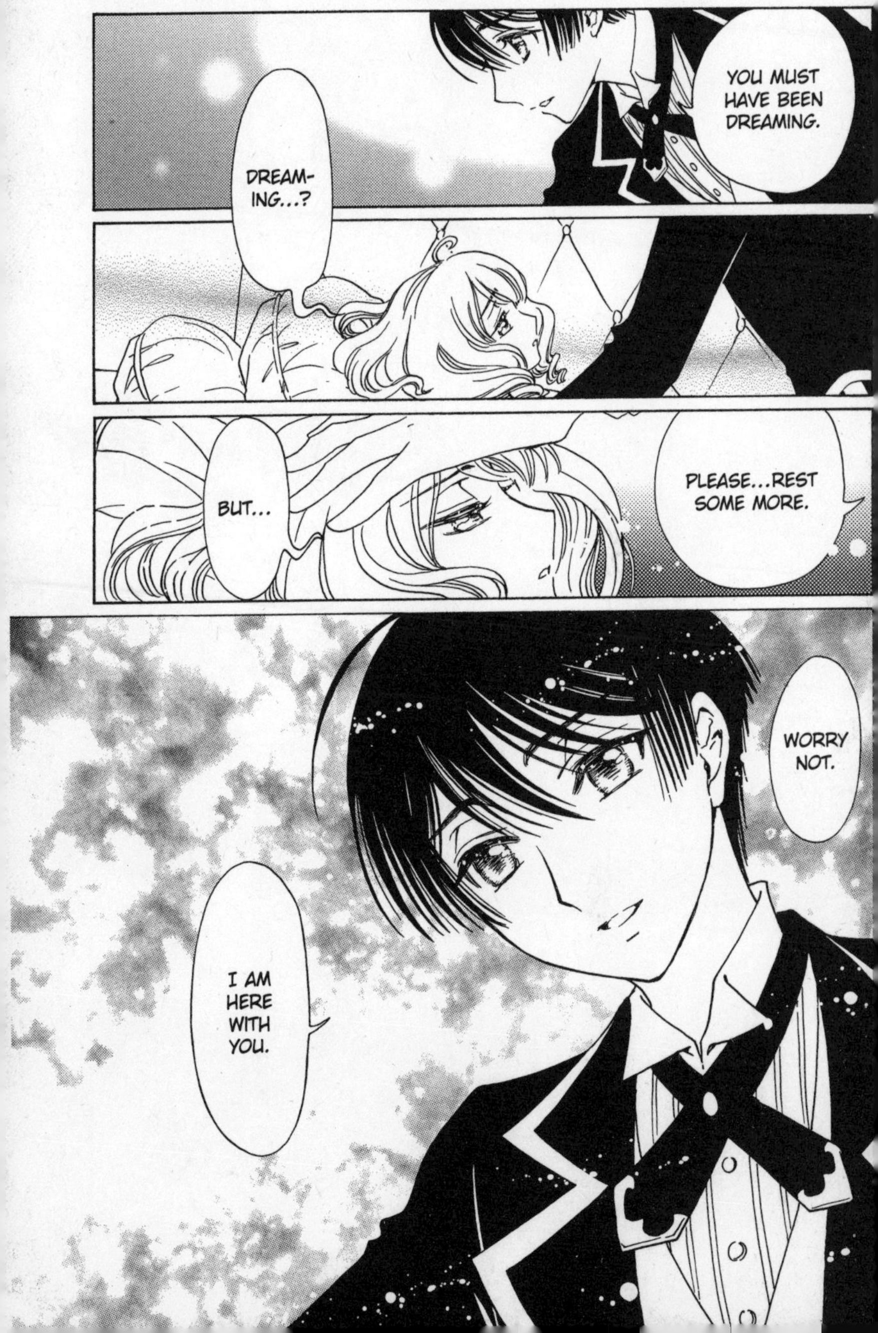
YOU MUST HAVE BEEN DREAMING.
DREAMING...?
PLEASE...REST SOME MORE.
BUT...
WORRY NOT.
I AM HERE WITH YOU.

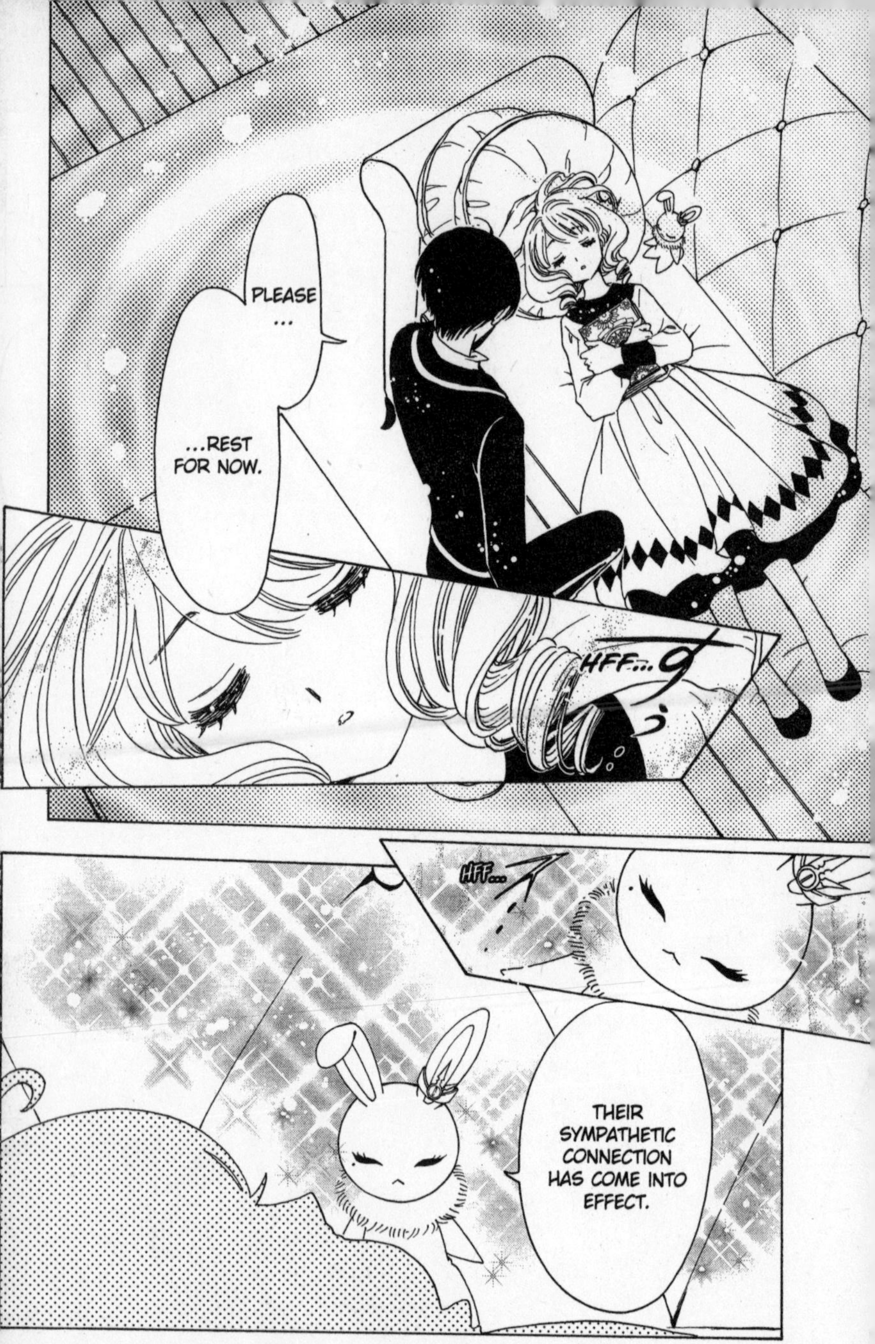
PLEASE ...
...REST FOR NOW.
HFF...
HFF...
THEIR SYMPATHETIC CONNECTION HAS COME INTO EFFECT.

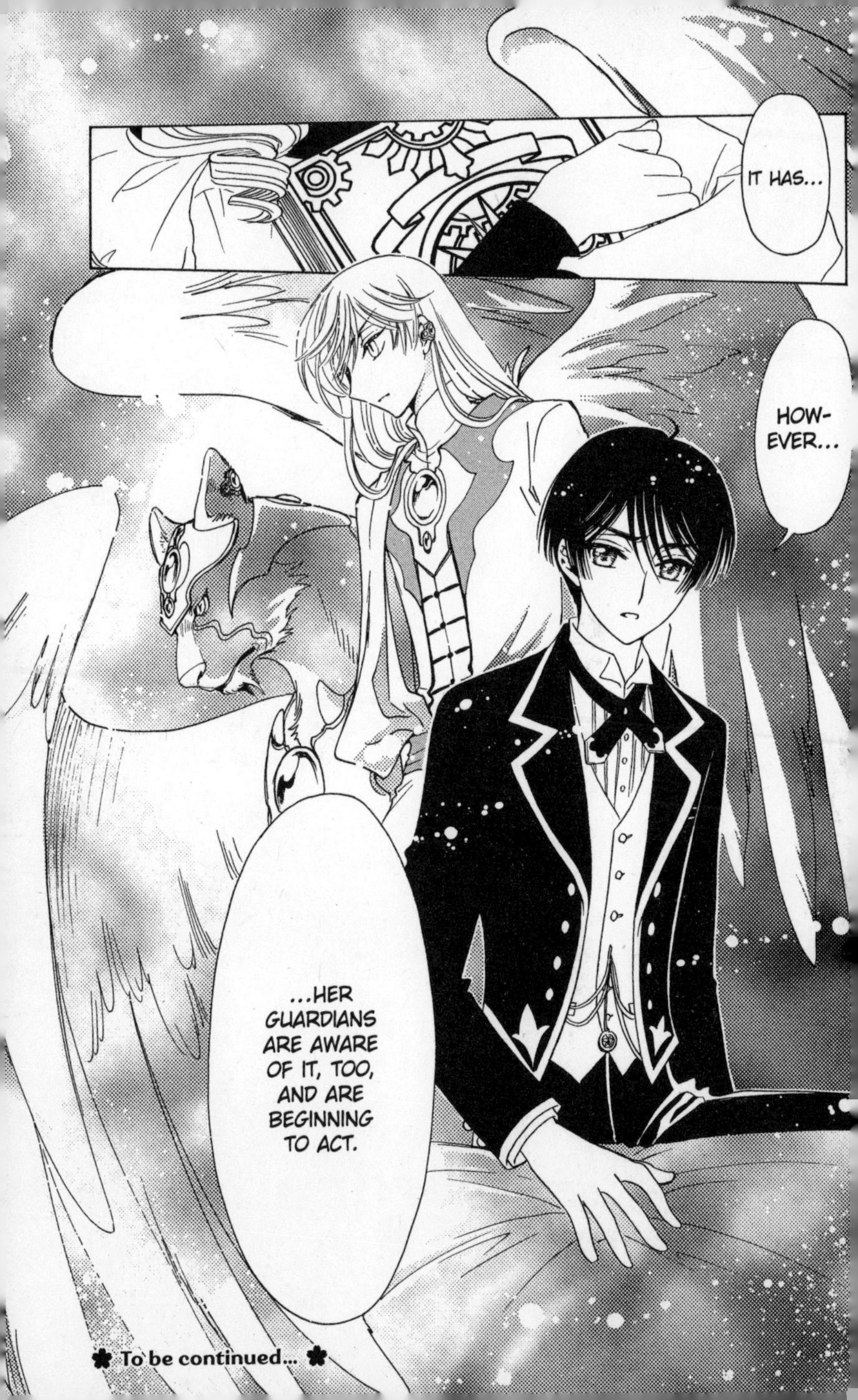
IT HAS...
HOW-EVER...
...HER GUARDIANS ARE AWARE OF IT, TOO, AND ARE BEGINNING TO ACT.
To be continued...

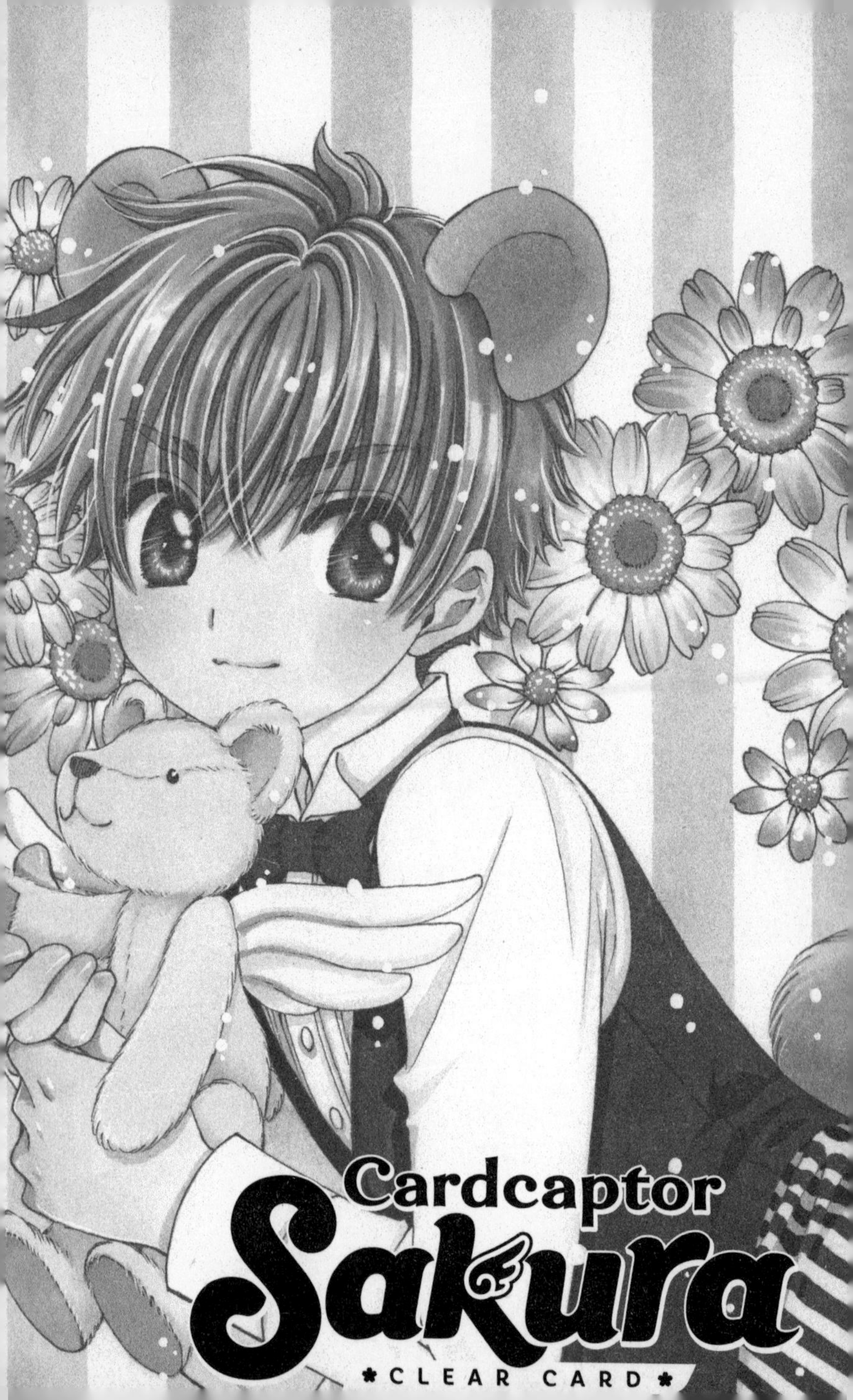
Cardcaptor
Sakura
CLEAR CARD

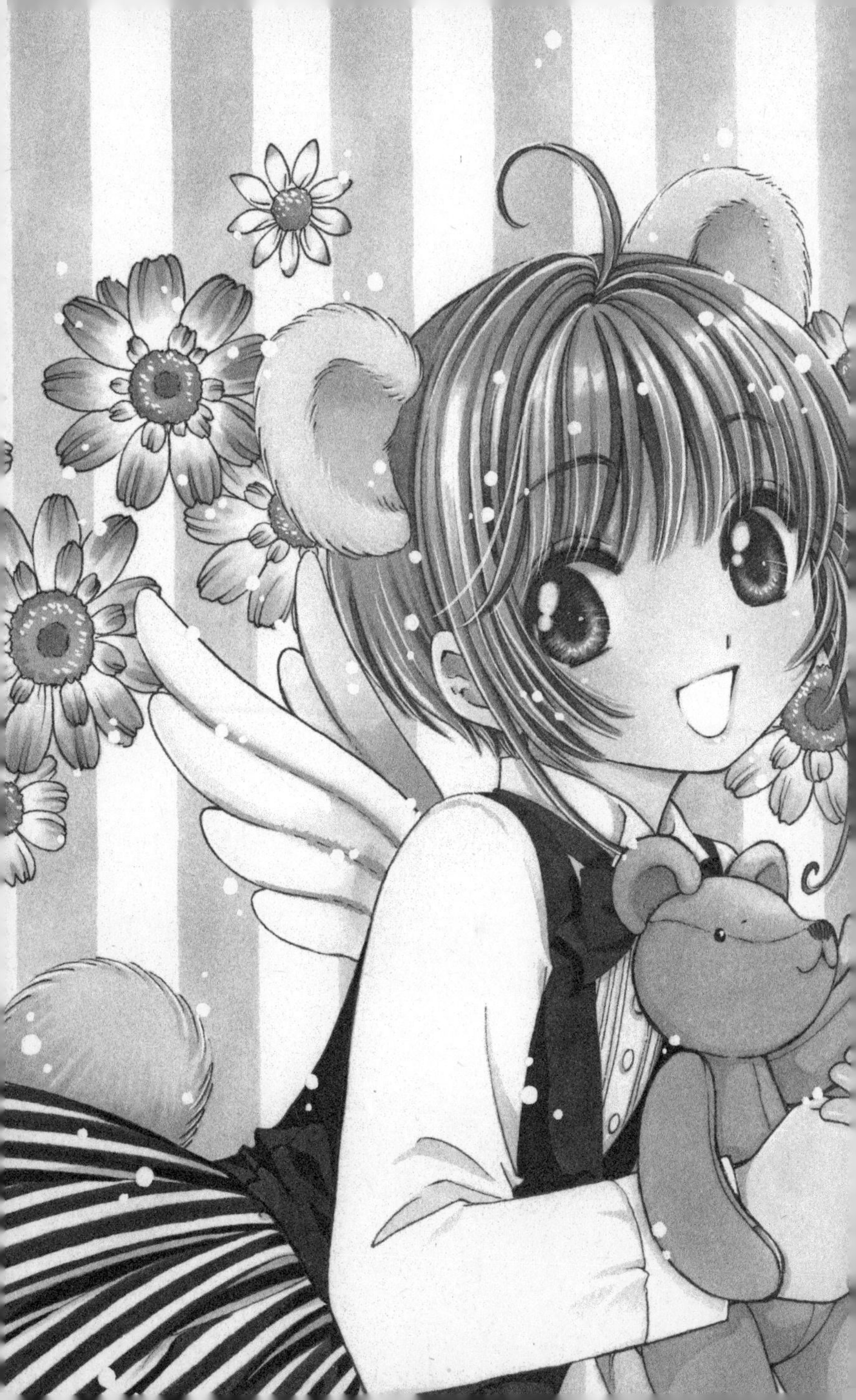

Cardcaptor Sakura
CLEAR CARD

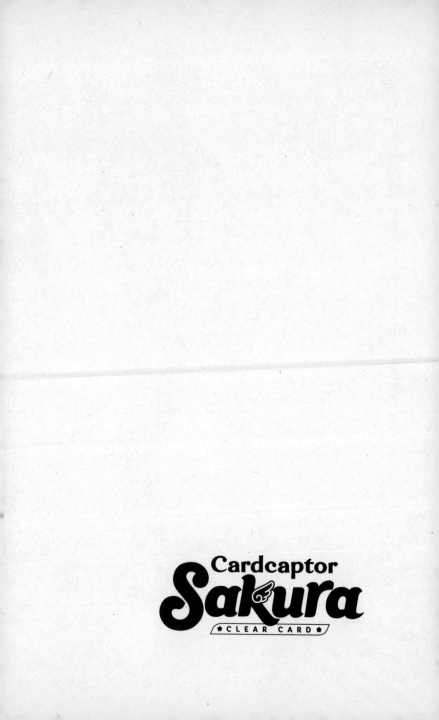

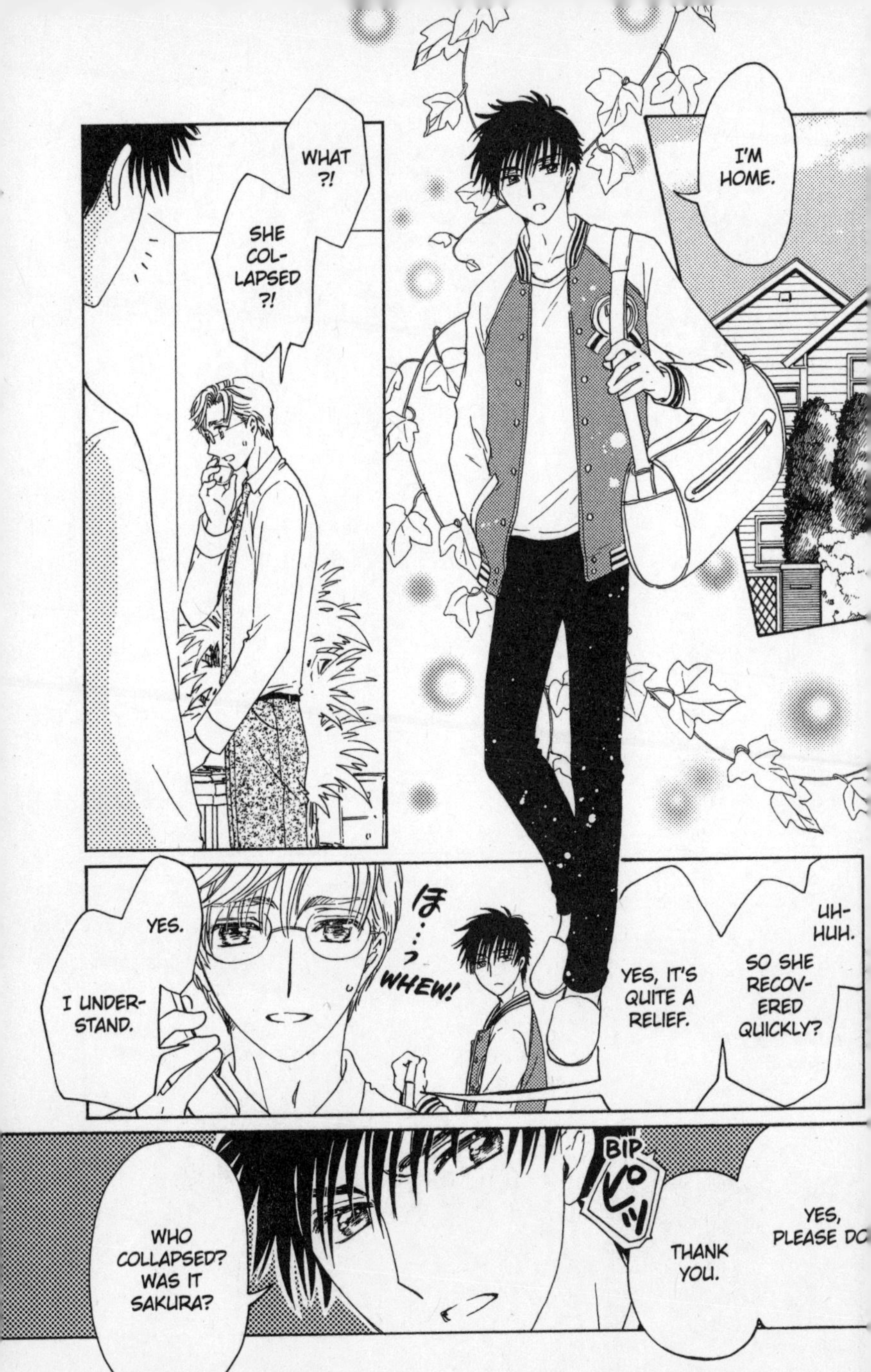
I'M HOME.
WHAT ?!
SHE COL-LAPSED ?!
UH-HUH.
SO SHE RECOV-ERED QUICKLY?
YES, IT'S QUITE A RELIEF.
ほ…っ
WHEW!
YES.
I UNDER-STAND.
BIP
ピッ
YES, PLEASE DO
THANK YOU.
WHO COLLAPSED? WAS IT SAKURA?

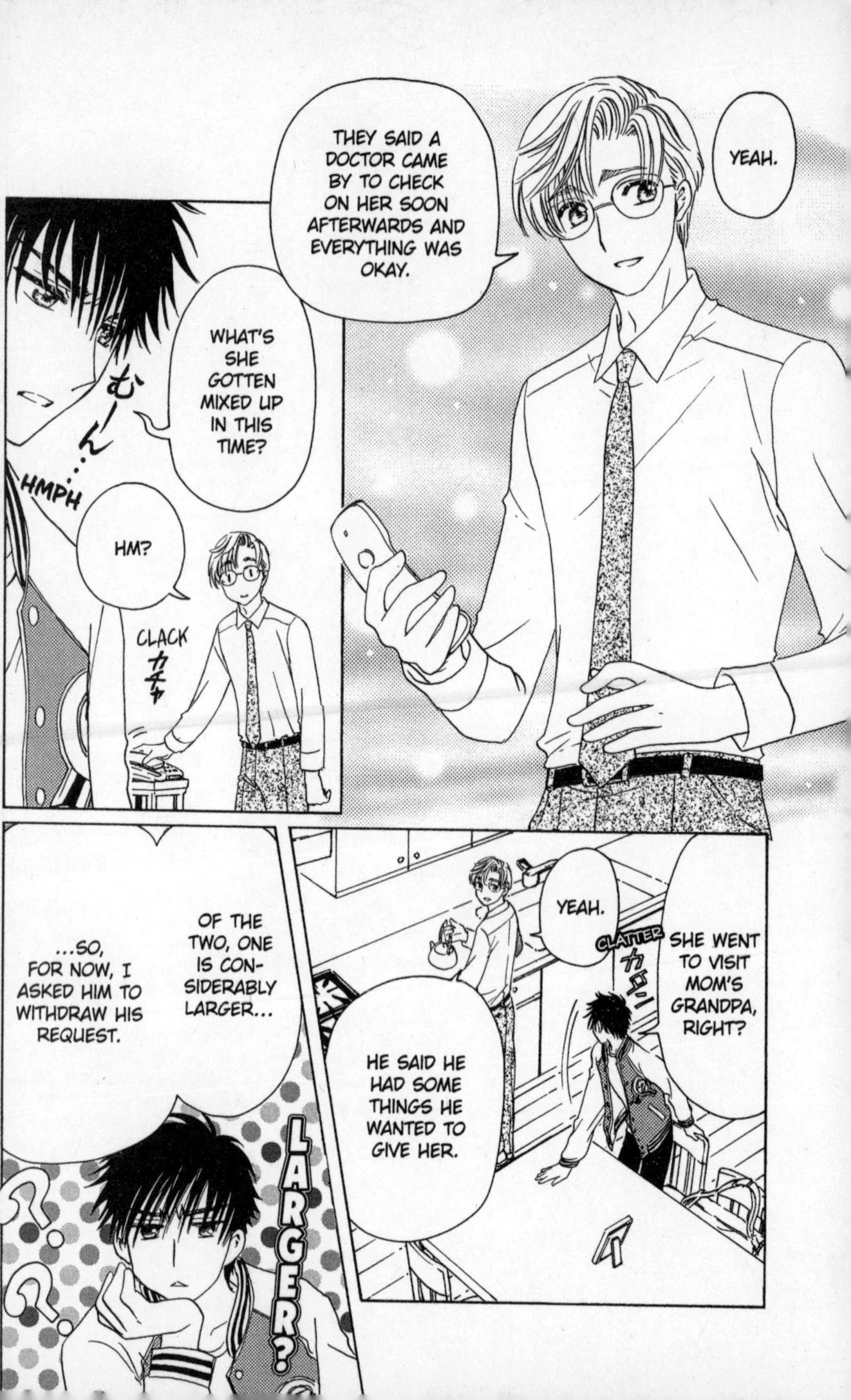
YEAH.
THEY SAID A DOCTOR CAME BY TO CHECK ON HER SOON AFTERWARDS AND EVERYTHING WAS OKAY.
WHAT'S SHE GOTTEN MIXED UP IN THIS TIME?
むーん…
HMPH
HM?
CLACK
カチャ
SHE WENT TO VISIT MOM'S GRANDPA, RIGHT?
CLATTER
ガタッ
YEAH.
HE SAID HE HAD SOME THINGS HE WANTED TO GIVE HER.
OF THE TWO, ONE IS CON-SIDERABLY LARGER...
...SO, FOR NOW, I ASKED HIM TO WITHDRAW HIS REQUEST.
LARGER?

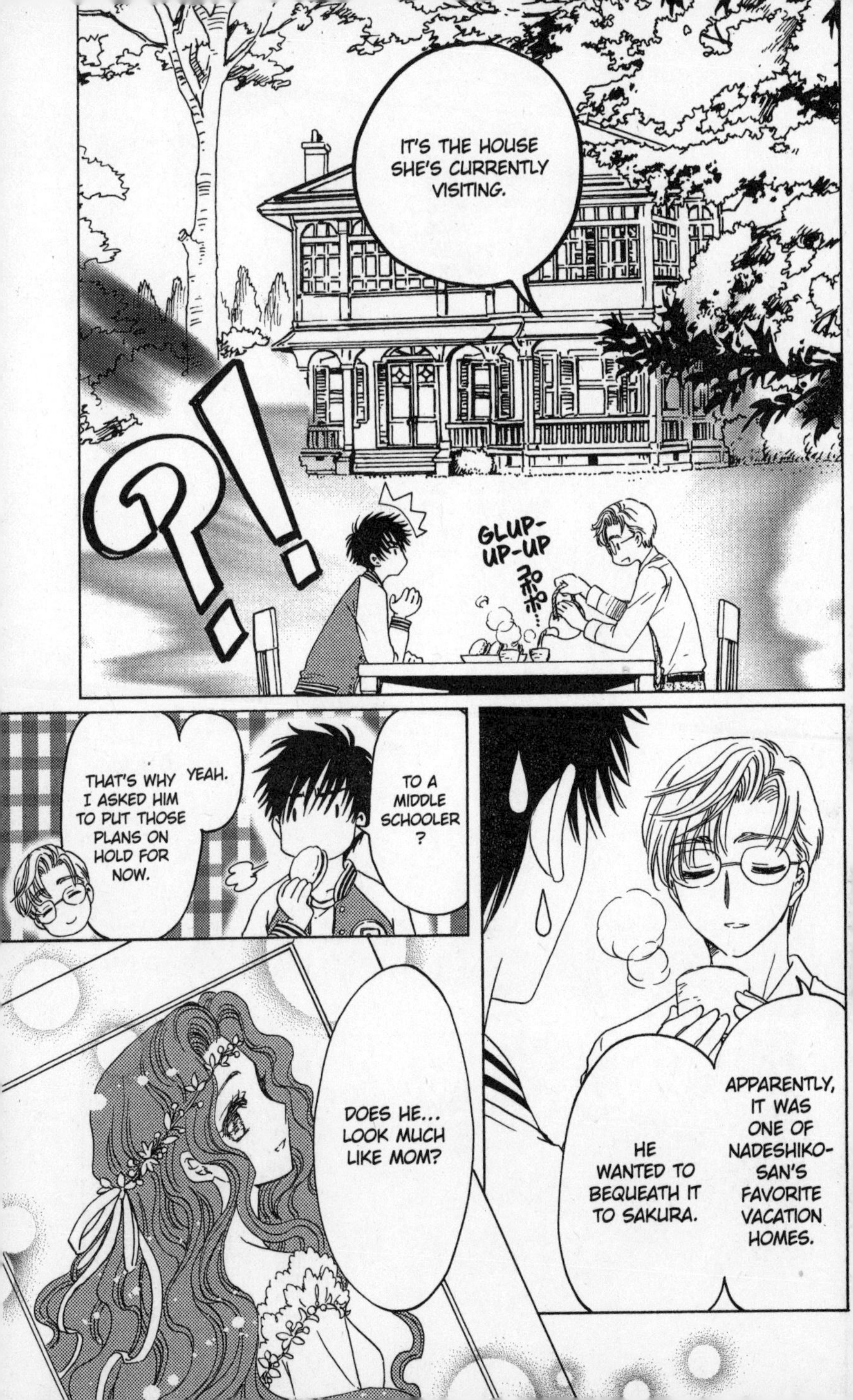
IT'S THE HOUSE SHE'S CURRENTLY VISITING.
?!
GLUP-UP-UP
コポポ…
APPARENTLY, IT WAS ONE OF NADESHIKO-SAN'S FAVORITE VACATION HOMES.
HE WANTED TO BEQUEATH IT TO SAKURA.
TO A MIDDLE SCHOOLER?
YEAH.
THAT'S WHY I ASKED HIM TO PUT THOSE PLANS ON HOLD FOR NOW.
DOES HE... LOOK MUCH LIKE MOM?

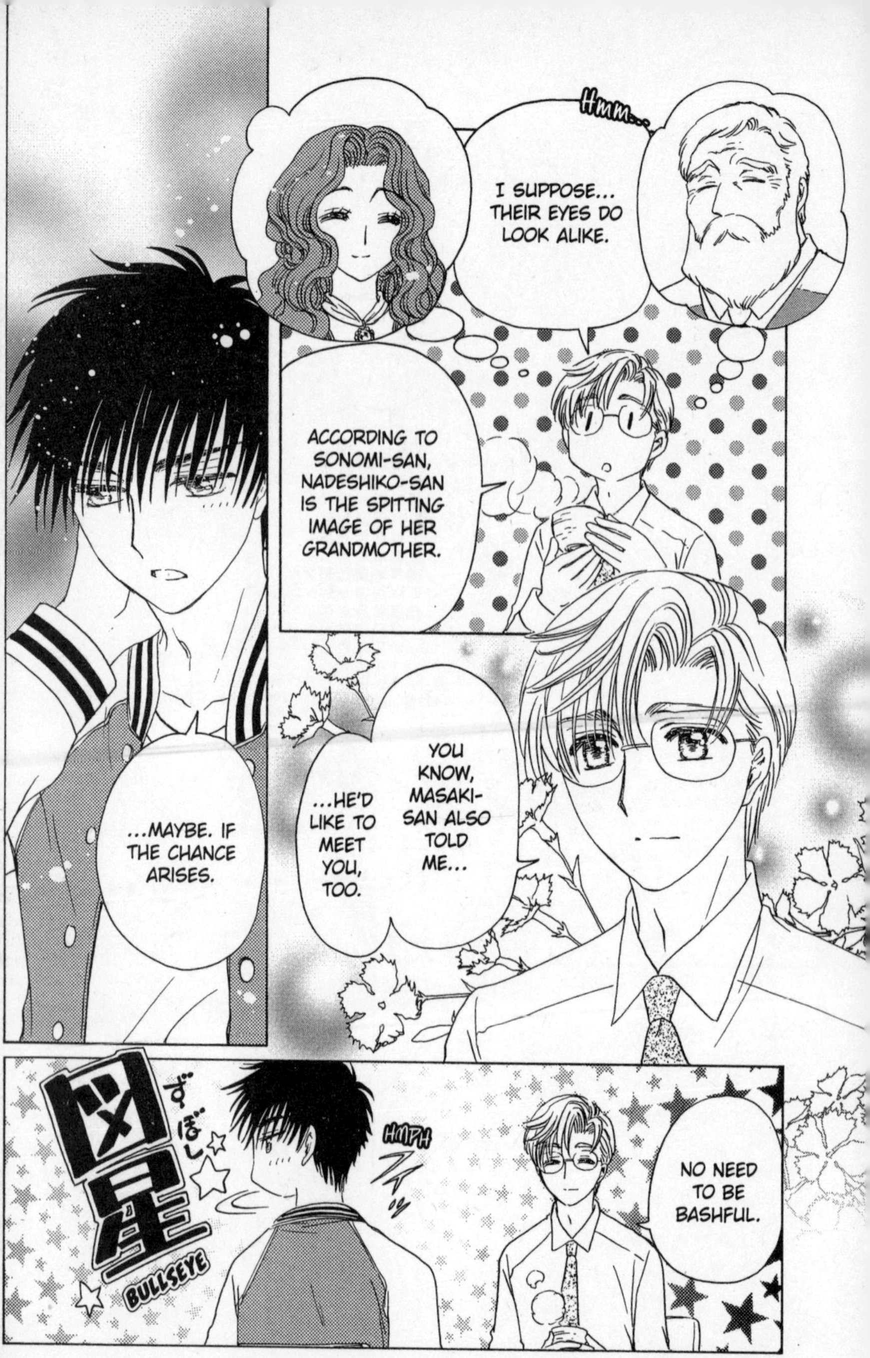
Hmm...
I SUPPOSE... THEIR EYES DO LOOK ALIKE.
ACCORDING TO SONOMI-SAN, NADESHIKO-SAN IS THE SPITTING IMAGE OF HER GRANDMOTHER.
YOU KNOW, MASAKI-SAN ALSO TOLD ME...
...HE'D LIKE TO MEET YOU, TOO.
...MAYBE. IF THE CHANCE ARISES.
NO NEED TO BE BASHFUL.
HMPH
ずぼし
図星
BULLSEYE

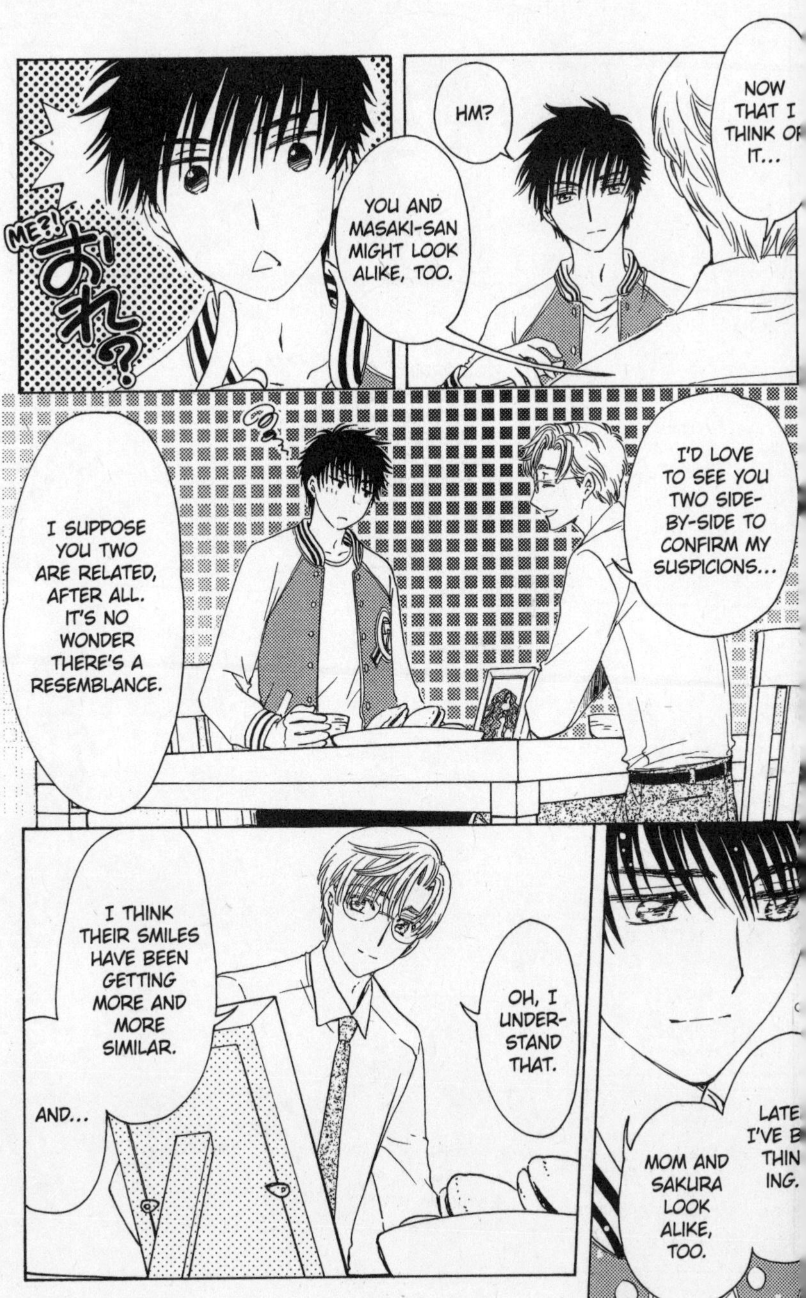
NOW THAT I THINK OF IT...
HM?
YOU AND MASAKI-SAN MIGHT LOOK ALIKE, TOO.
ME?! おれ?
I'D LOVE TO SEE YOU TWO SIDE-BY-SIDE TO CONFIRM MY SUSPICIONS...
I SUPPOSE YOU TWO ARE RELATED, AFTER ALL. IT'S NO WONDER THERE'S A RESEMBLANCE.
LATE I'VE B THIN ING.
MOM AND SAKURA LOOK ALIKE, TOO.
OH, I UNDERSTAND THAT.
I THINK THEIR SMILES HAVE BEEN GETTING MORE AND MORE SIMILAR.
AND...

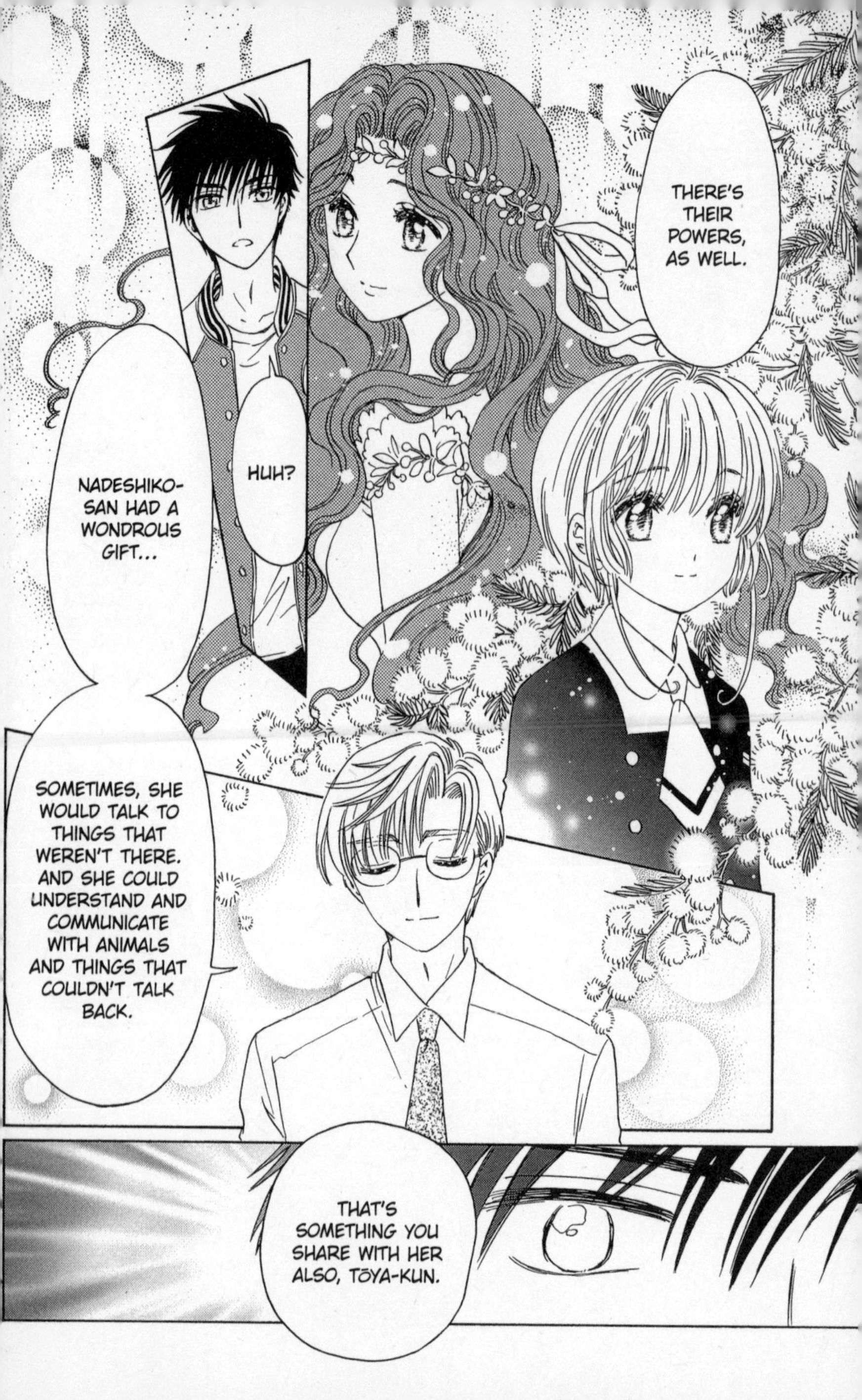
THERE'S THEIR POWERS, AS WELL.
HUH?
NADESHIKO-SAN HAD A WONDROUS GIFT...
SOMETIMES, SHE WOULD TALK TO THINGS THAT WEREN'T THERE. AND SHE COULD UNDERSTAND AND COMMUNICATE WITH ANIMALS AND THINGS THAT COULDN'T TALK BACK.
THAT'S SOMETHING YOU SHARE WITH HER ALSO, TŌYA-KUN.

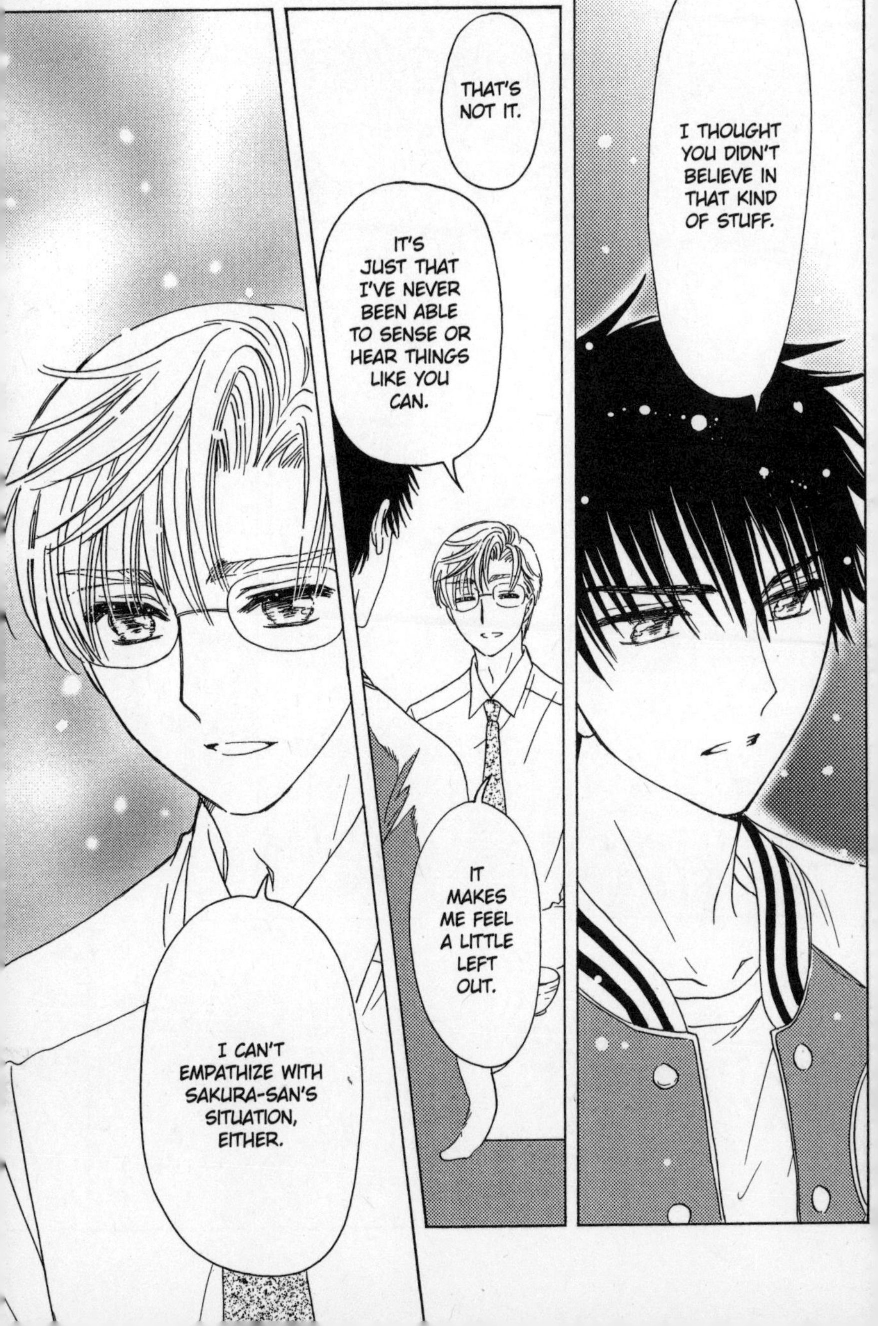
I THOUGHT YOU DIDN'T BELIEVE IN THAT KIND OF STUFF.
THAT'S NOT IT.
IT'S JUST THAT I'VE NEVER BEEN ABLE TO SENSE OR HEAR THINGS LIKE YOU CAN.
IT MAKES ME FEEL A LITTLE LEFT OUT.
I CAN'T EMPATHIZE WITH SAKURA-SAN'S SITUATION, EITHER.

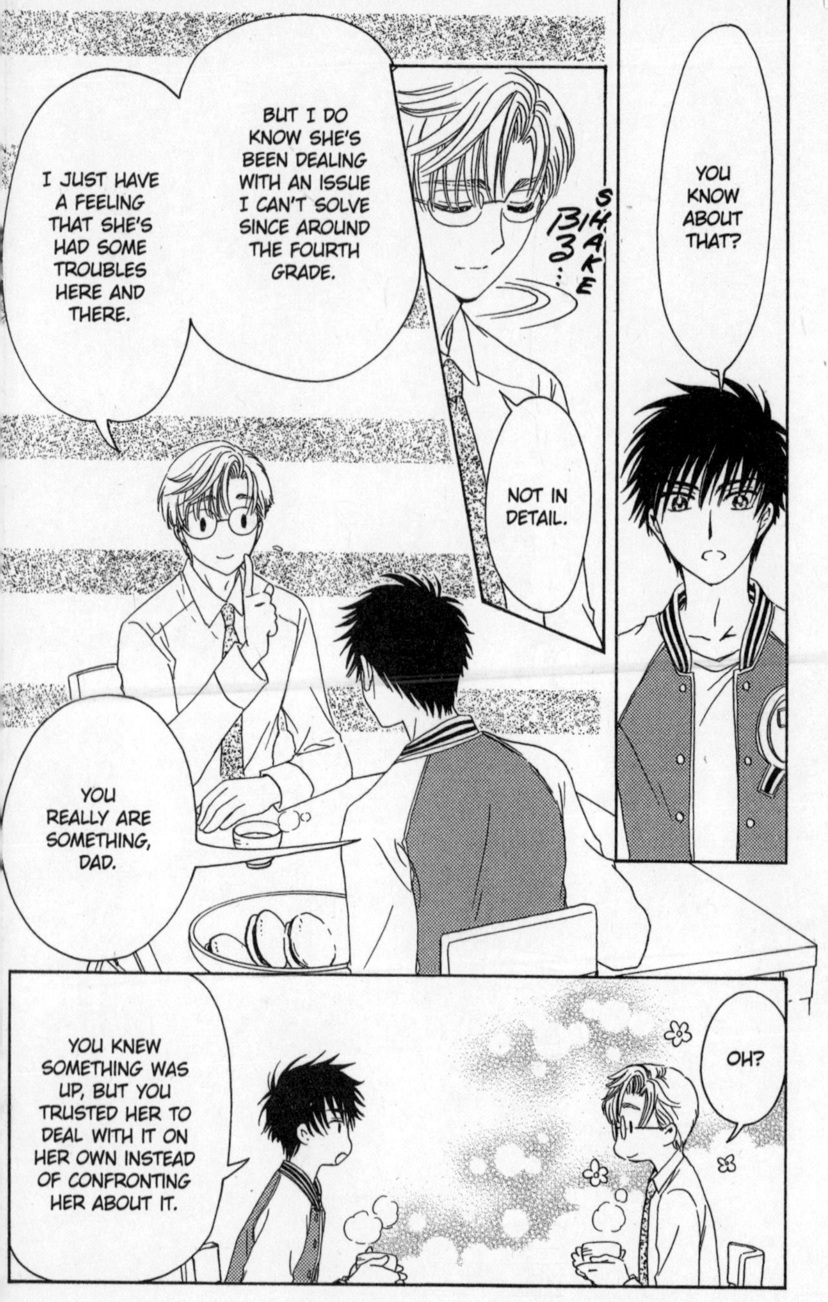
YOU KNOW ABOUT THAT?
NOT IN DETAIL.
SHAKE
BUT I DO KNOW SHE'S BEEN DEALING WITH AN ISSUE I CAN'T SOLVE SINCE AROUND THE FOURTH GRADE.
I JUST HAVE A FEELING THAT SHE'S HAD SOME TROUBLES HERE AND THERE.
YOU REALLY ARE SOMETHING, DAD.
YOU KNEW SOMETHING WAS UP, BUT YOU TRUSTED HER TO DEAL WITH IT ON HER OWN INSTEAD OF CONFRONTING HER ABOUT IT.
OH?

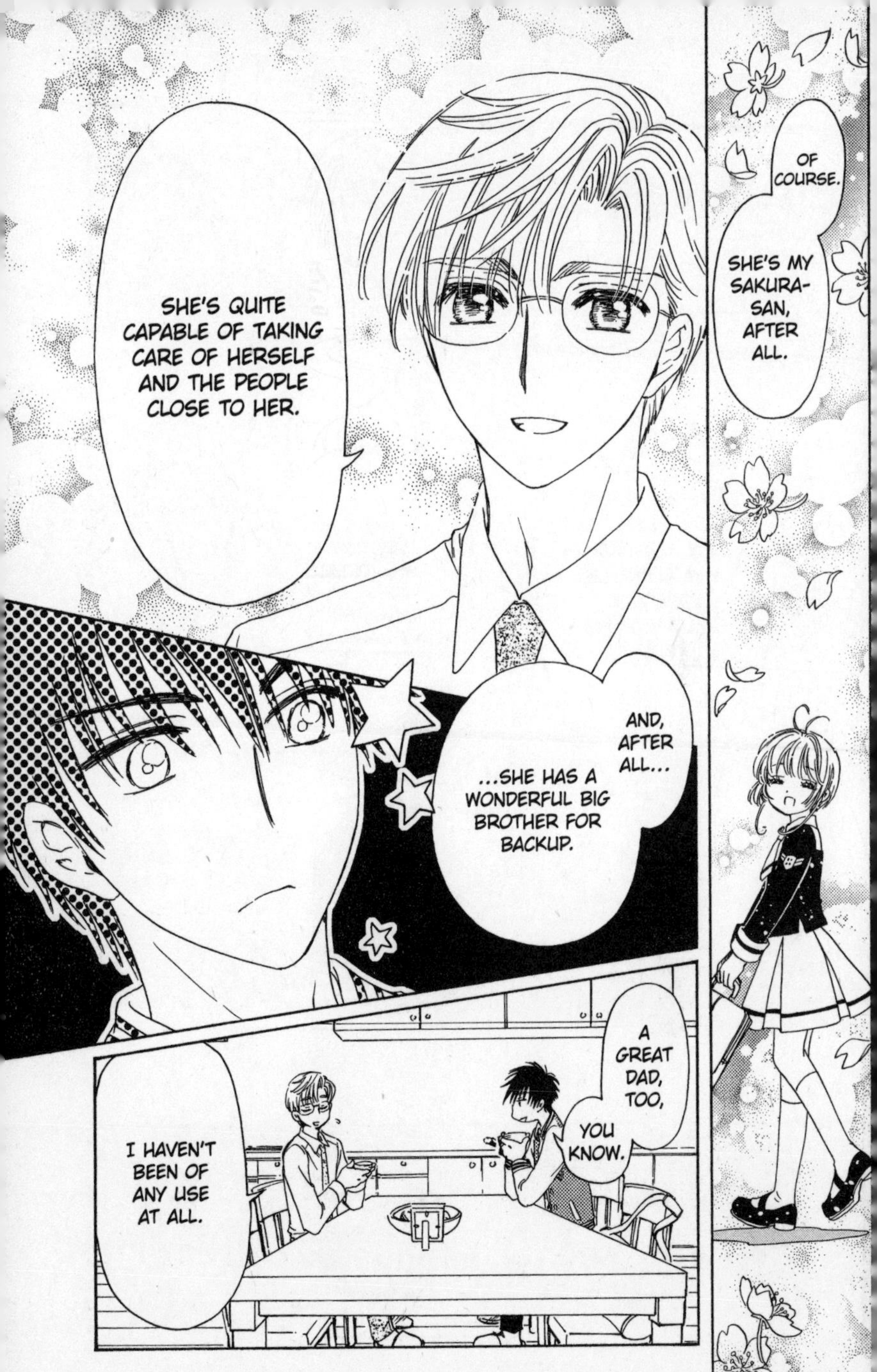
OF COURSE.
SHE'S MY SAKURA-SAN, AFTER ALL.
SHE'S QUITE CAPABLE OF TAKING CARE OF HERSELF AND THE PEOPLE CLOSE TO HER.
AND, AFTER ALL...
...SHE HAS A WONDERFUL BIG BROTHER FOR BACKUP.
A GREAT DAD, TOO,
YOU KNOW.
I HAVEN'T BEEN OF ANY USE AT ALL.

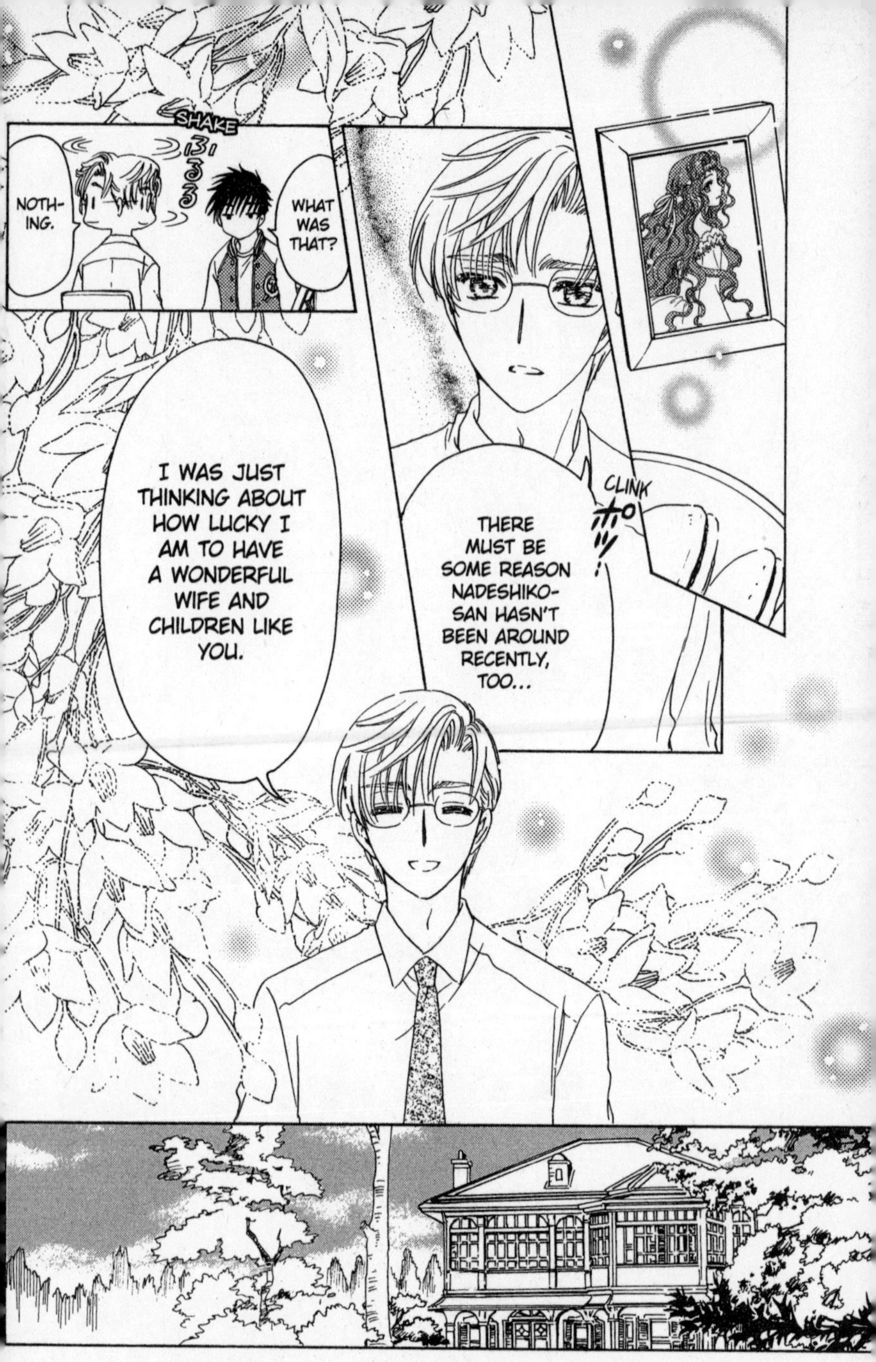
CLINK
THERE MUST BE SOME REASON NADESHIKO-SAN HASN'T BEEN AROUND RECENTLY, TOO...
WHAT WAS THAT?
SHAKE
NOTH-ING.
I WAS JUST THINKING ABOUT HOW LUCKY I AM TO HAVE A WONDERFUL WIFE AND CHILDREN LIKE YOU.

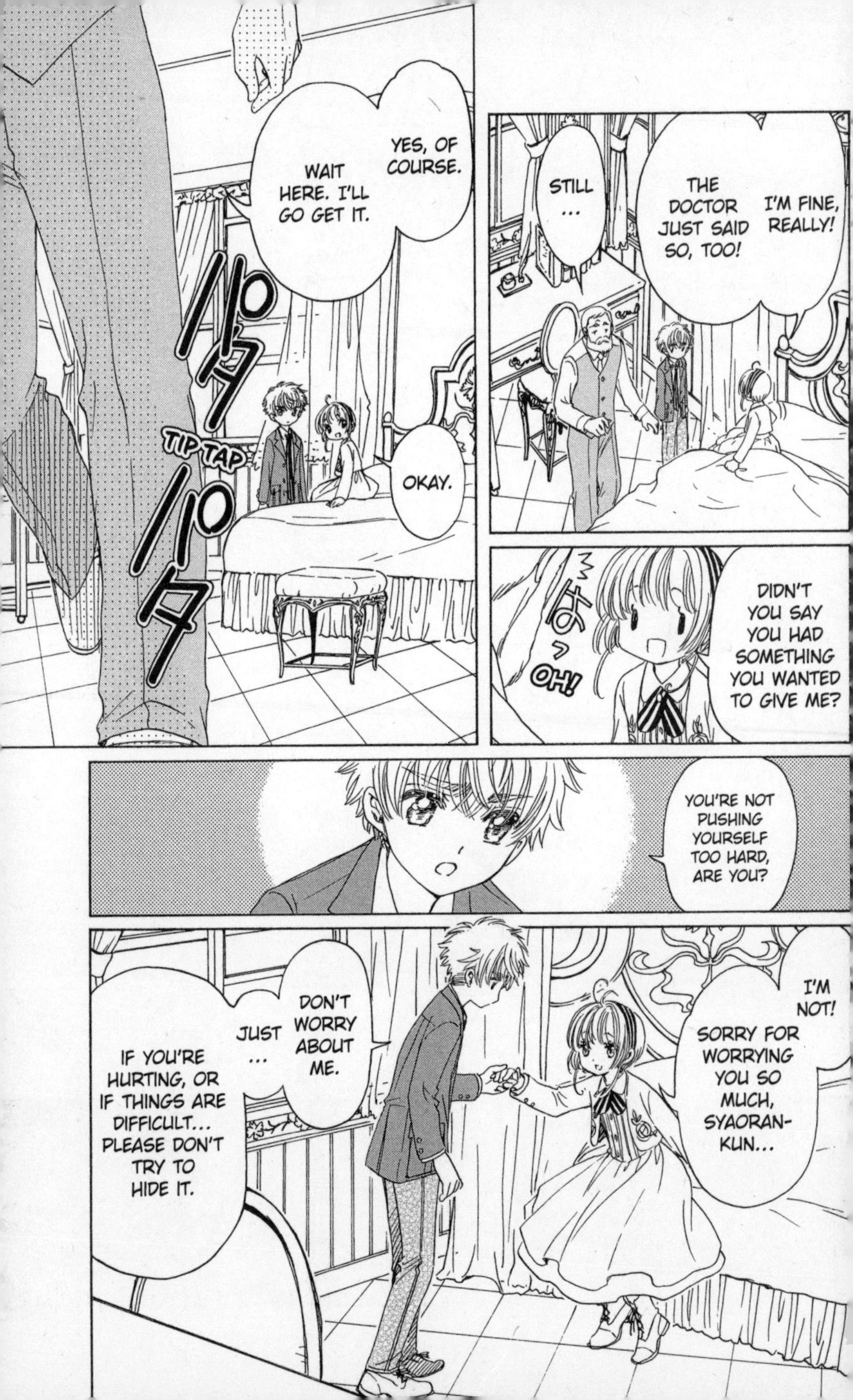
I'M FINE, REALLY!
THE DOCTOR JUST SAID SO, TOO!
STILL...
はっ
OH!
DIDN'T YOU SAY YOU HAD SOMETHING YOU WANTED TO GIVE ME?
YES, OF COURSE.
WAIT HERE. I'LL GO GET IT.
OKAY.
パタパタ
TIP TAP
YOU'RE NOT PUSHING YOURSELF TOO HARD, ARE YOU?
I'M NOT!
SORRY FOR WORRYING YOU SO MUCH, SYAORAN-KUN...
DON'T WORRY ABOUT ME.
JUST...
IF YOU'RE HURTING, OR IF THINGS ARE DIFFICULT... PLEASE DON'T TRY TO HIDE IT.

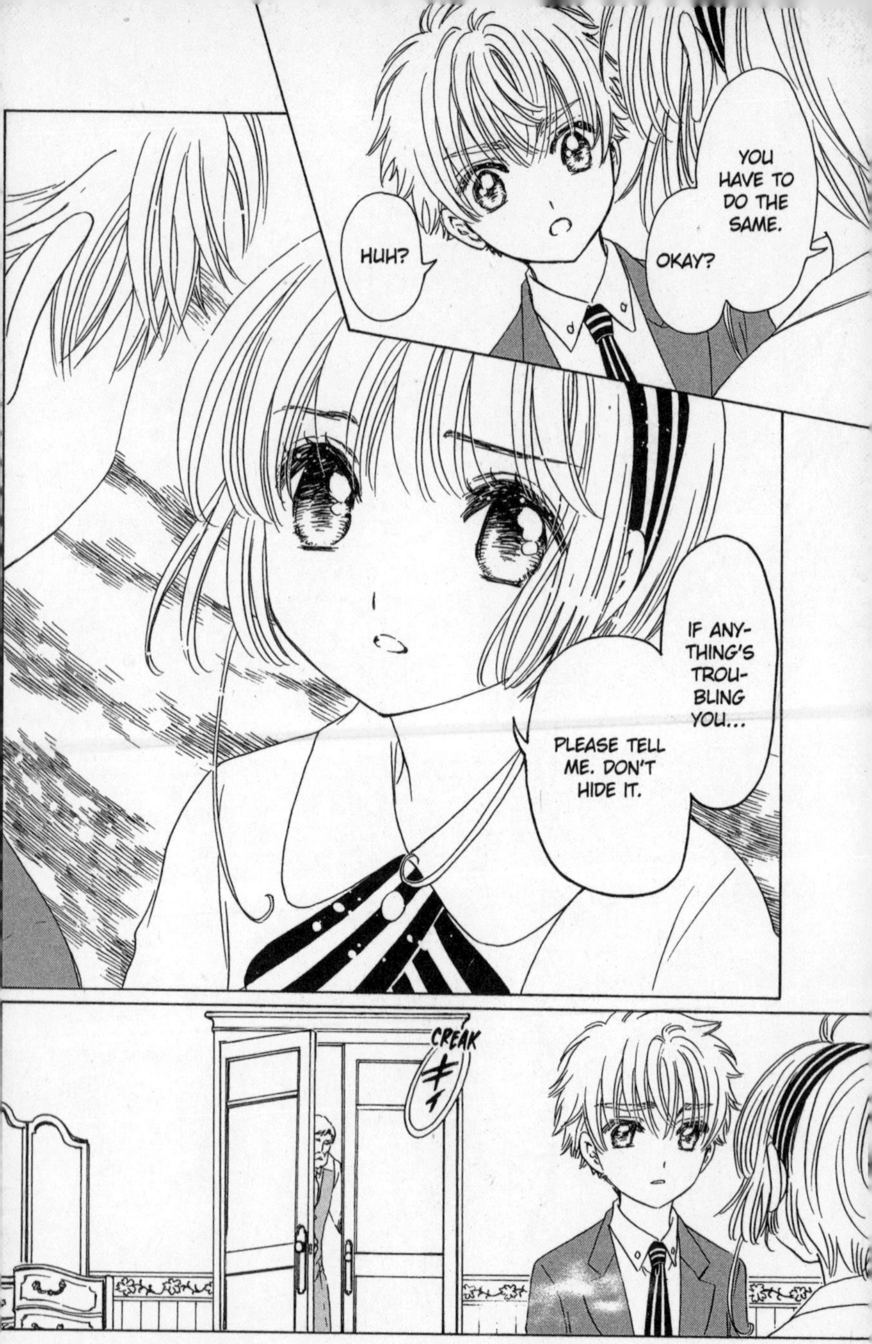
YOU HAVE TO DO THE SAME.
OKAY?
HUH?
IF ANYTHING'S TROUBLING YOU...
PLEASE TELL ME. DON'T HIDE IT.
CREAK

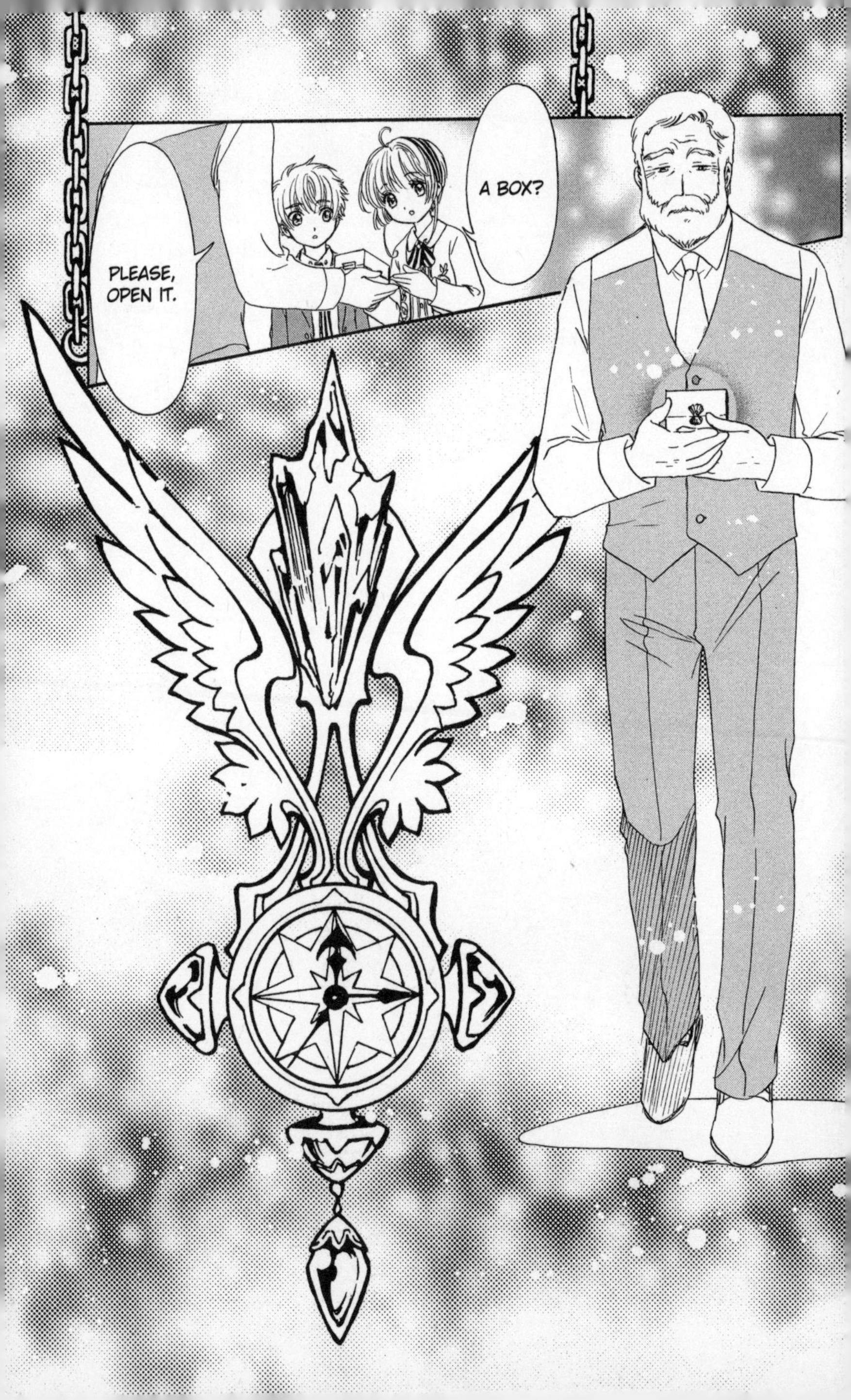
A BOX?
PLEASE, OPEN IT.

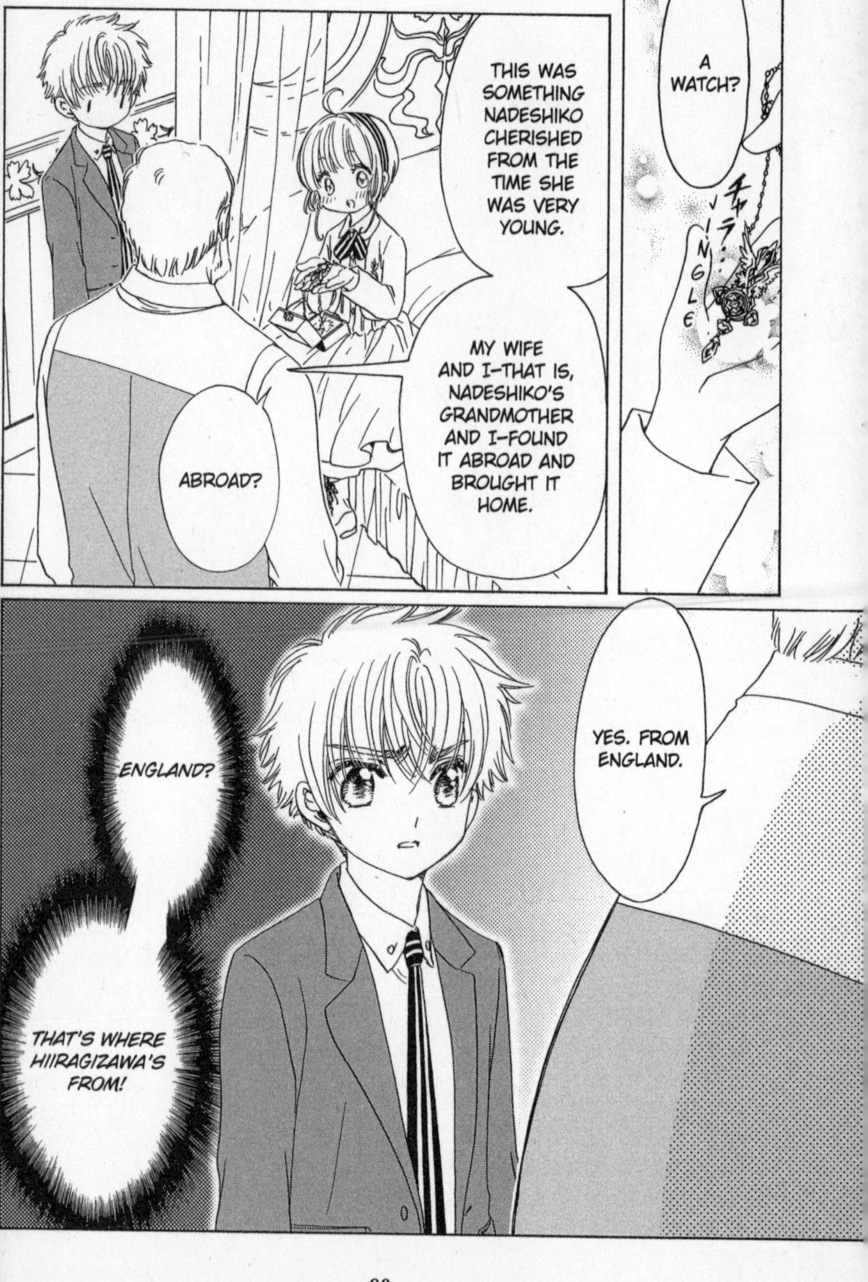
A WATCH?
チャラ
JINGLE
THIS WAS SOMETHING NADESHIKO CHERISHED FROM THE TIME SHE WAS VERY YOUNG.
MY WIFE AND I–THAT IS, NADESHIKO'S GRANDMOTHER AND I–FOUND IT ABROAD AND BROUGHT IT HOME.
ABROAD?
YES. FROM ENGLAND.
ENGLAND?
THAT'S WHERE HIIRAGIZAWA'S FROM!

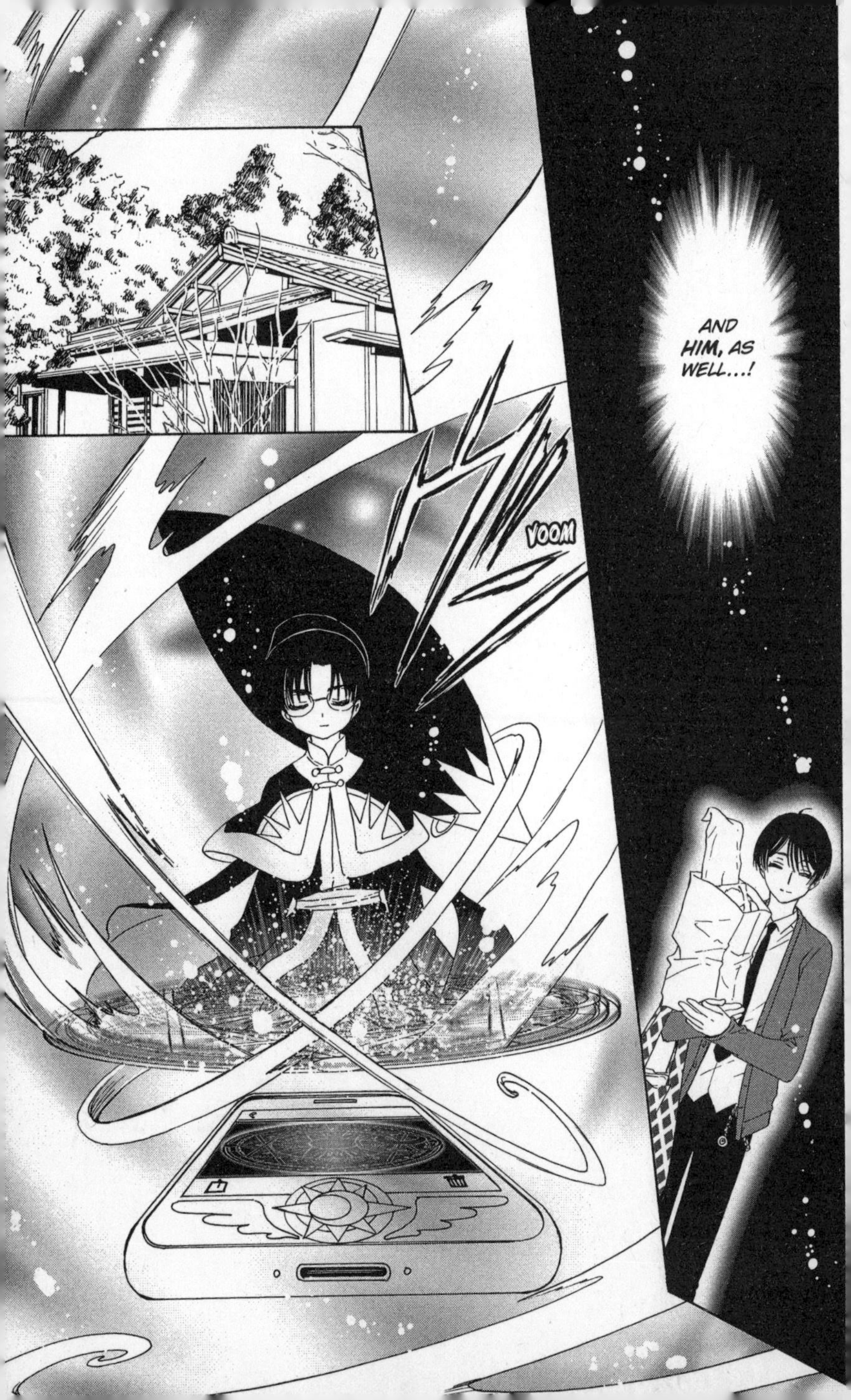
AND HIM, AS WELL...!
VOOM

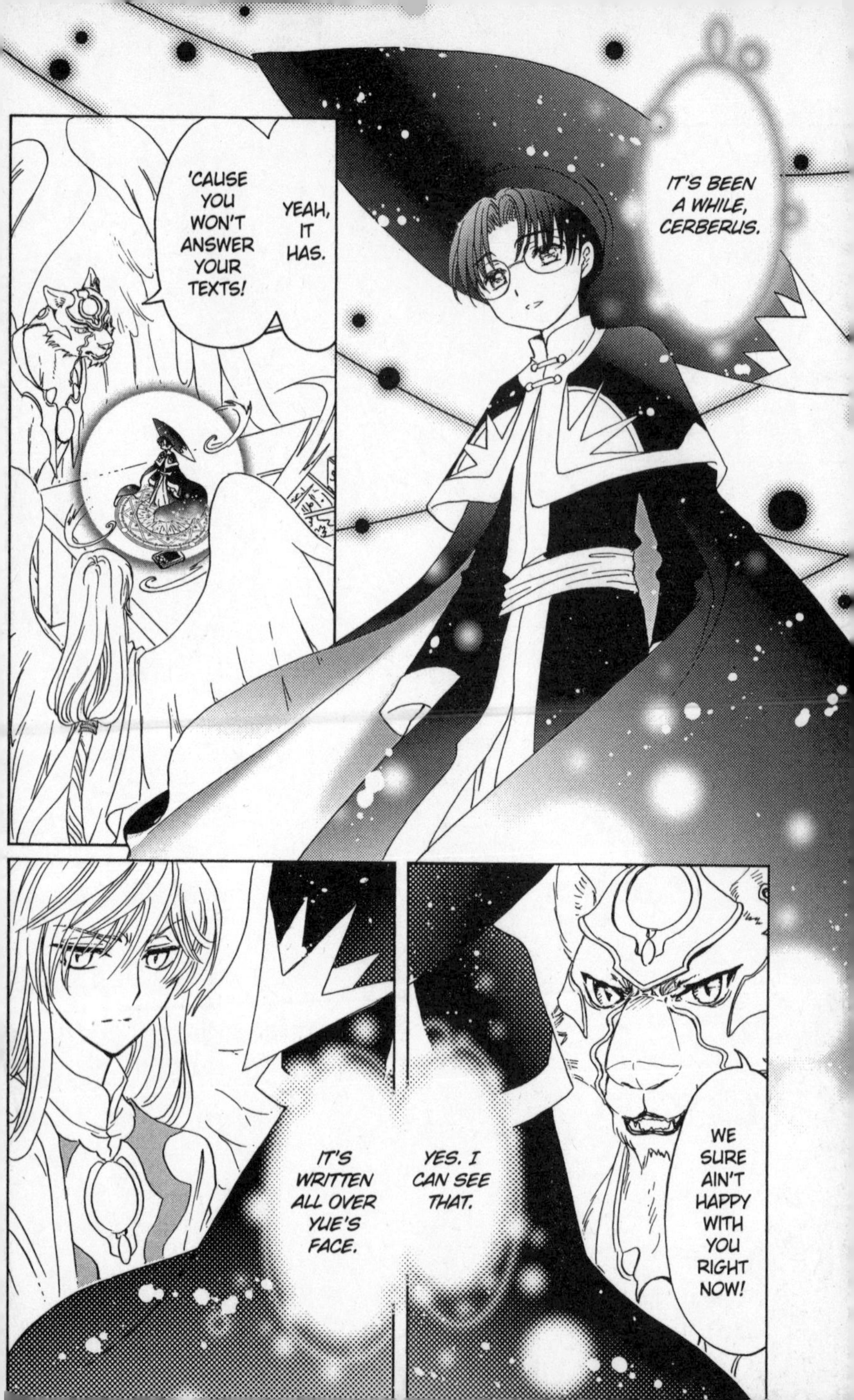
IT'S BEEN A WHILE, CERBERUS.
YEAH, IT HAS.
'CAUSE YOU WON'T ANSWER YOUR TEXTS!
WE SURE AIN'T HAPPY WITH YOU RIGHT NOW!
YES. I CAN SEE THAT.
IT'S WRITTEN ALL OVER YUE'S FACE.

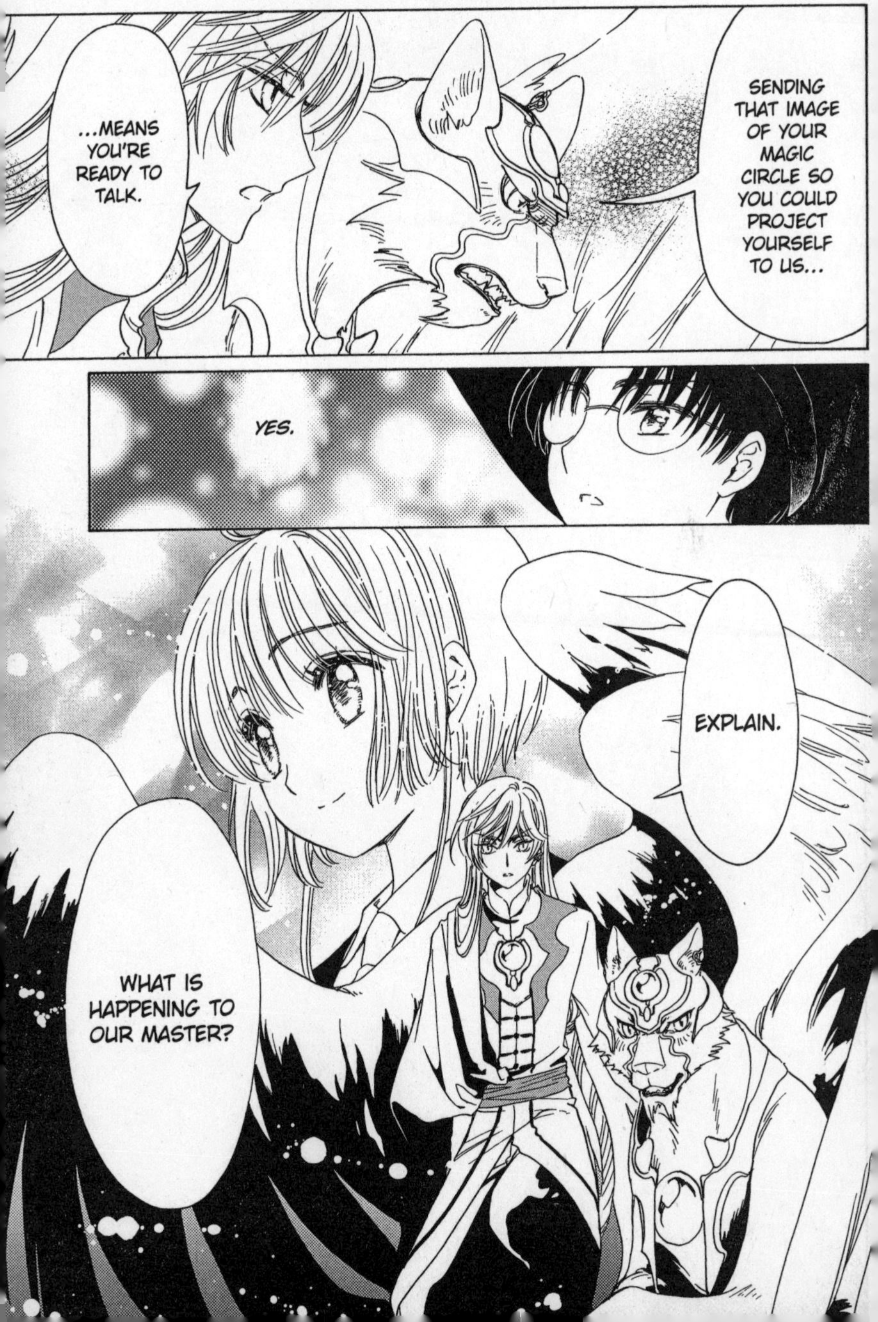
SENDING THAT IMAGE OF YOUR MAGIC CIRCLE SO YOU COULD PROJECT YOURSELF TO US...
...MEANS YOU'RE READY TO TALK.
YES.
EXPLAIN.
WHAT IS HAPPENING TO OUR MASTER?

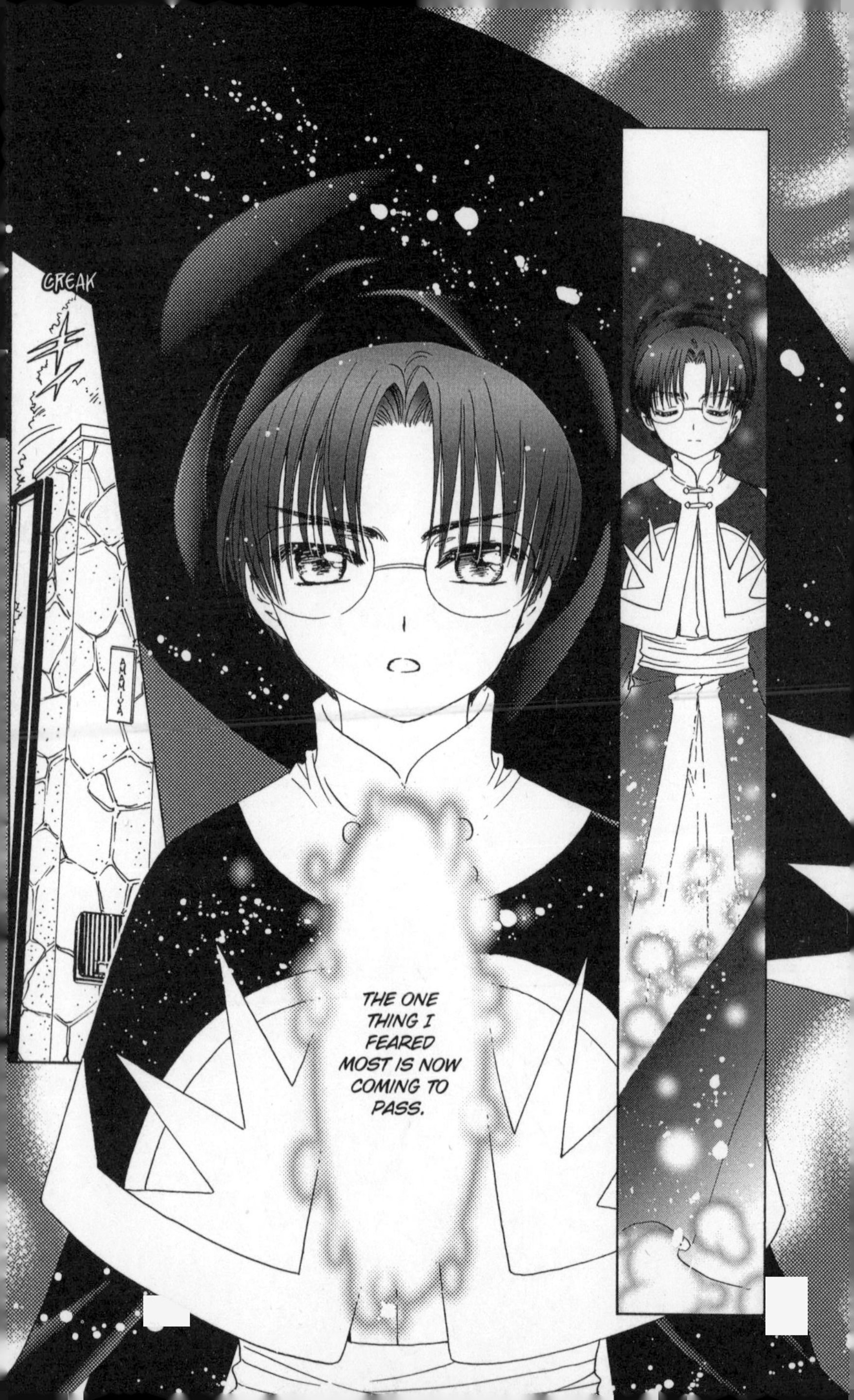
CREAK
AMAMIYA
THE ONE THING I FEARED MOST IS NOW COMING TO PASS.

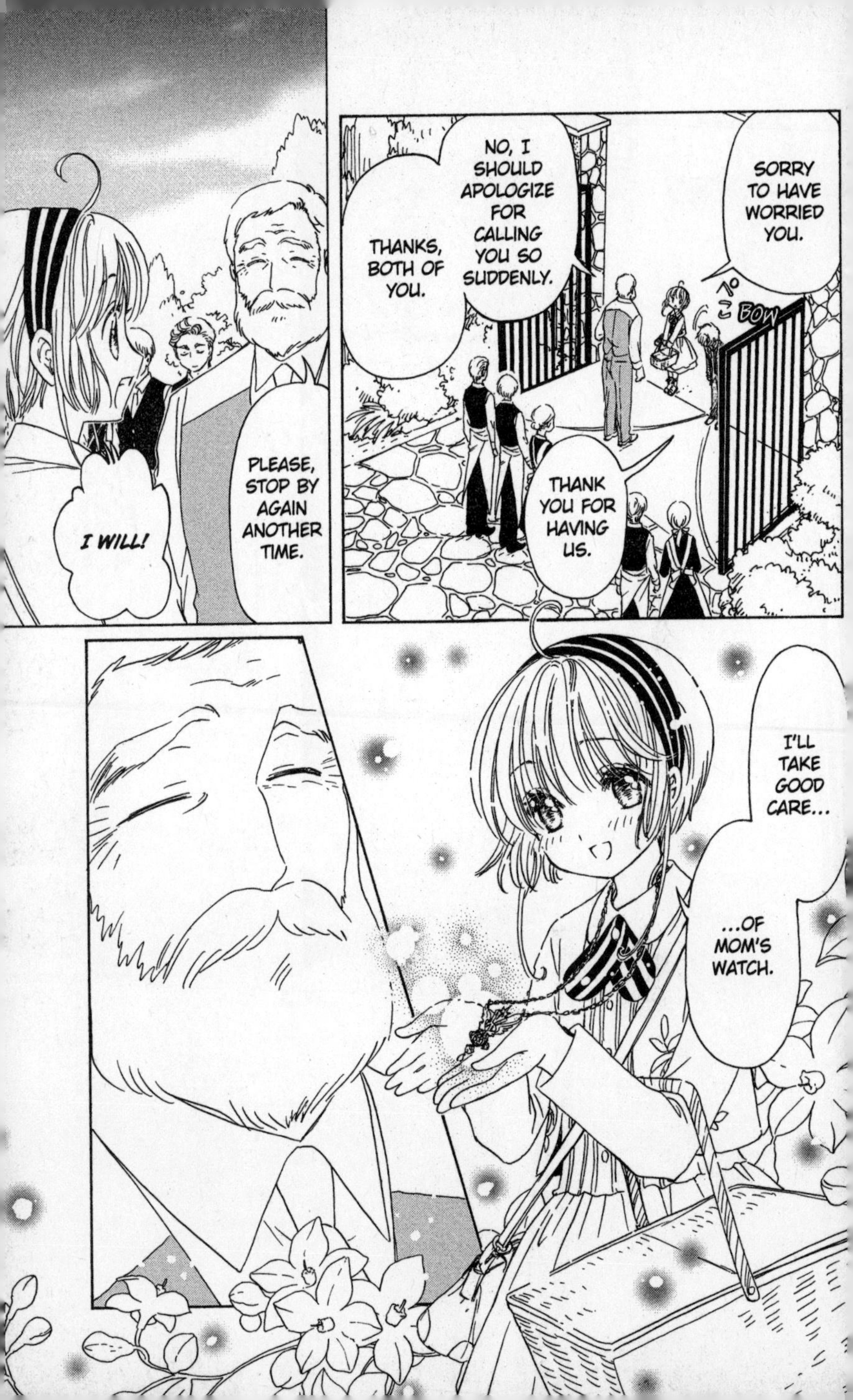
SORRY TO HAVE WORRIED YOU.
BOW
NO, I SHOULD APOLOGIZE FOR CALLING YOU SO SUDDENLY.
THANKS, BOTH OF YOU.
THANK YOU FOR HAVING US.
PLEASE, STOP BY AGAIN ANOTHER TIME.
I WILL!
I'LL TAKE GOOD CARE...
...OF MOM'S WATCH.

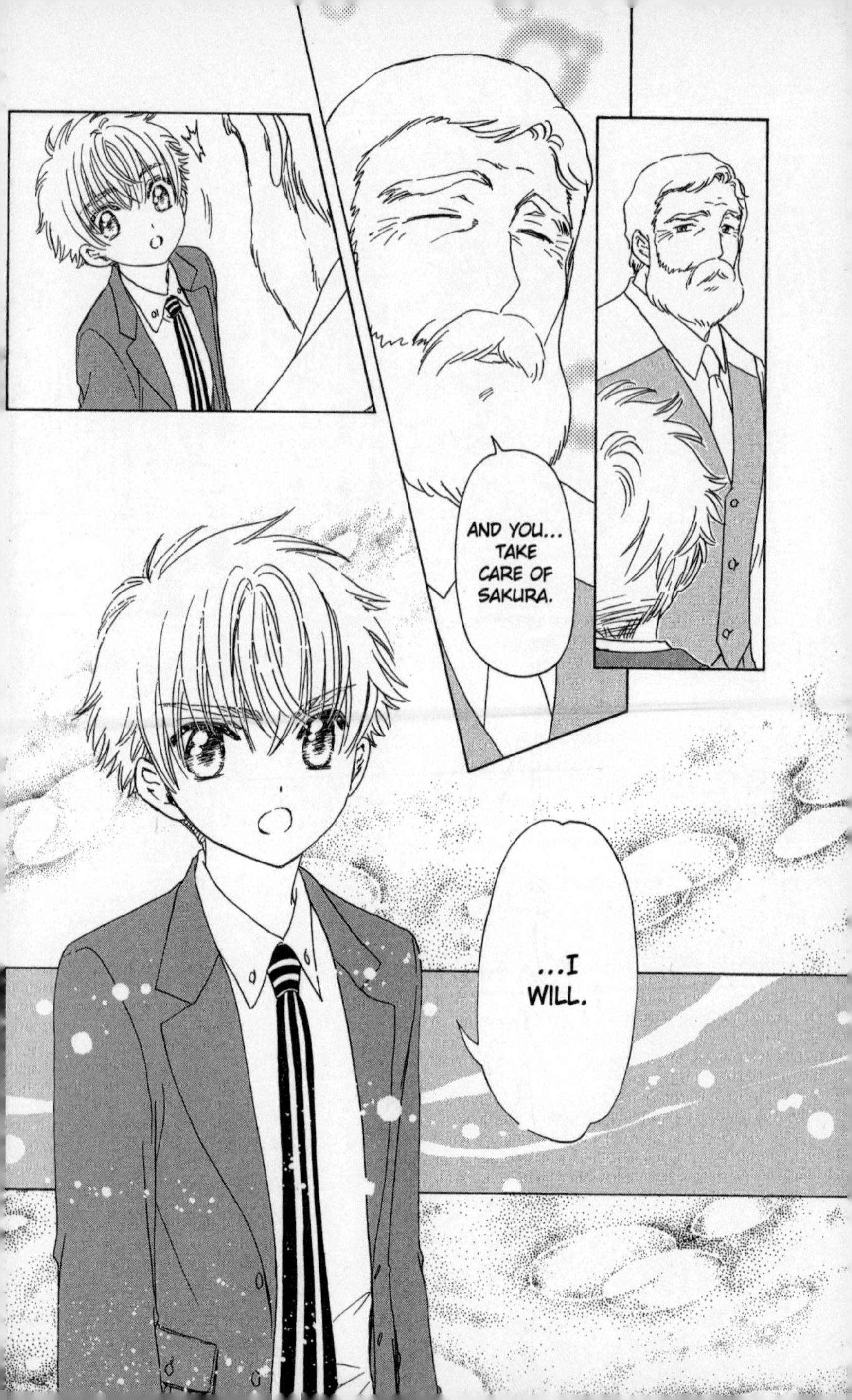
AND YOU... TAKE CARE OF SAKURA.
...I WILL.

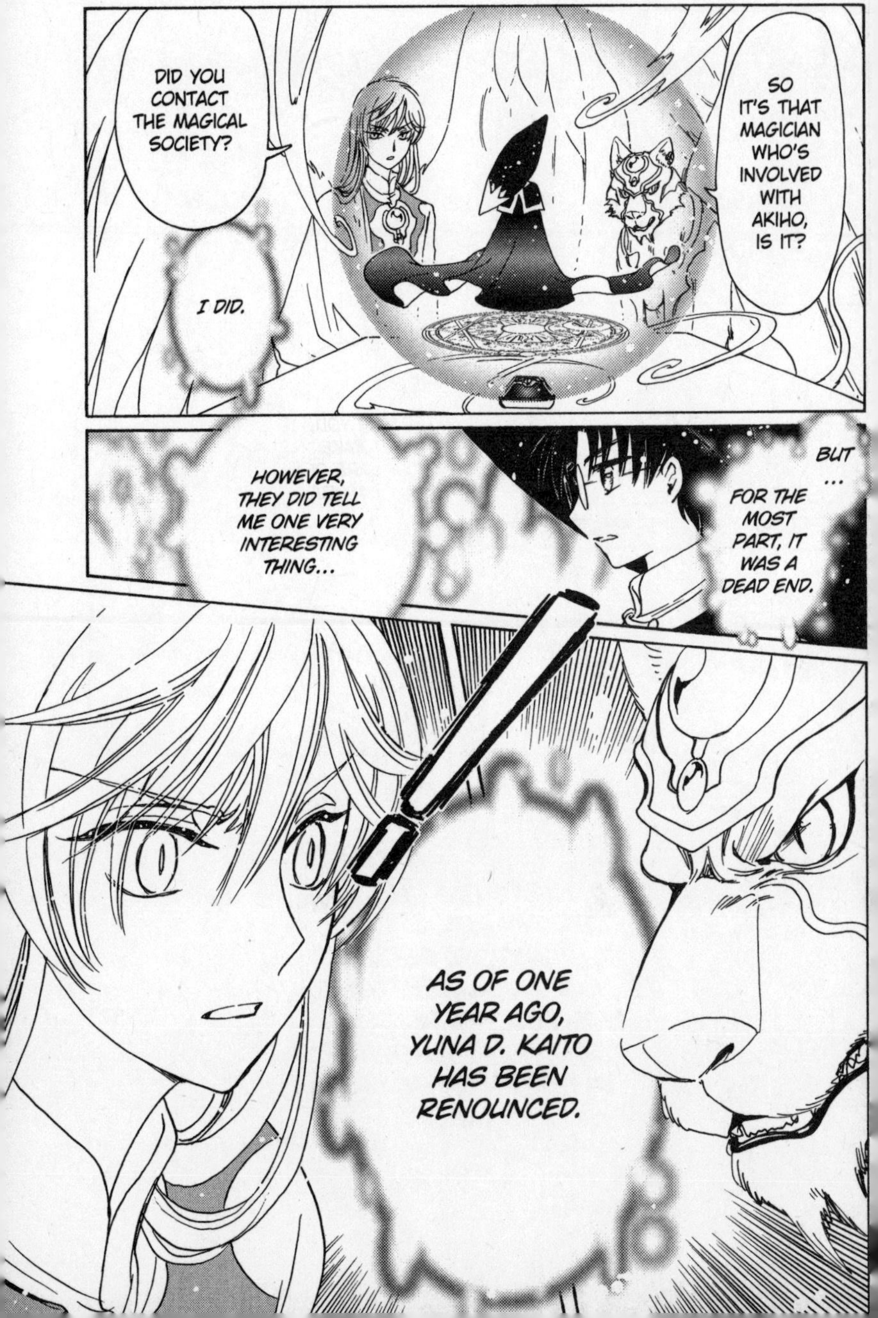
SO IT'S THAT MAGICIAN WHO'S INVOLVED WITH AKIHO, IS IT?
DID YOU CONTACT THE MAGICAL SOCIETY?
I DID.
BUT...
FOR THE MOST PART, IT WAS A DEAD END.
HOWEVER, THEY DID TELL ME ONE VERY INTERESTING THING...
AS OF ONE YEAR AGO, YUNA D. KAITO HAS BEEN RENOUNCED.

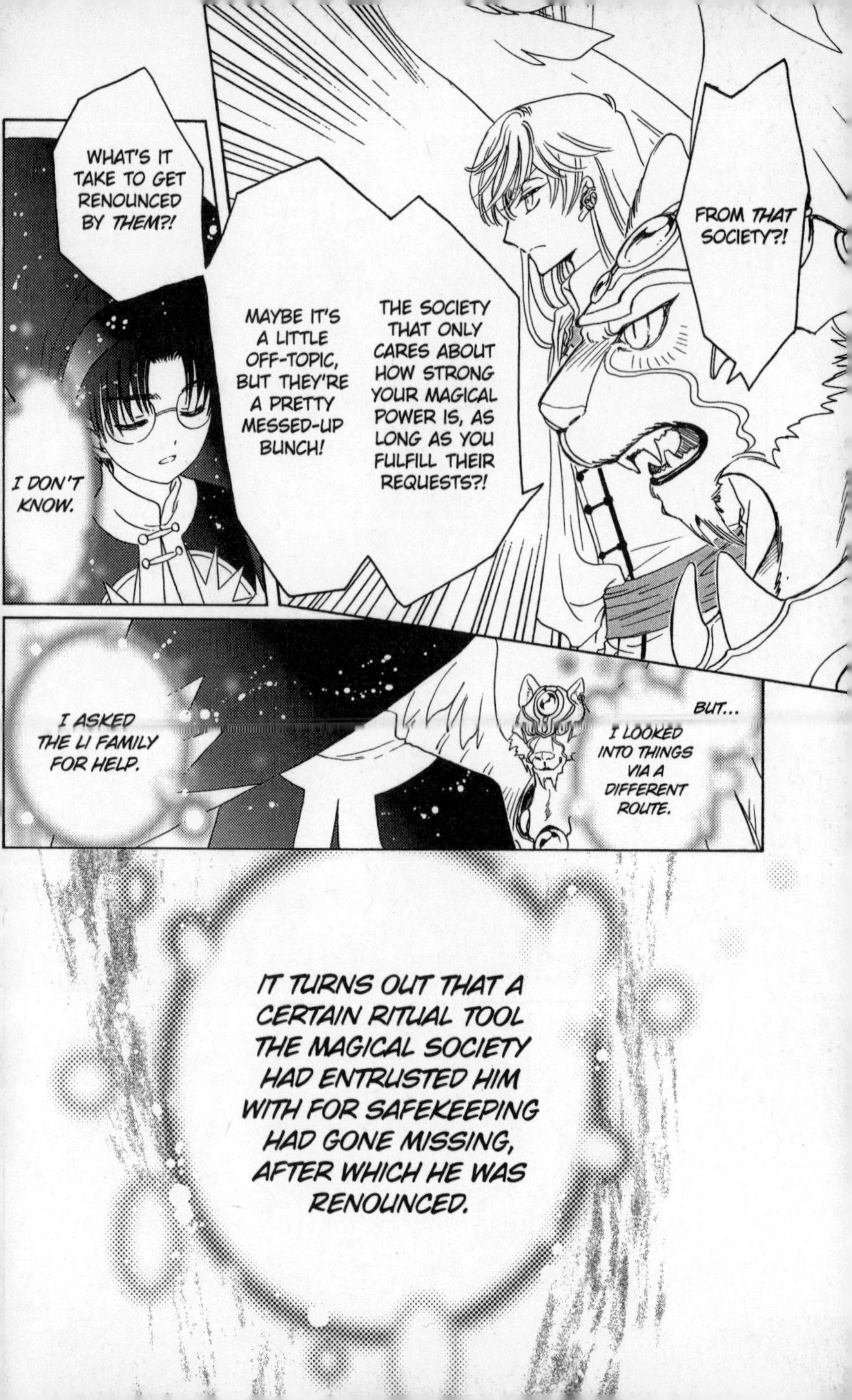
FROM THAT SOCIETY?!
THE SOCIETY THAT ONLY CARES ABOUT HOW STRONG YOUR MAGICAL POWER IS, AS LONG AS YOU FULFILL THEIR REQUESTS?!
MAYBE IT'S A LITTLE OFF-TOPIC, BUT THEY'RE A PRETTY MESSED-UP BUNCH!
WHAT'S IT TAKE TO GET RENOUNCED BY THEM?!
I DON'T KNOW.
BUT...
I LOOKED INTO THINGS VIA A DIFFERENT ROUTE.
I ASKED THE LI FAMILY FOR HELP.
IT TURNS OUT THAT A CERTAIN RITUAL TOOL THE MAGICAL SOCIETY HAD ENTRUSTED HIM WITH FOR SAFEKEEPING HAD GONE MISSING, AFTER WHICH HE WAS RENOUNCED.

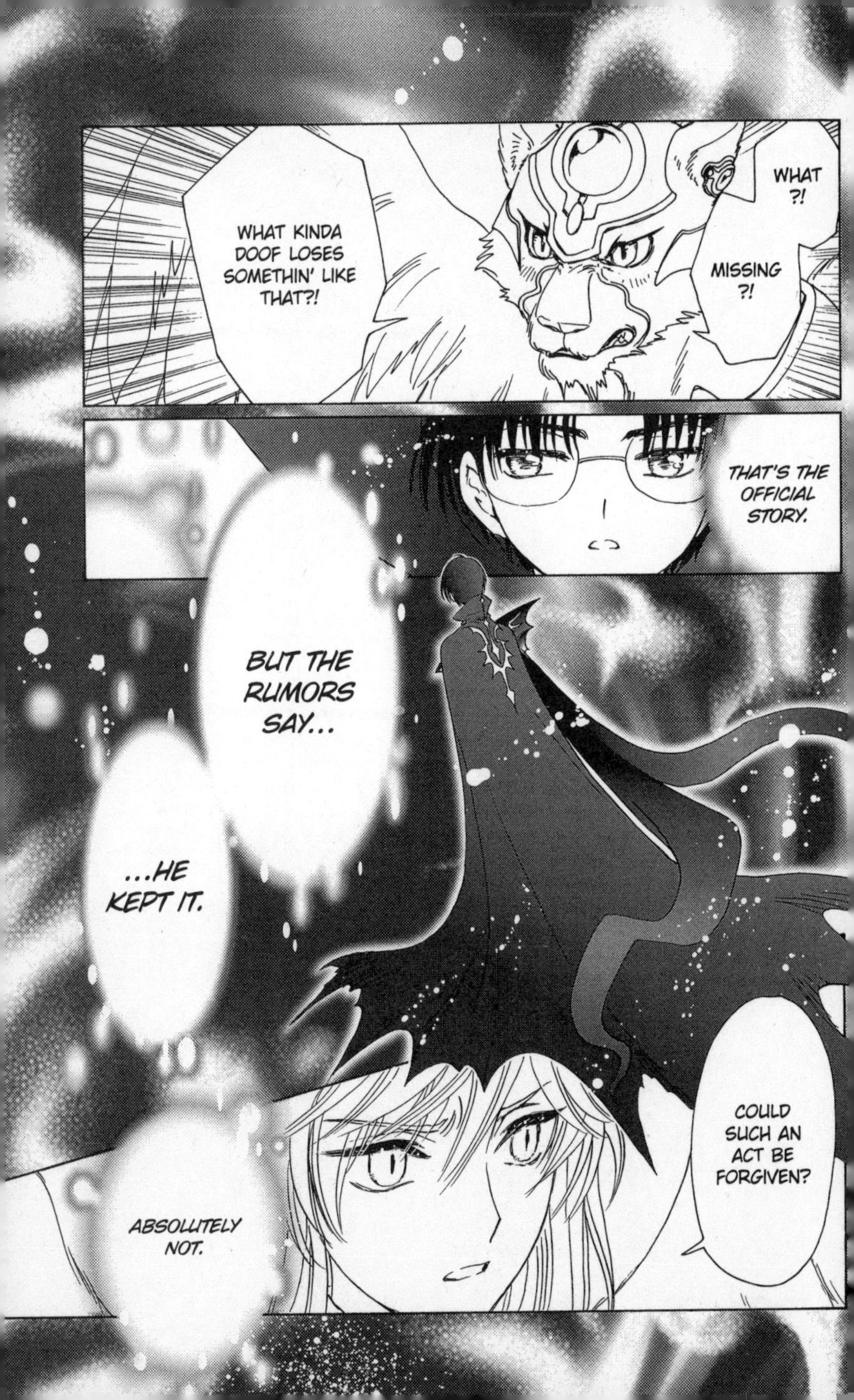
WHAT ?!
MISSING ?!
WHAT KINDA DOOF LOSES SOMETHIN' LIKE THAT?!
THAT'S THE OFFICIAL STORY.
BUT THE RUMORS SAY...
...HE KEPT IT.
COULD SUCH AN ACT BE FORGIVEN?
ABSOLUTELY NOT.

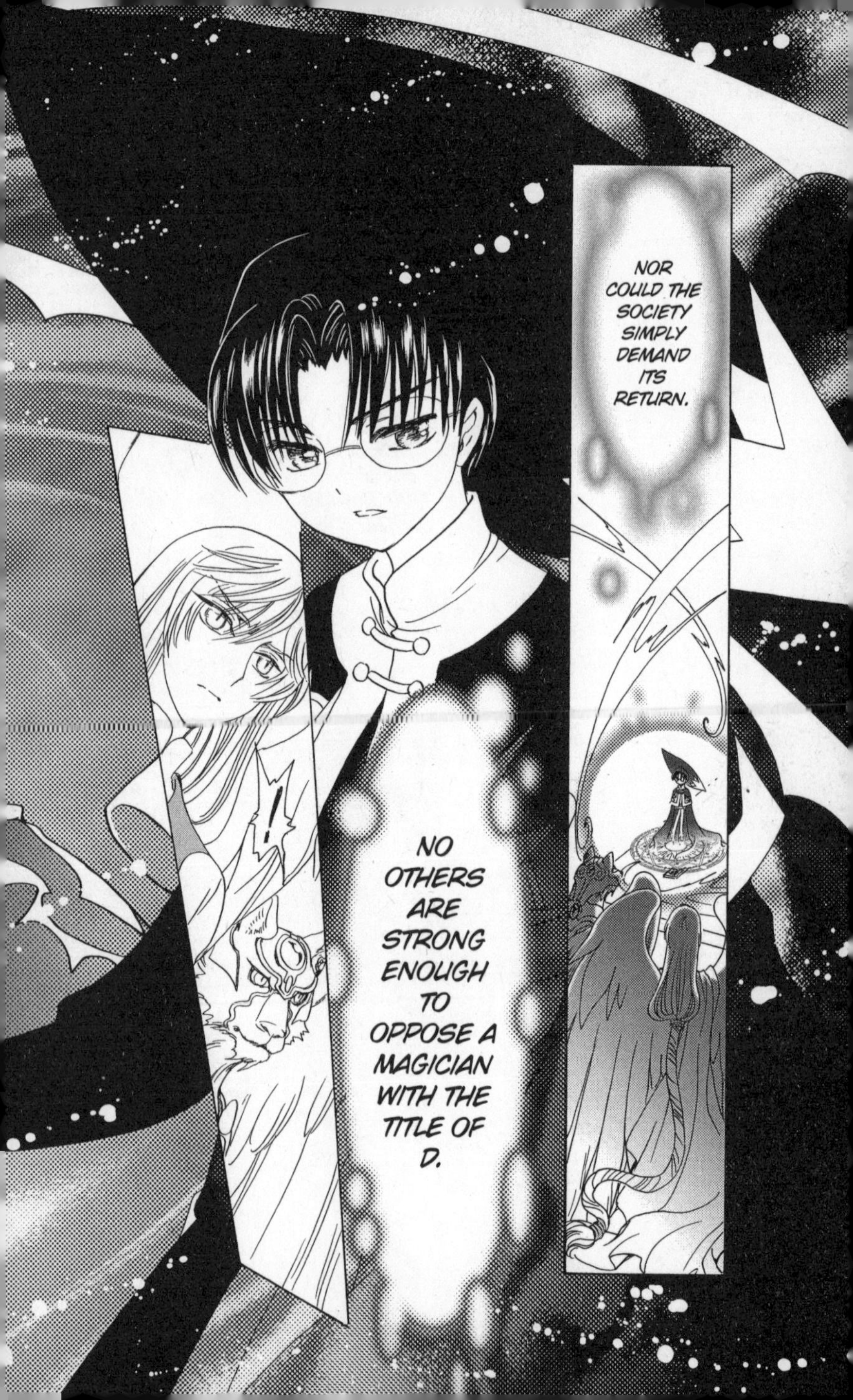
NOR COULD THE SOCIETY SIMPLY DEMAND ITS RETURN.
NO OTHERS ARE STRONG ENOUGH TO OPPOSE A MAGICIAN WITH THE TITLE OF D.
!

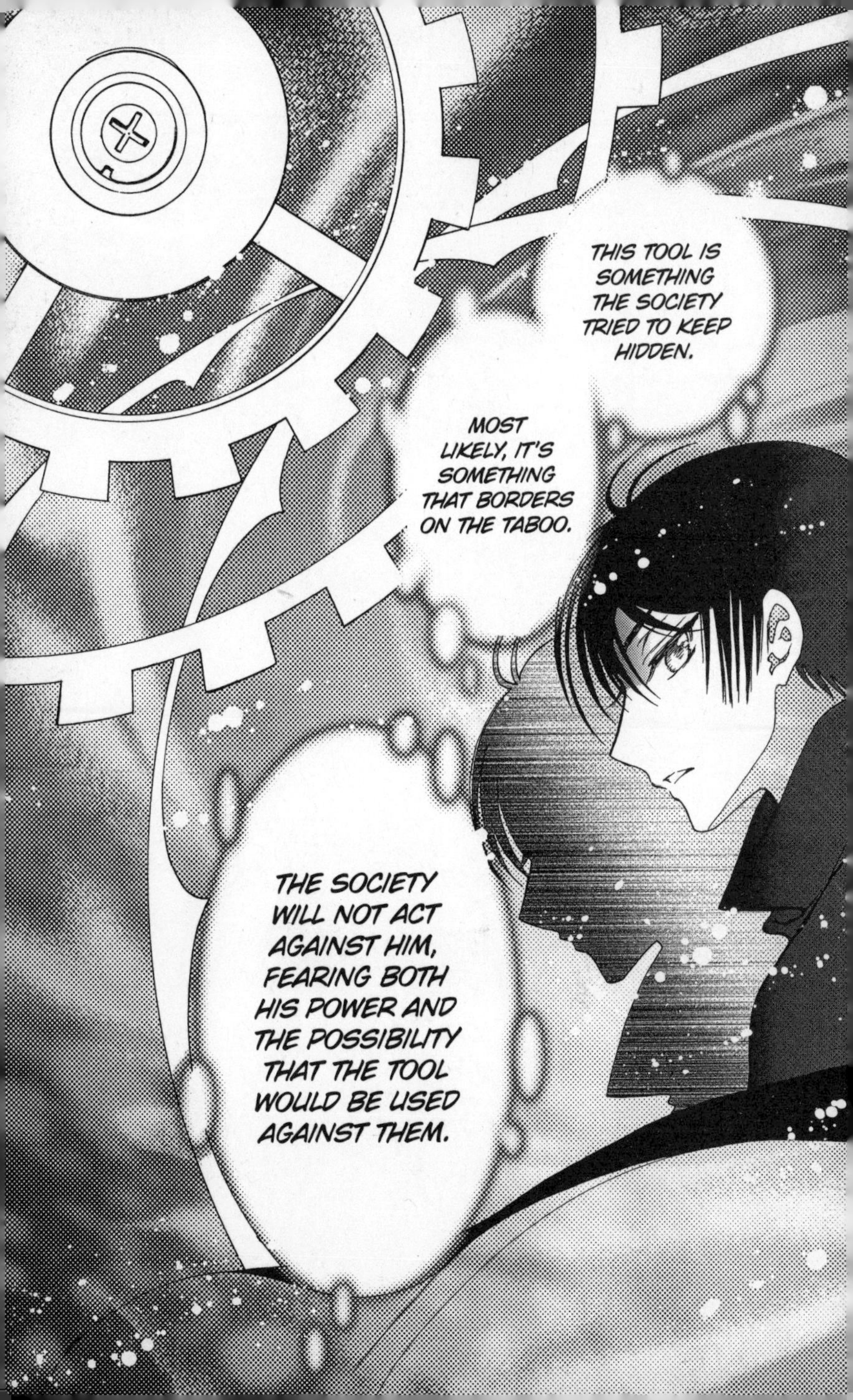
THIS TOOL IS SOMETHING THE SOCIETY TRIED TO KEEP HIDDEN.
MOST LIKELY, IT'S SOMETHING THAT BORDERS ON THE TABOO.
THE SOCIETY WILL NOT ACT AGAINST HIM, FEARING BOTH HIS POWER AND THE POSSIBILITY THAT THE TOOL WOULD BE USED AGAINST THEM.

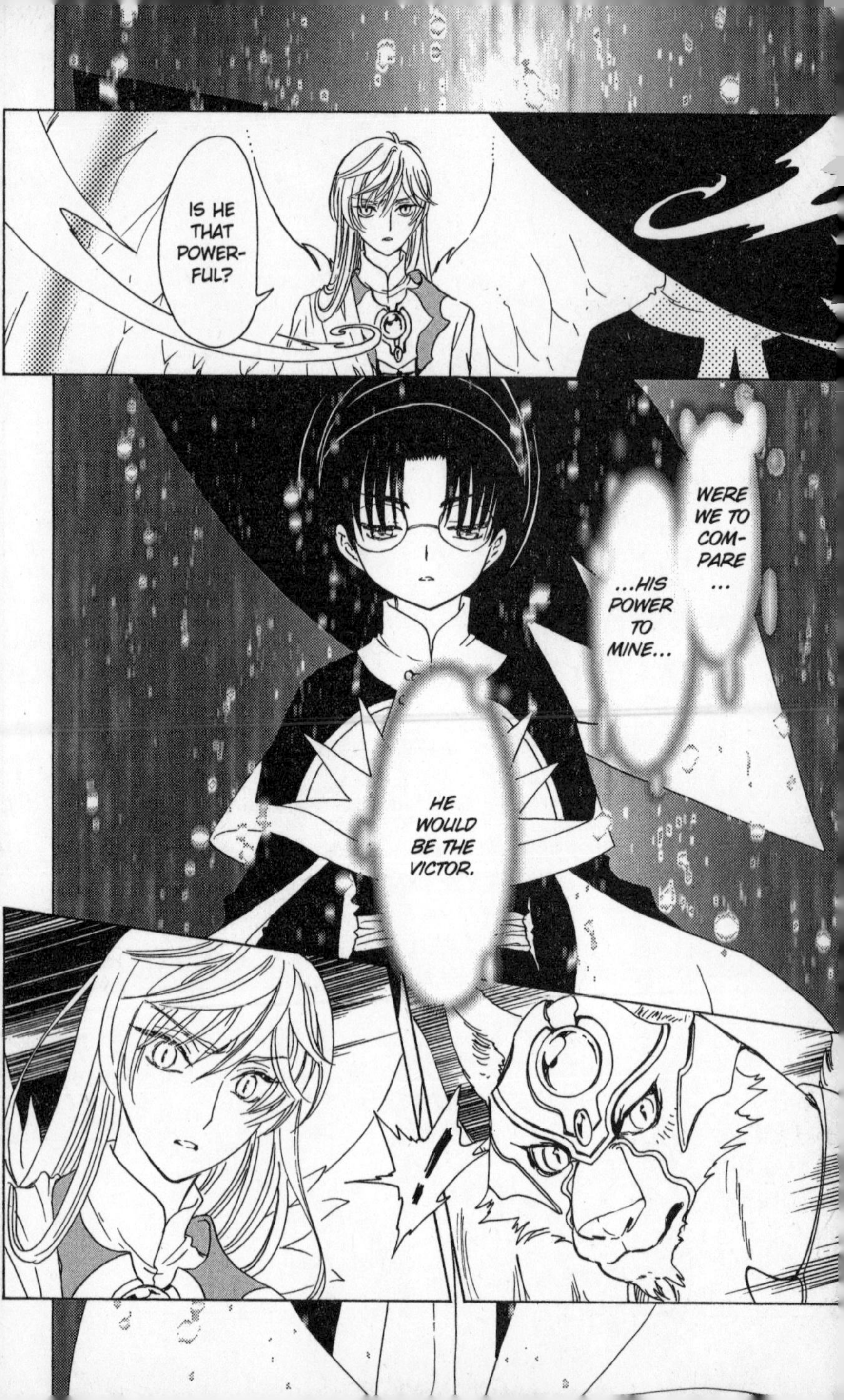
IS HE THAT POWER-FUL?
WERE WE TO COM-PARE ...
...HIS POWER TO MINE...
HE WOULD BE THE VICTOR.

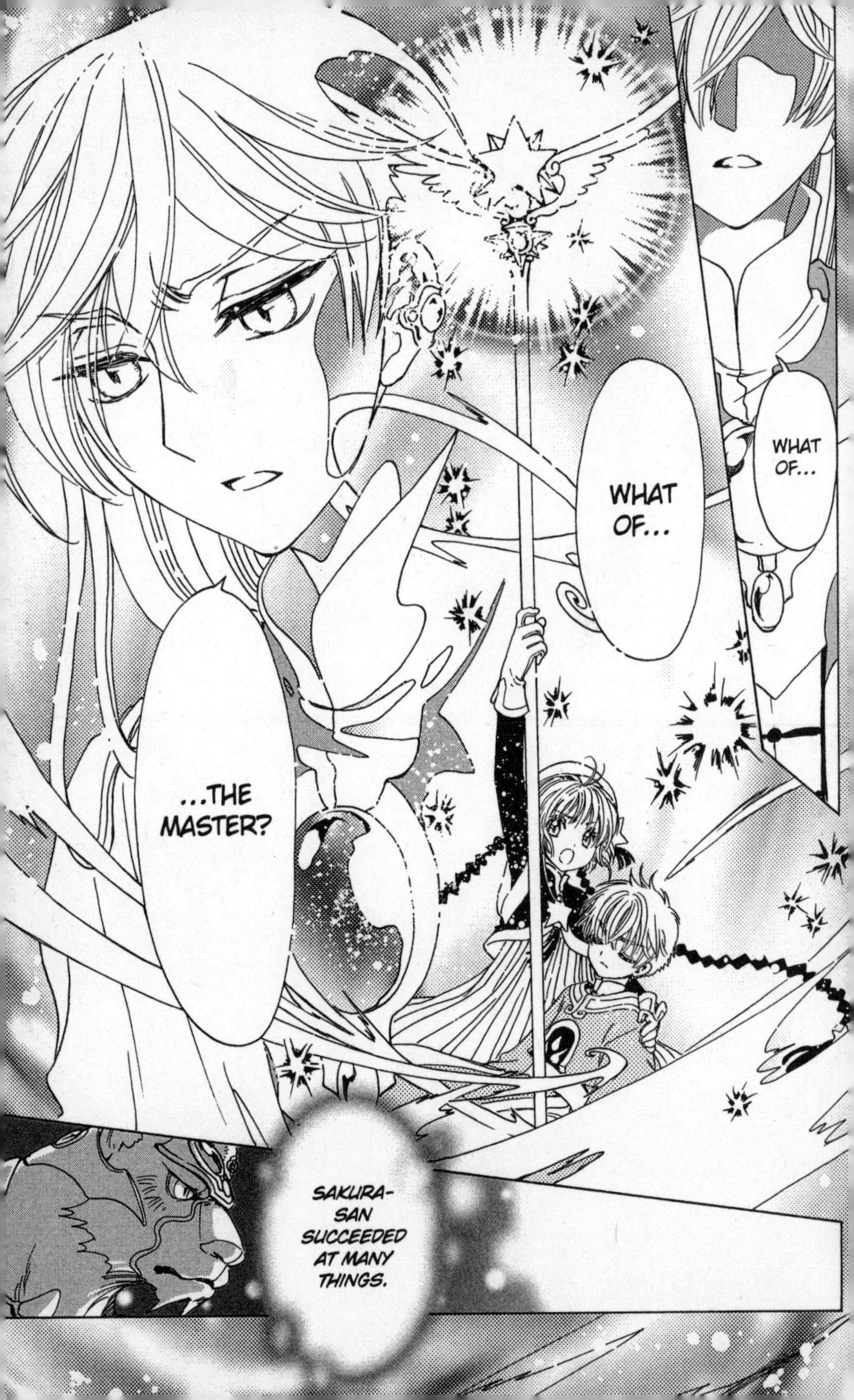
WHAT OF...
WHAT OF...
...THE MASTER?
SAKURA-SAN SUCCEEDED AT MANY THINGS.

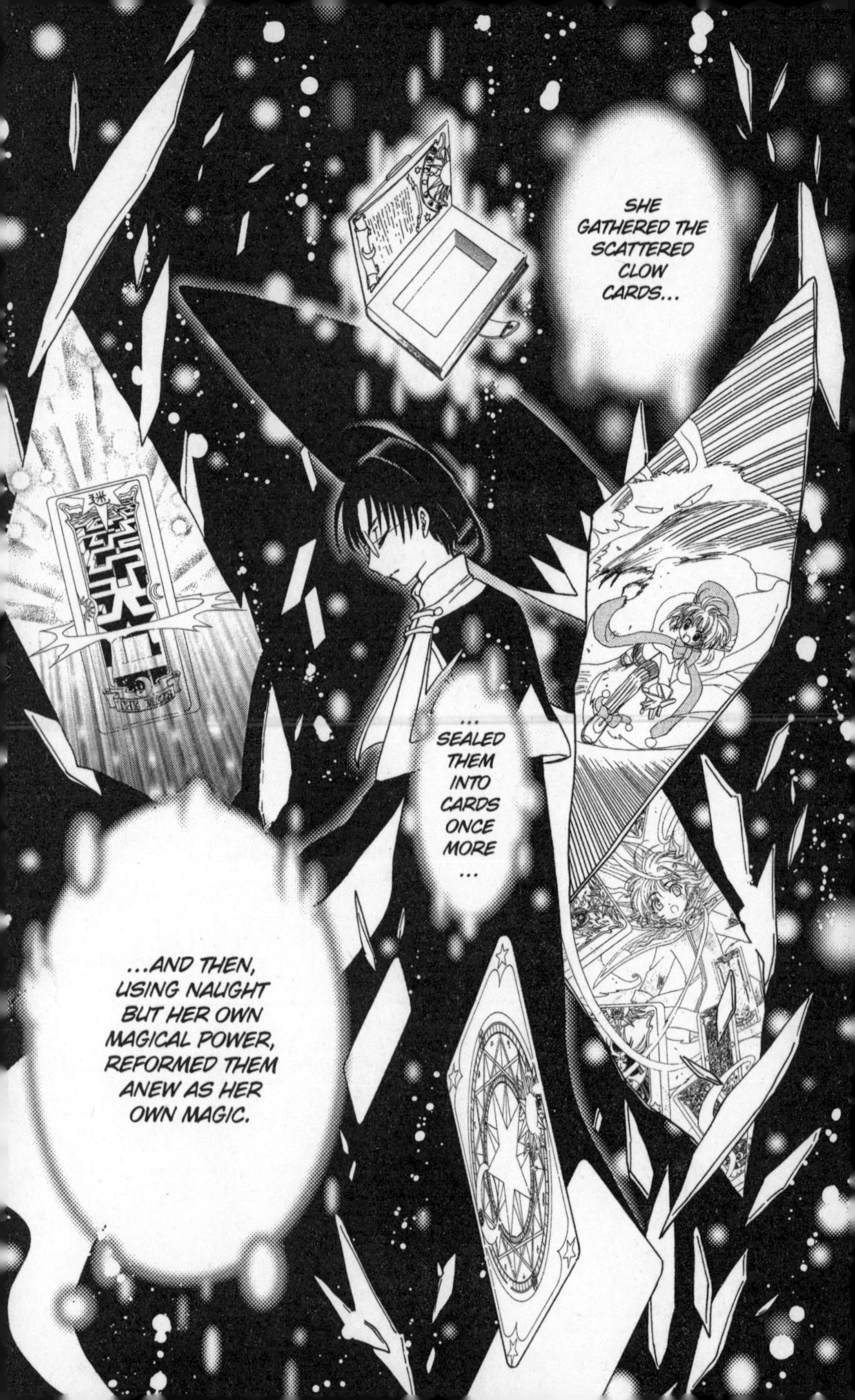
SHE GATHERED THE SCATTERED CLOW CARDS...
...SEALED THEM INTO CARDS ONCE MORE...
...AND THEN, USING NAUGHT BUT HER OWN MAGICAL POWER, REFORMED THEM ANEW AS HER OWN MAGIC.

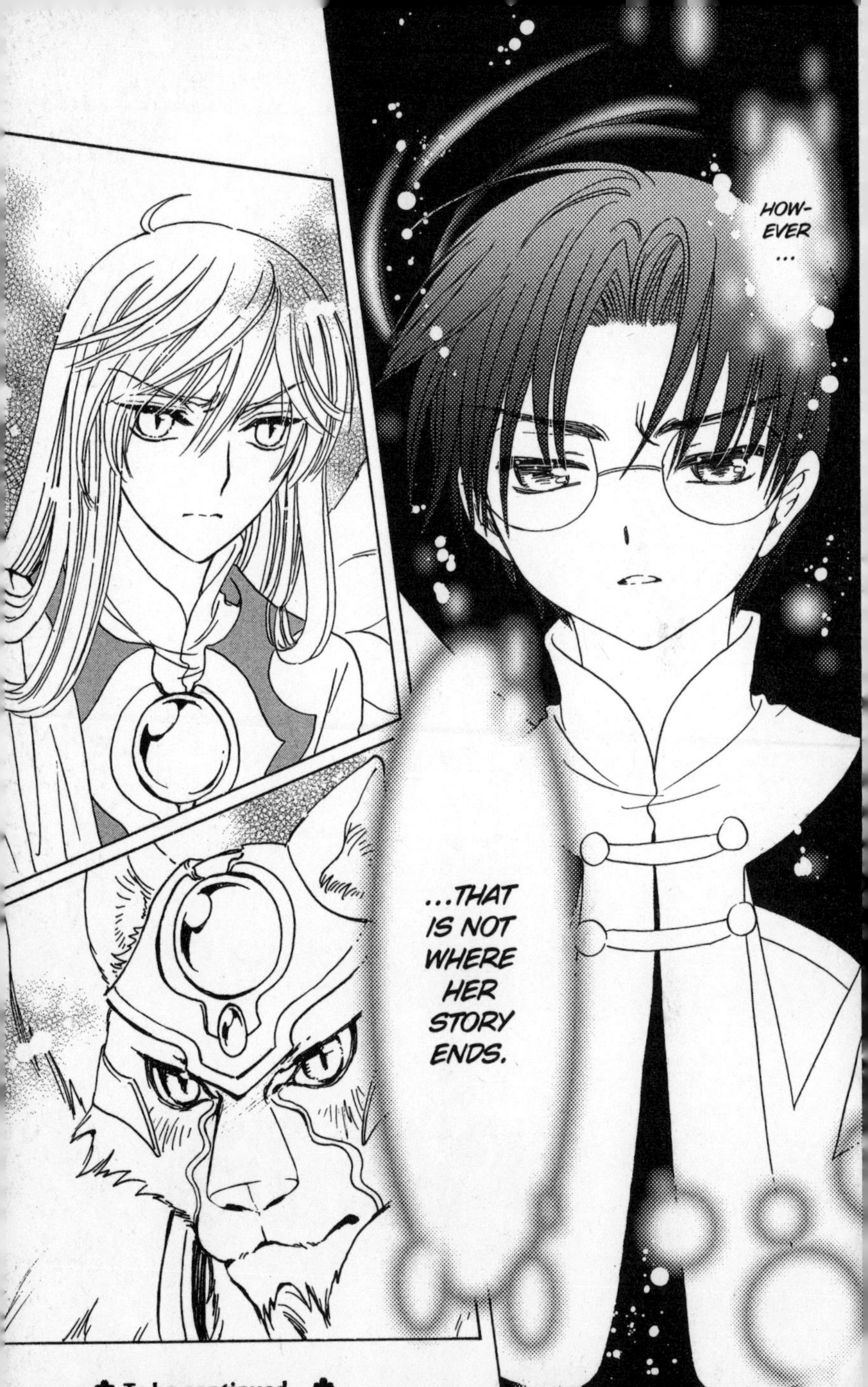
HOW-EVER ...
...THAT IS NOT WHERE HER STORY ENDS.

✿ To be continued... ✿

Cardcaptor Sakura

CLEAR CARD

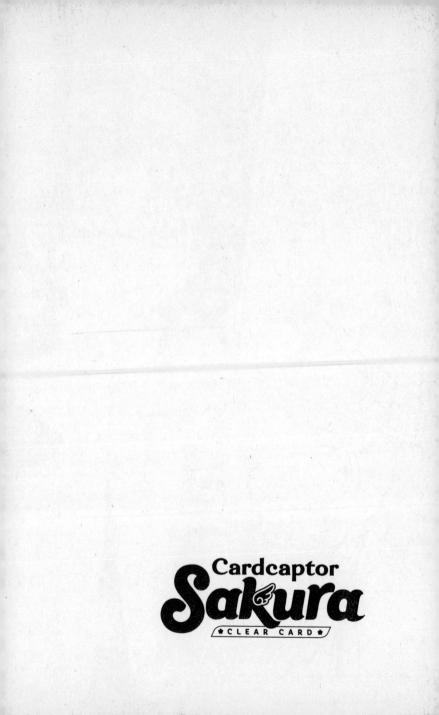

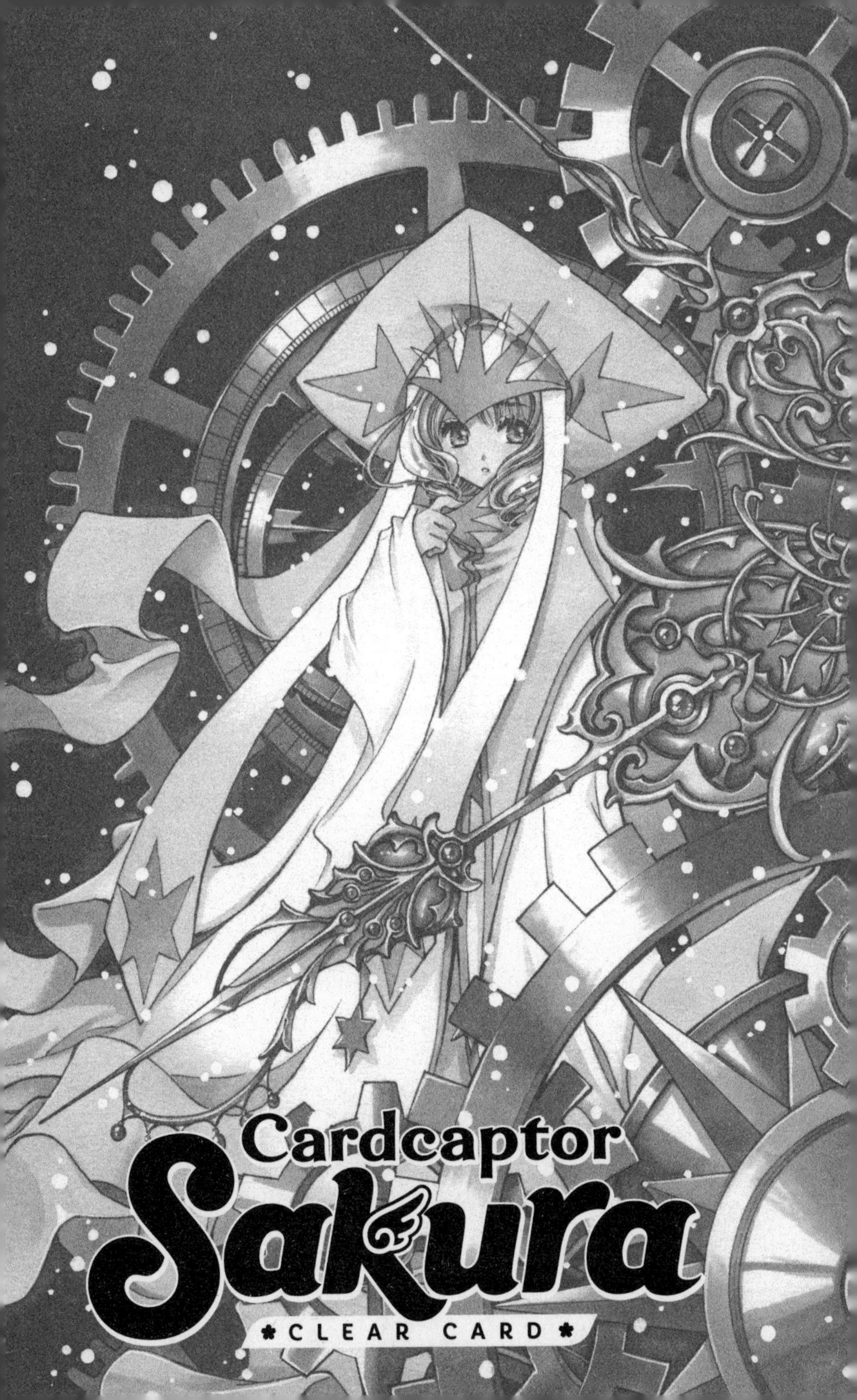
Cardcaptor
Sakura
CLEAR CARD

Cardcaptor Sakura
CLEAR CARD

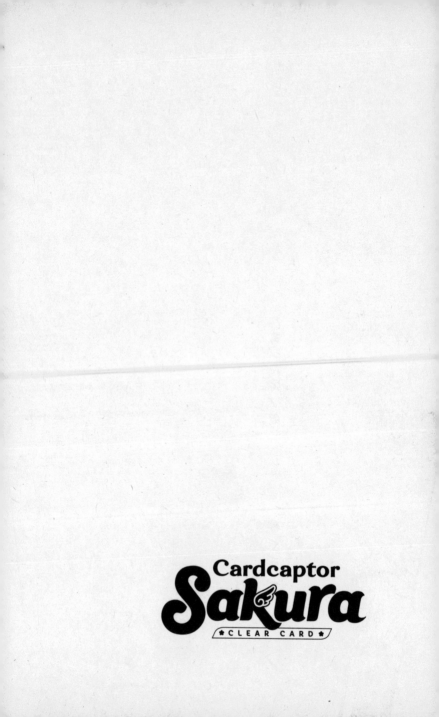

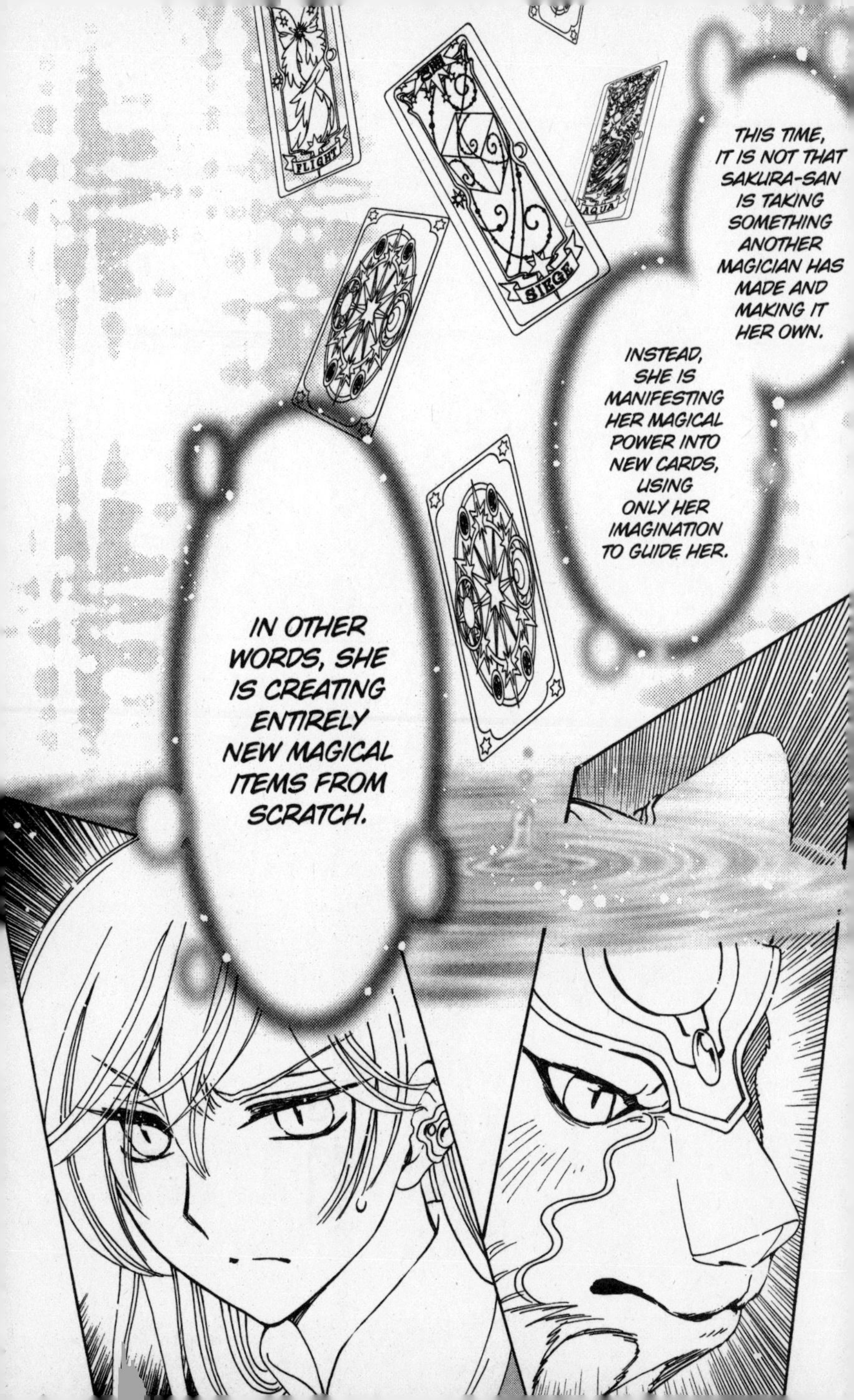
THIS TIME, IT IS NOT THAT SAKURA-SAN IS TAKING SOMETHING ANOTHER MAGICIAN HAS MADE AND MAKING IT HER OWN.
INSTEAD, SHE IS MANIFESTING HER MAGICAL POWER INTO NEW CARDS, USING ONLY HER IMAGINATION TO GUIDE HER.
IN OTHER WORDS, SHE IS CREATING ENTIRELY NEW MAGICAL ITEMS FROM SCRATCH.
FLIGHT
SIEGE
AQUA

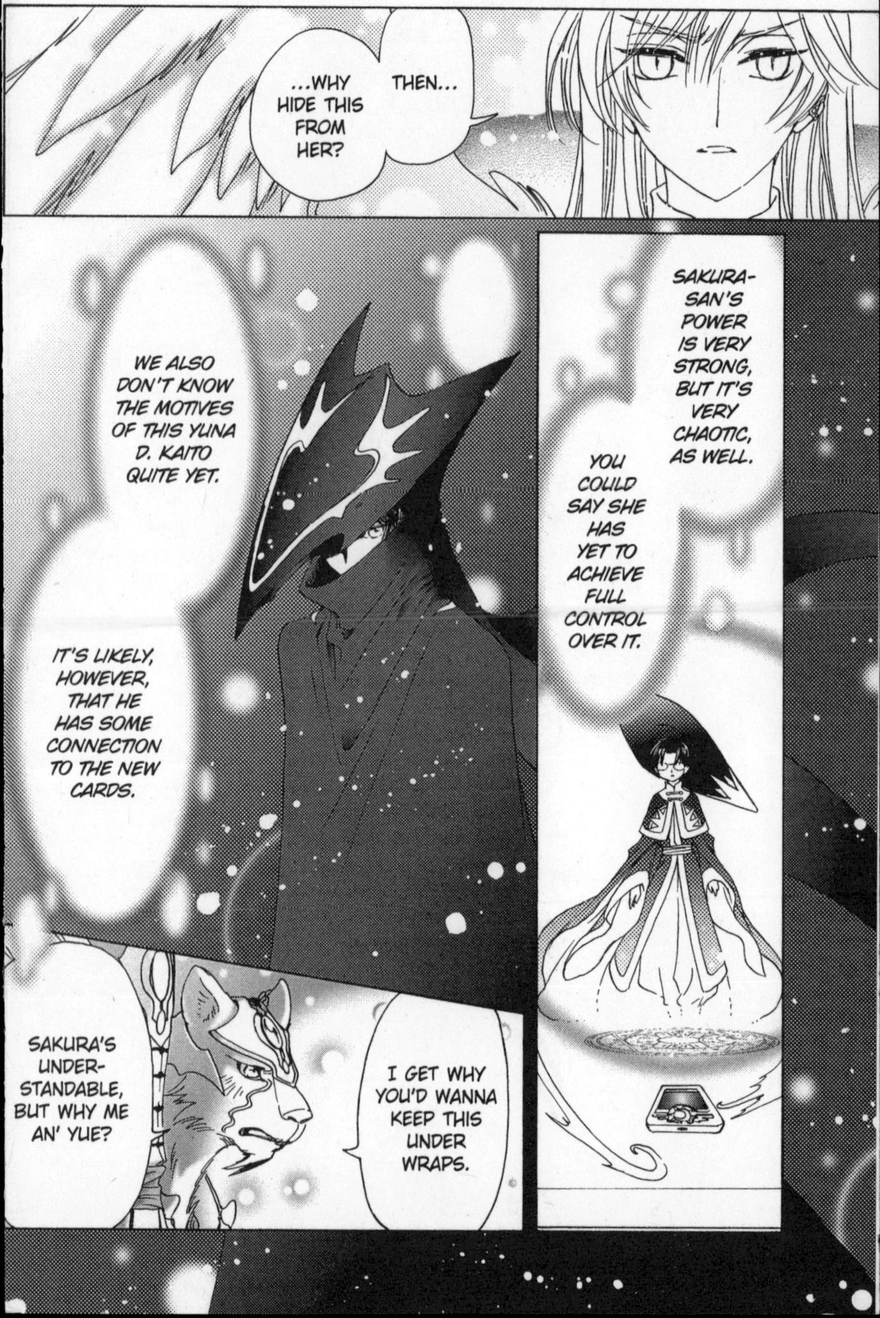
THEN... ...WHY HIDE THIS FROM HER?
SAKURA-SAN'S POWER IS VERY STRONG, BUT IT'S VERY CHAOTIC, AS WELL.
YOU COULD SAY SHE HAS YET TO ACHIEVE FULL CONTROL OVER IT.
WE ALSO DON'T KNOW THE MOTIVES OF THIS YUNA D. KAITO QUITE YET.
IT'S LIKELY, HOWEVER, THAT HE HAS SOME CONNECTION TO THE NEW CARDS.
I GET WHY YOU'D WANNA KEEP THIS UNDER WRAPS.
SAKURA'S UNDERSTANDABLE, BUT WHY ME AN' YUE?

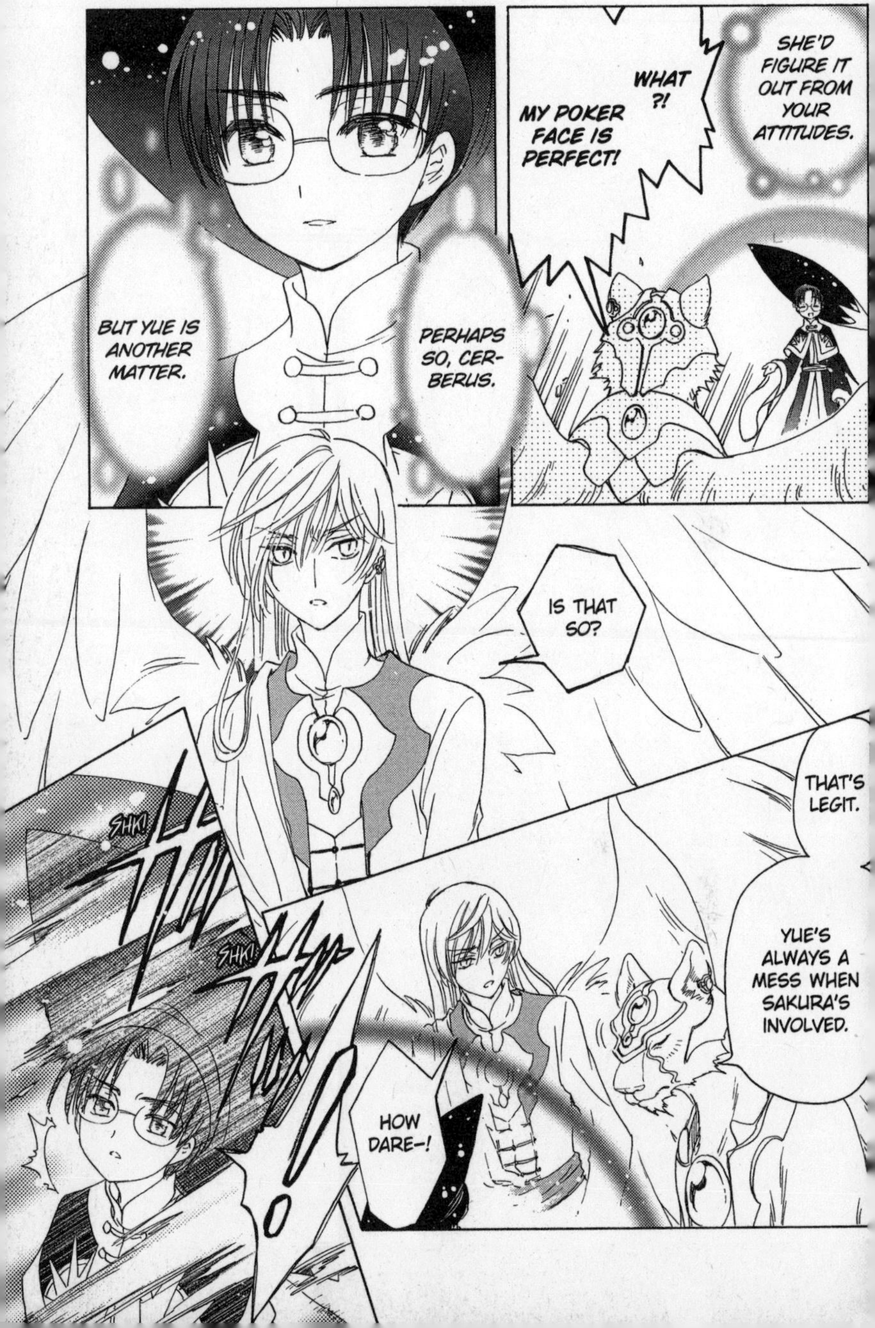
SHE'D FIGURE IT OUT FROM YOUR ATTITUDES.
WHAT ?!
MY POKER FACE IS PERFECT!
PERHAPS SO, CER-BERUS.
BUT YUE IS ANOTHER MATTER.
IS THAT SO?
THAT'S LEGIT.
YUE'S ALWAYS A MESS WHEN SAKURA'S INVOLVED.
SHK!
SHK!
HOW DARE-!

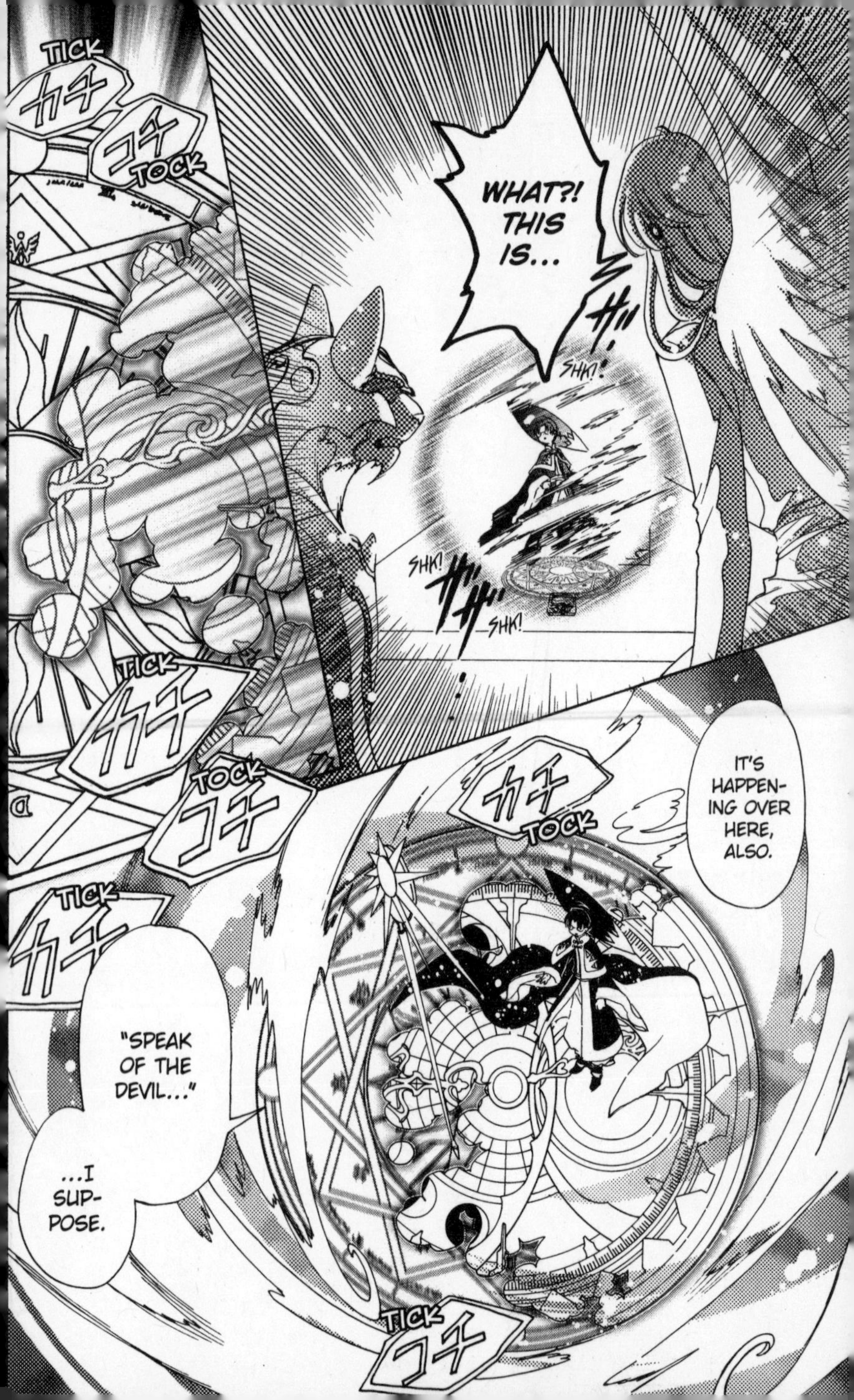
WHAT?! THIS IS...
ザッ SHK!
ザザ SHK! SHK!
TICK カチ
コチ TOCK
TICK カチ
TOCK コチ
カチ TOCK
IT'S HAPPENING OVER HERE, ALSO.
TICK カチ
"SPEAK OF THE DEVIL..."
...I SUPPOSE.
TICK コチ

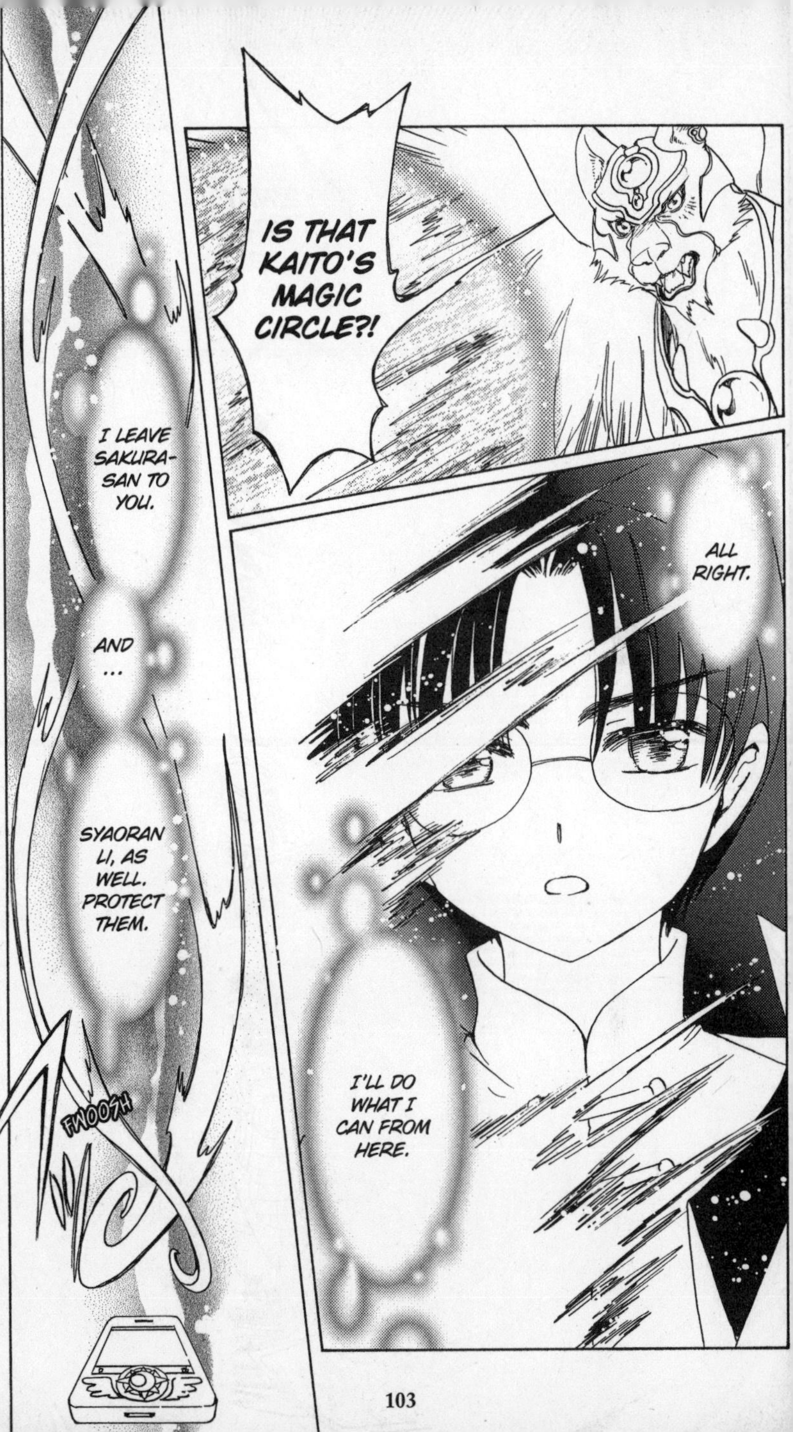
IS THAT KAITO'S MAGIC CIRCLE?!
ALL RIGHT.
I'LL DO WHAT I CAN FROM HERE.
I LEAVE SAKURA-SAN TO YOU.
AND ...
SYAORAN LI, AS WELL. PROTECT THEM.
FWOOSH

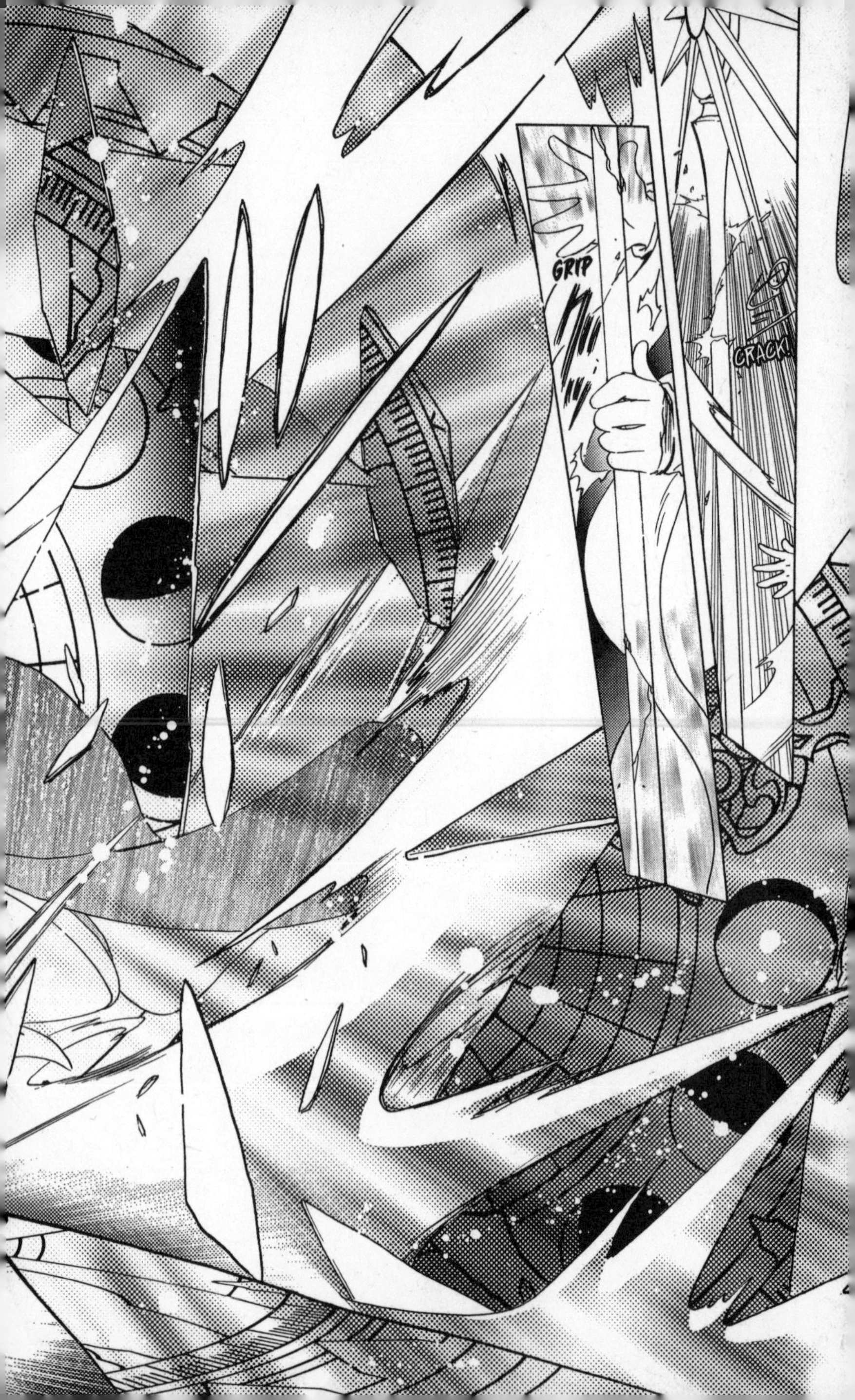
CRACK!
GRIP

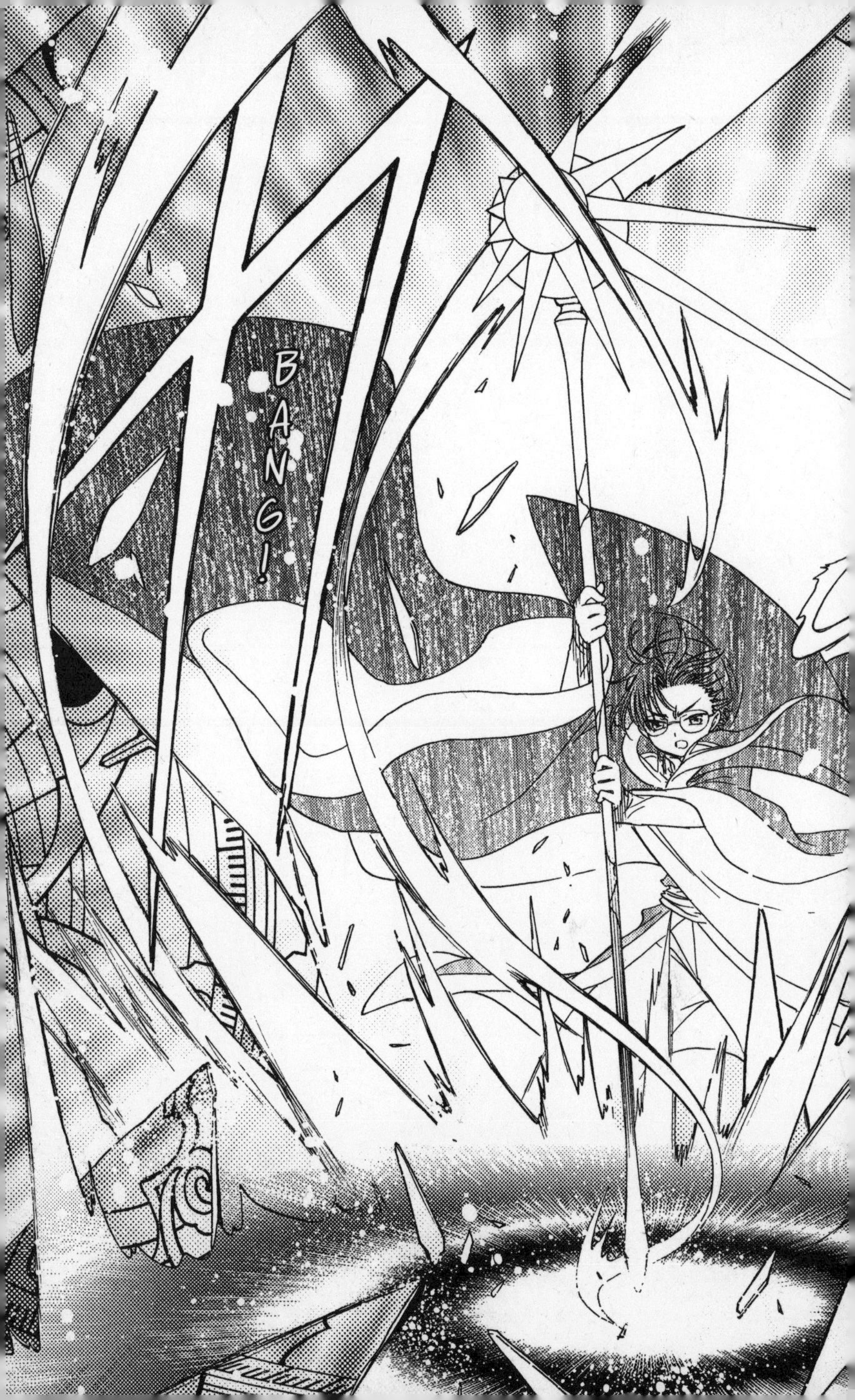
BANG!

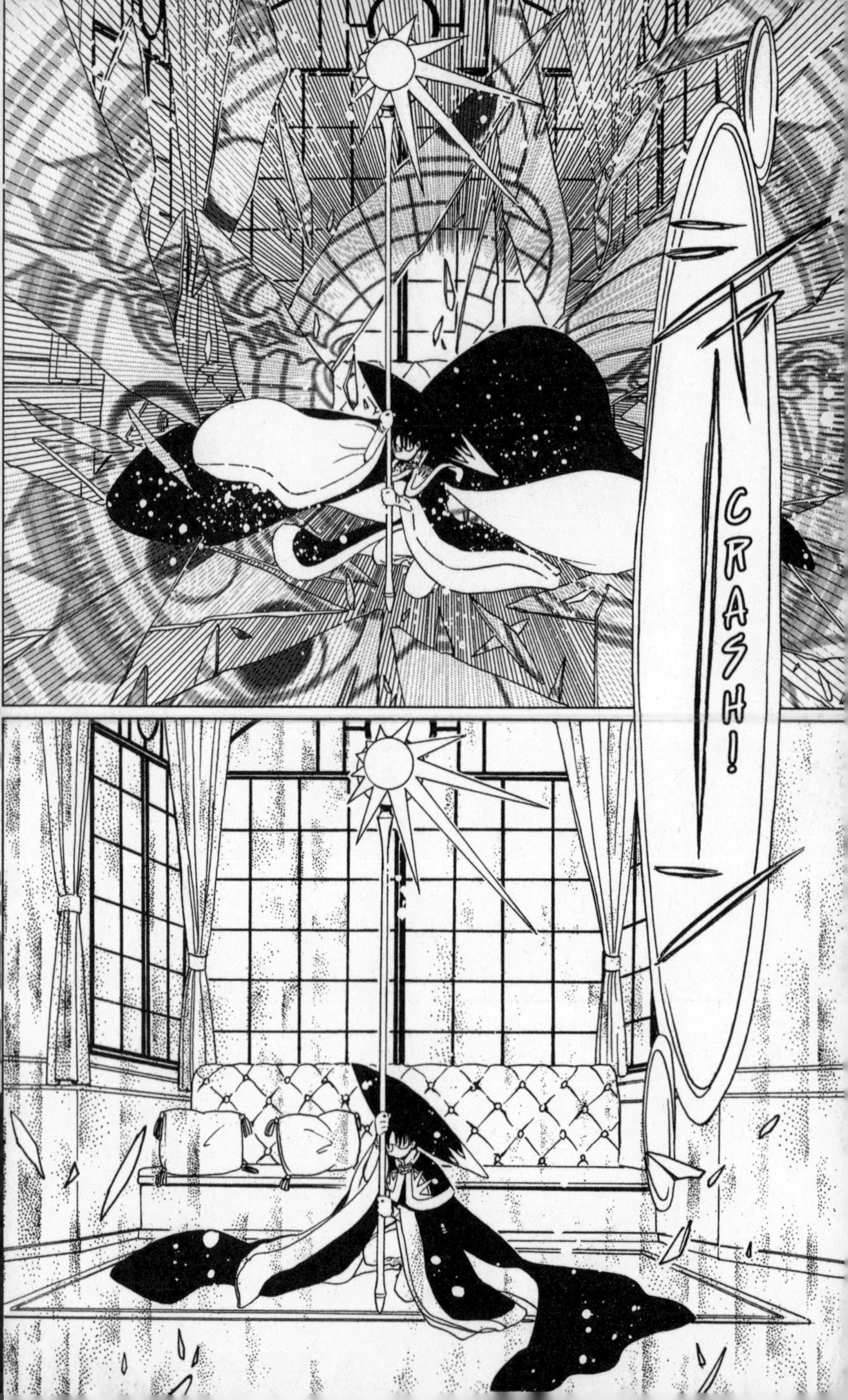
CRASH!

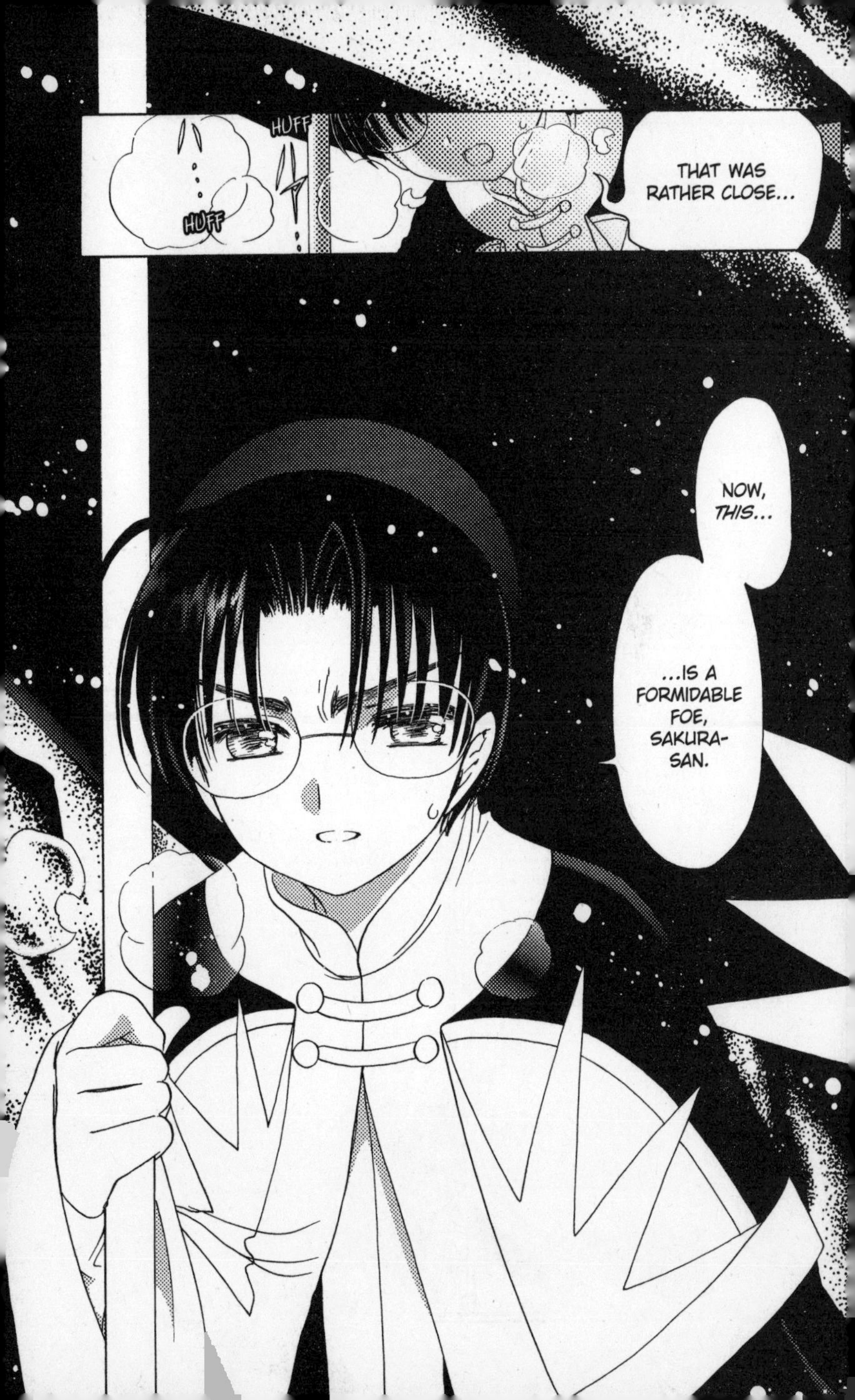
THAT WAS RATHER CLOSE...
HUFF
HUFF
NOW, THIS...
...IS A FORMIDABLE FOE, SAKURA-SAN.

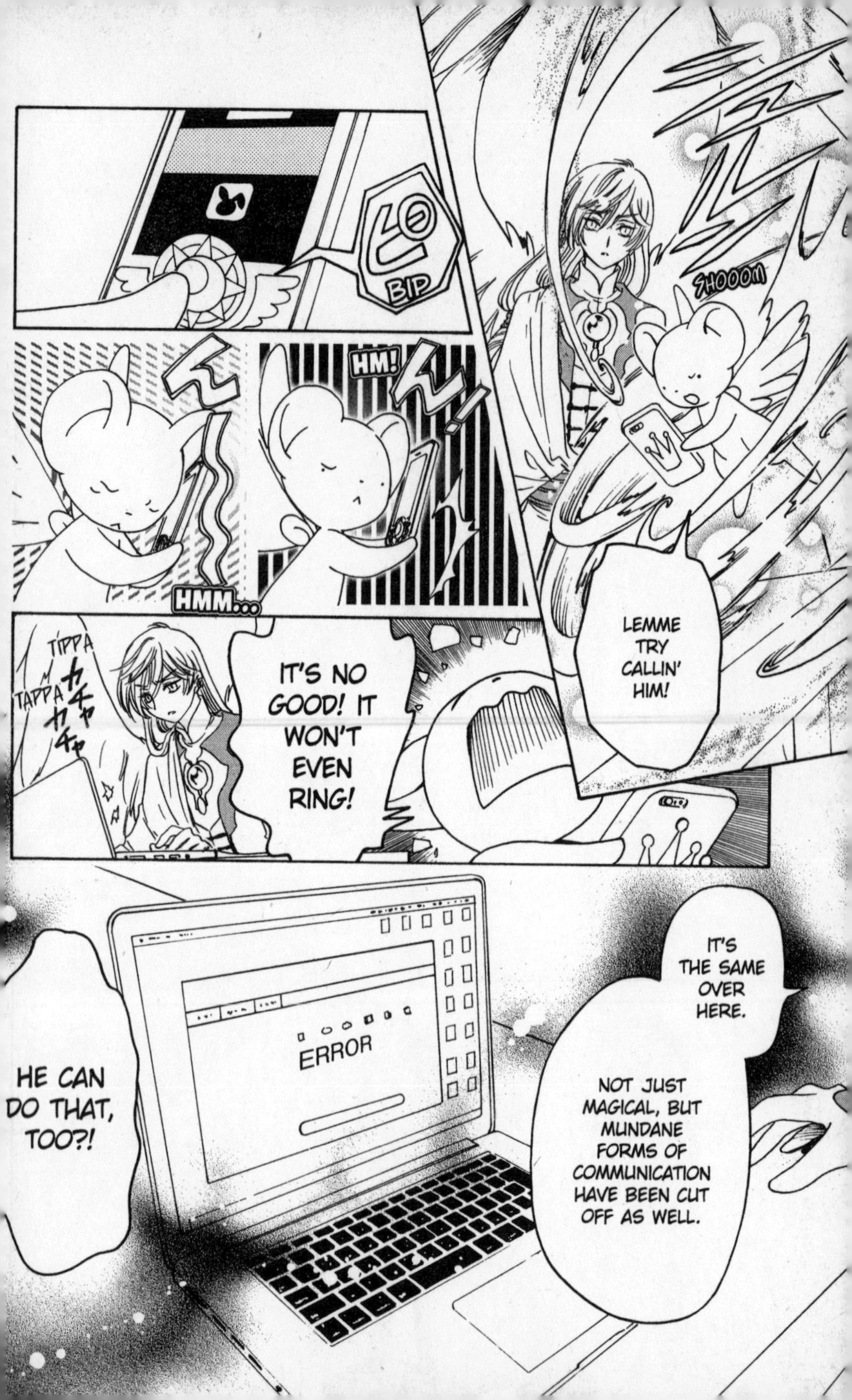
SHOOOM
LEMME TRY CALLIN' HIM!
BIP
HM!
ん!
ん
HMM...
TIPPA
TAPPA
カチャカチャ
IT'S NO GOOD! IT WON'T EVEN RING!
IT'S THE SAME OVER HERE.
NOT JUST MAGICAL, BUT MUNDANE FORMS OF COMMUNICATION HAVE BEEN CUT OFF AS WELL.
ERROR
HE CAN DO THAT, TOO?!

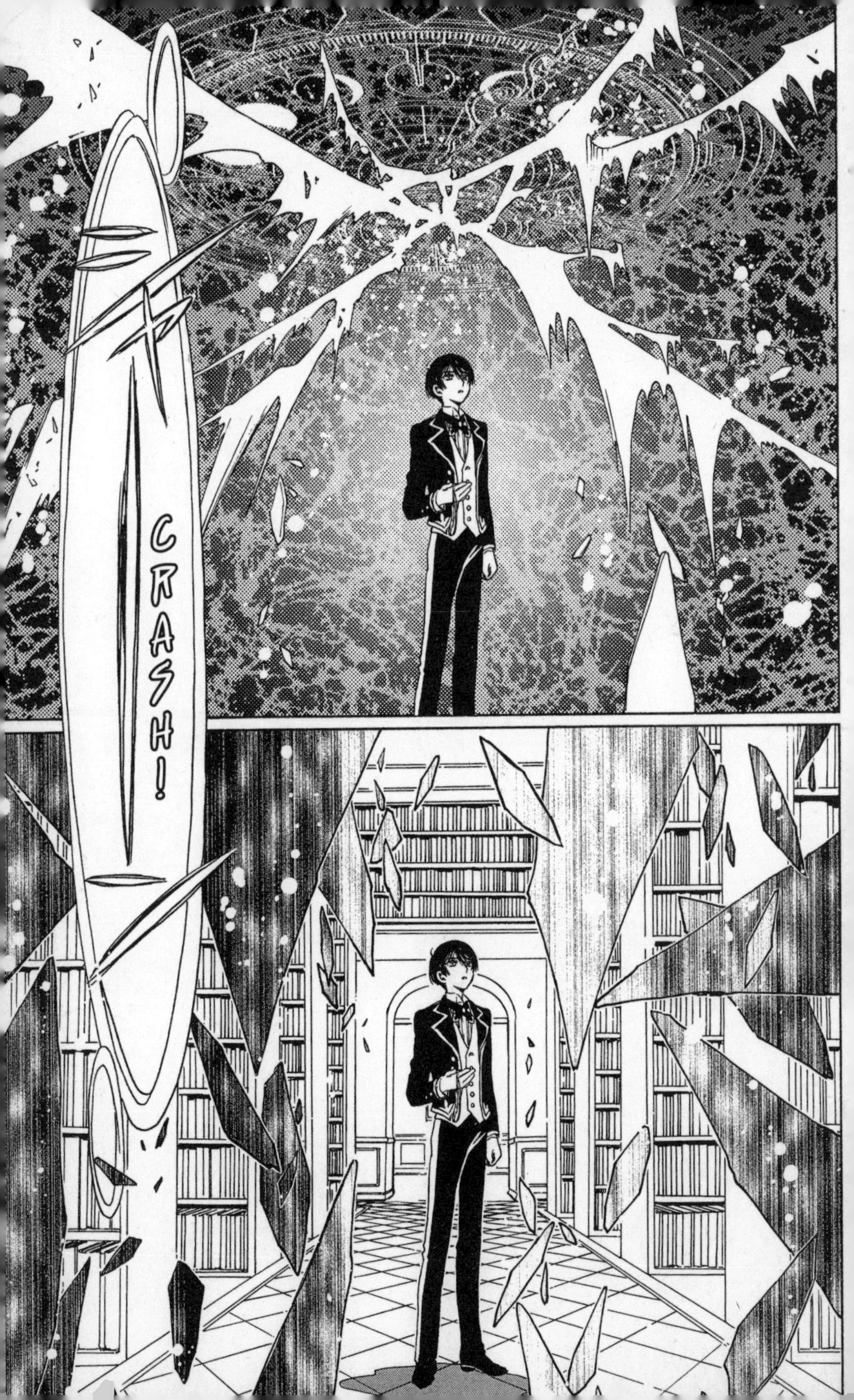
CRASH!

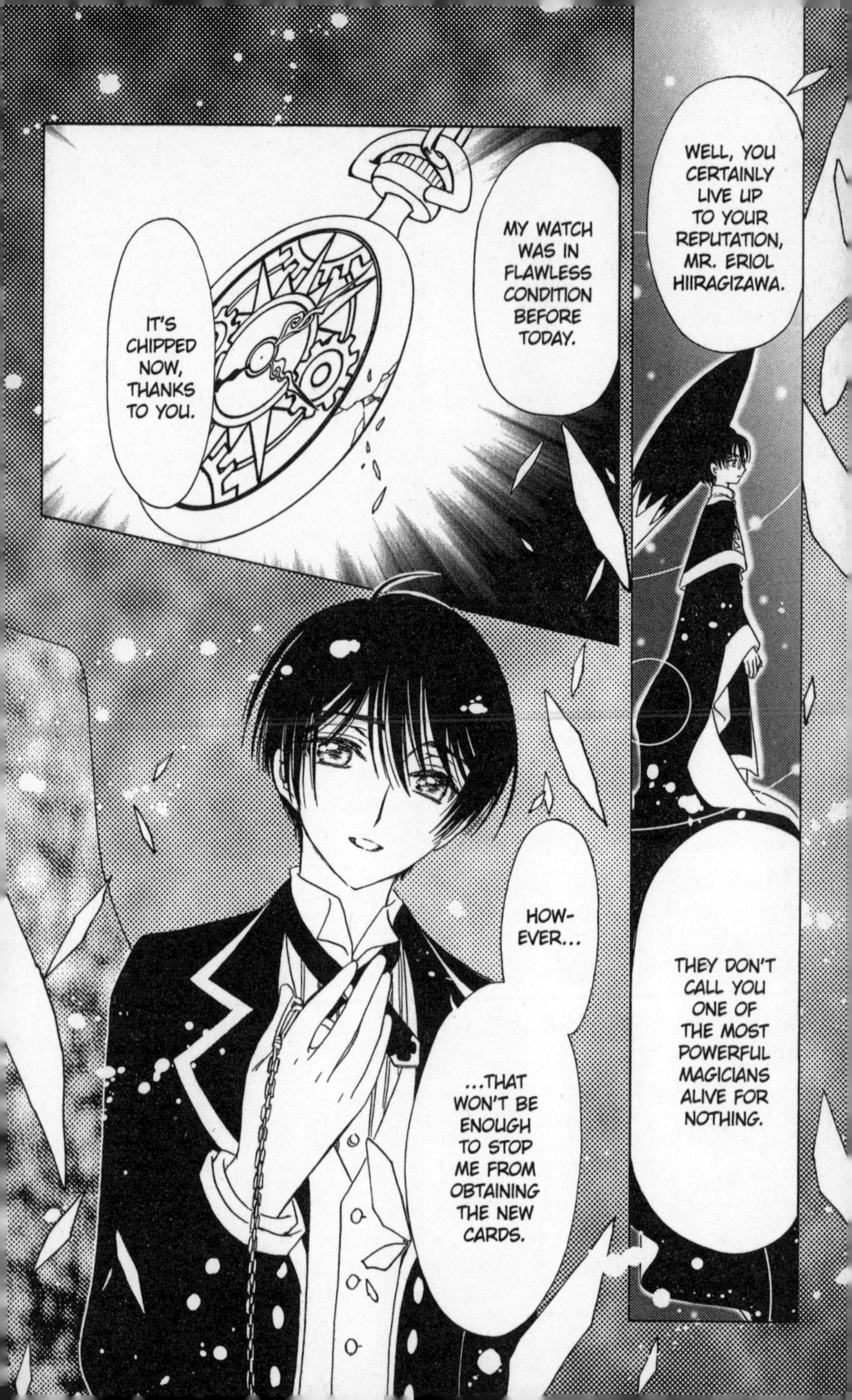
WELL, YOU CERTAINLY LIVE UP TO YOUR REPUTATION, MR. ERIOL HIIRAGIZAWA.
THEY DON'T CALL YOU ONE OF THE MOST POWERFUL MAGICIANS ALIVE FOR NOTHING.
MY WATCH WAS IN FLAWLESS CONDITION BEFORE TODAY.
IT'S CHIPPED NOW, THANKS TO YOU.
HOW-EVER...
...THAT WON'T BE ENOUGH TO STOP ME FROM OBTAINING THE NEW CARDS.

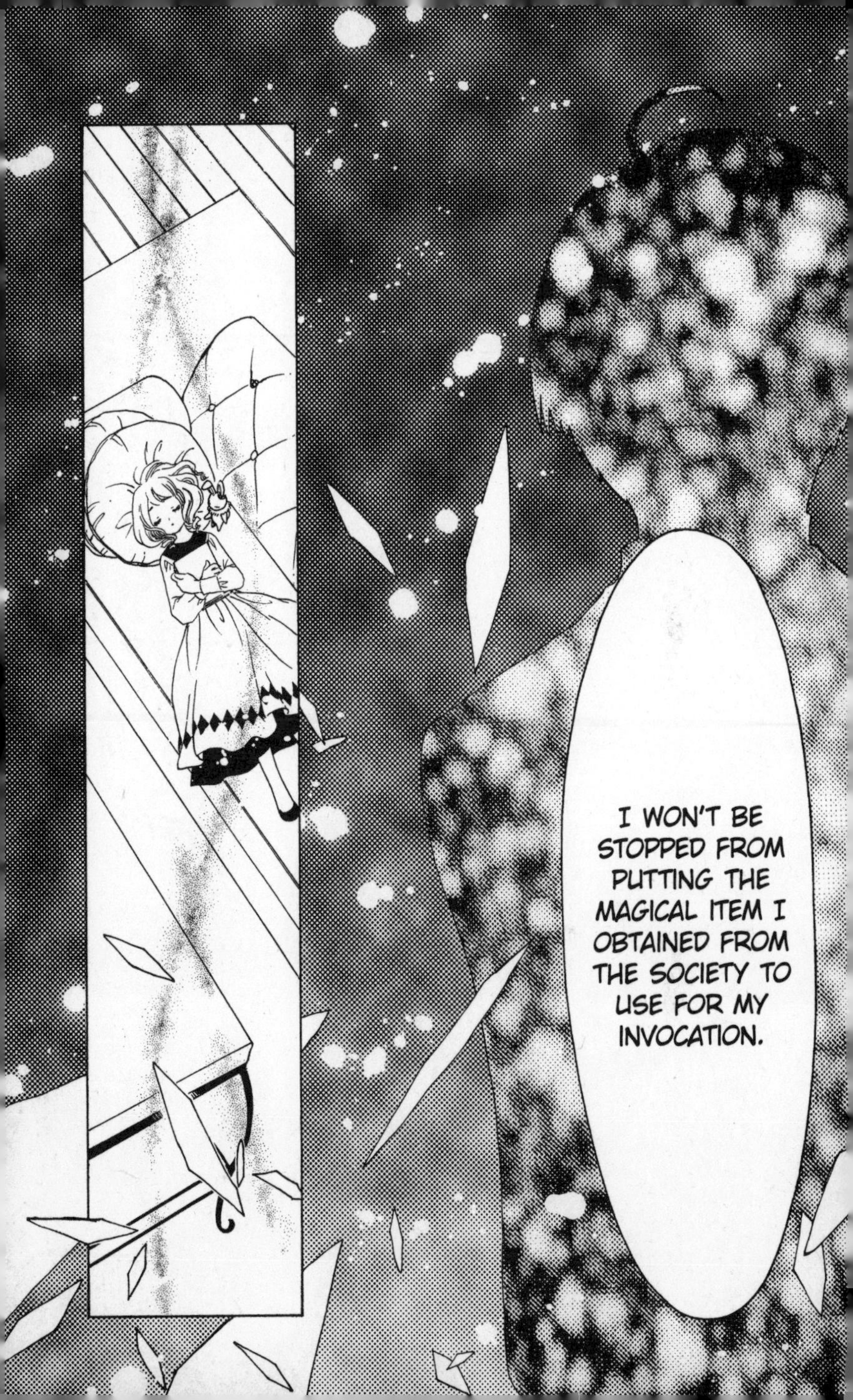
I WON'T BE STOPPED FROM PUTTING THE MAGICAL ITEM I OBTAINED FROM THE SOCIETY TO USE FOR MY INVOCATION.

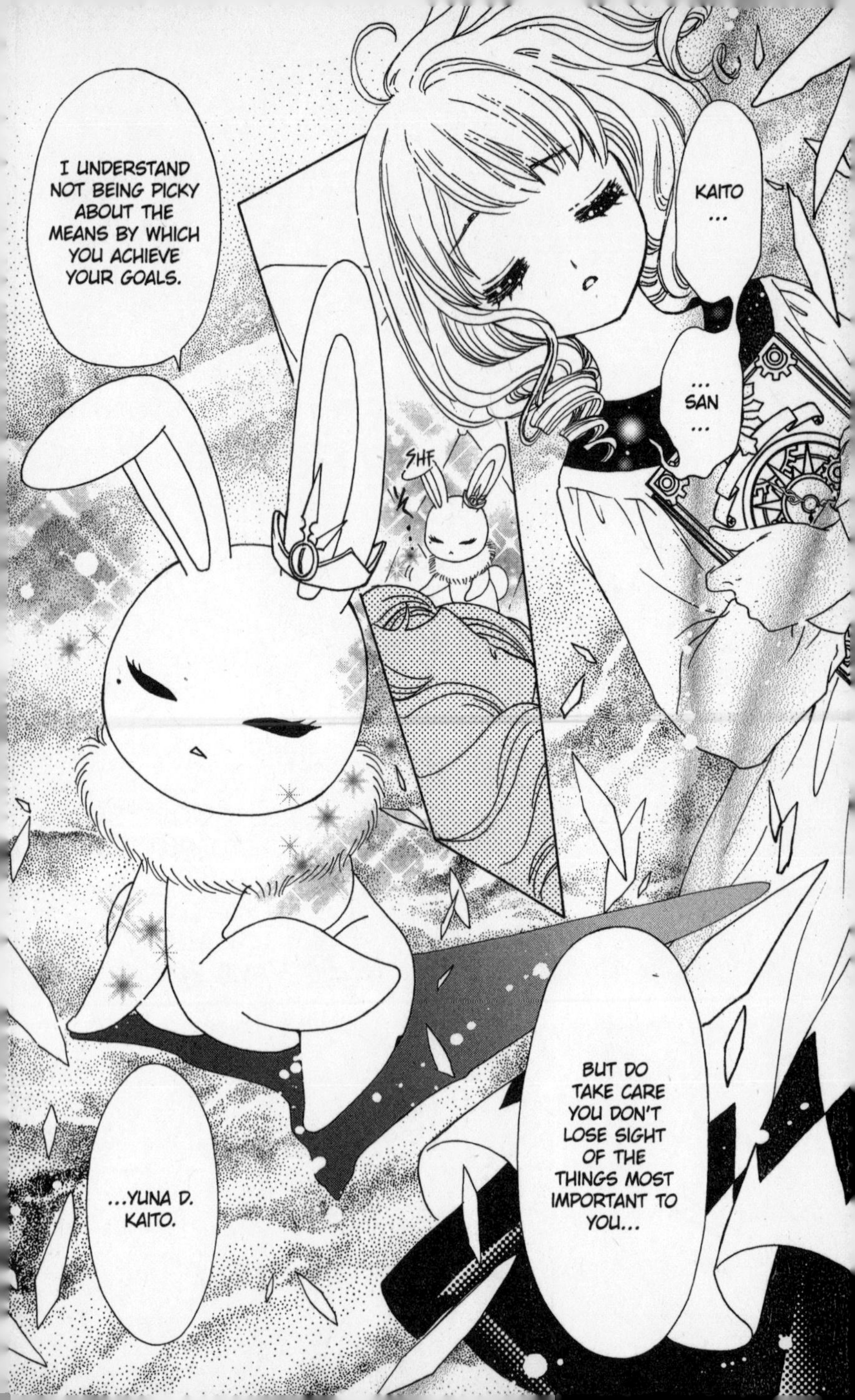
KAITO ...
... SAN ...
I UNDERSTAND NOT BEING PICKY ABOUT THE MEANS BY WHICH YOU ACHIEVE YOUR GOALS.
SHF
BUT DO TAKE CARE YOU DON'T LOSE SIGHT OF THE THINGS MOST IMPORTANT TO YOU...
...YUNA D. KAITO.

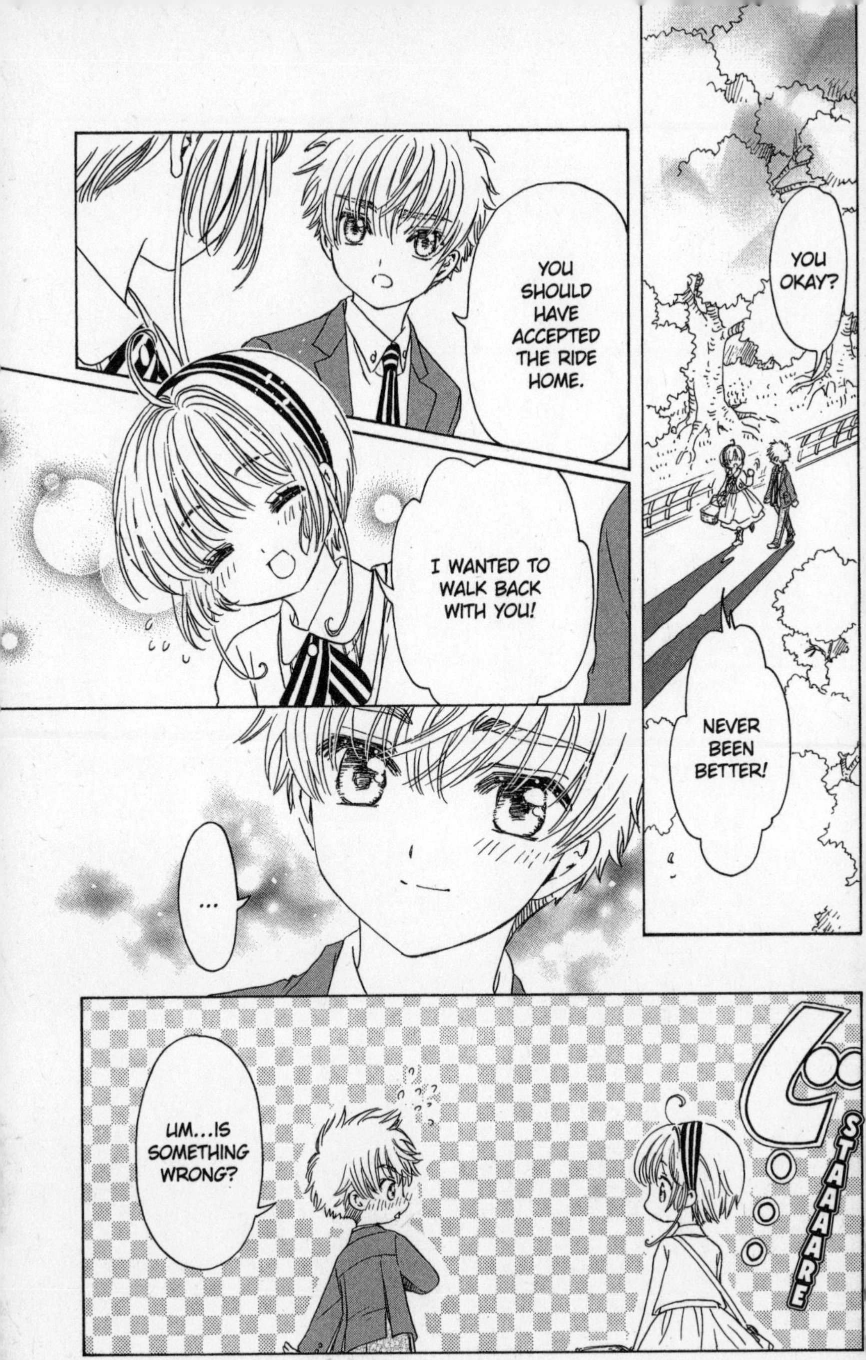
YOU OKAY?
NEVER BEEN BETTER!
YOU SHOULD HAVE ACCEPTED THE RIDE HOME.
I WANTED TO WALK BACK WITH YOU!
...
STAAAARE
UM...IS SOMETHING WRONG?

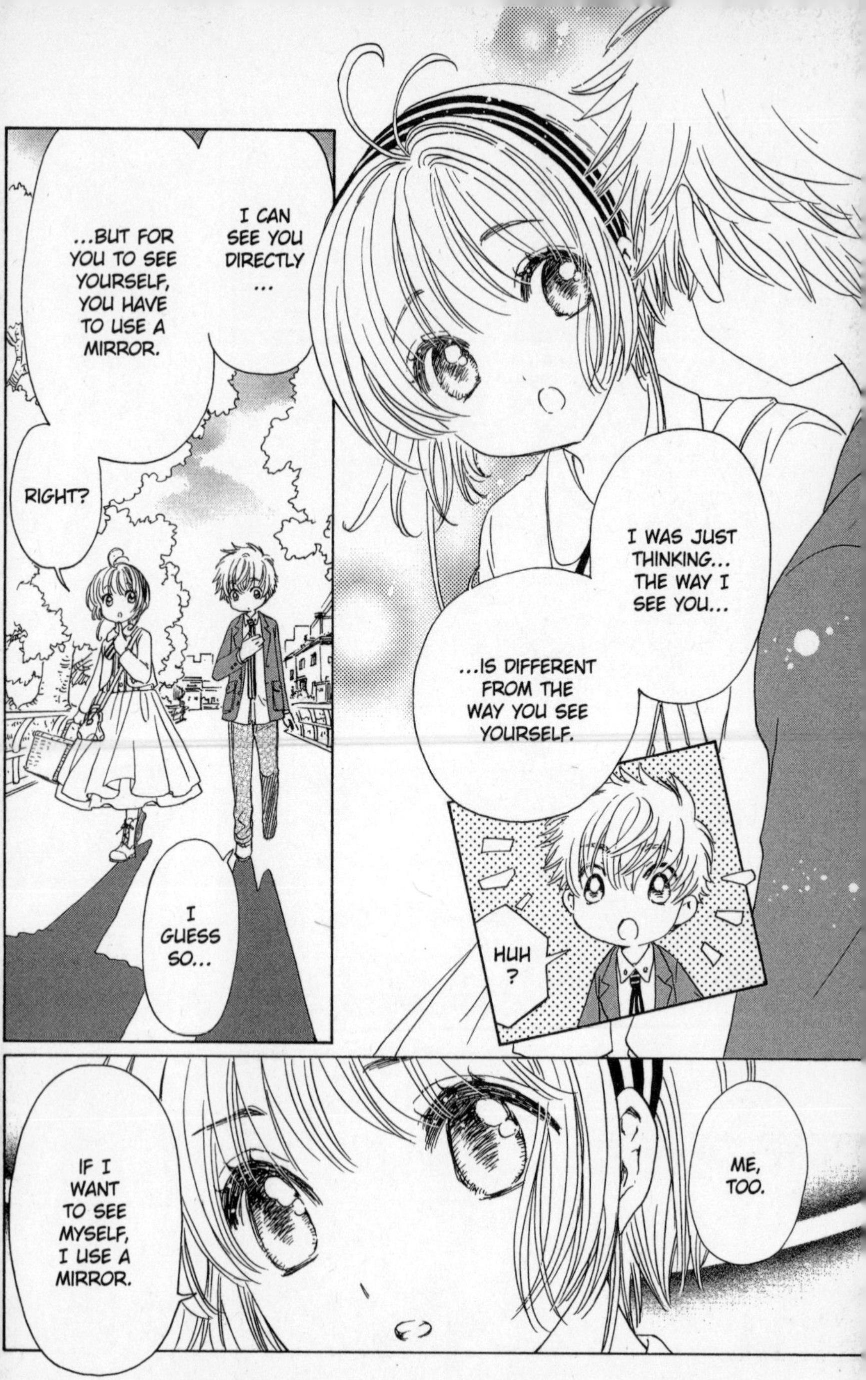
I WAS JUST THINKING... THE WAY I SEE YOU...
...IS DIFFERENT FROM THE WAY YOU SEE YOURSELF.
HUH?
I CAN SEE YOU DIRECTLY ...
...BUT FOR YOU TO SEE YOURSELF, YOU HAVE TO USE A MIRROR.
RIGHT?
I GUESS SO...
ME, TOO.
IF I WANT TO SEE MYSELF, I USE A MIRROR.

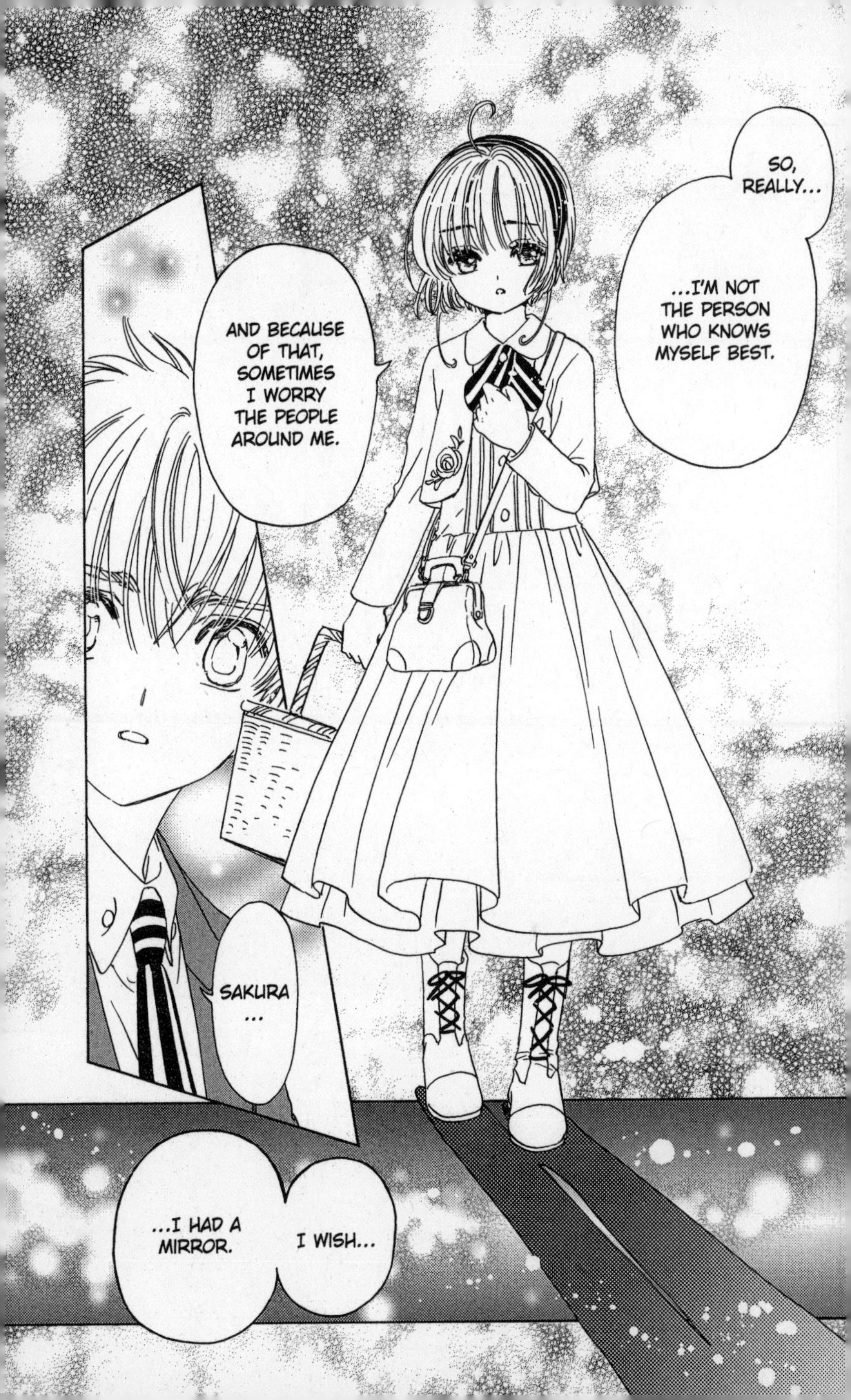
SO, REALLY...
...I'M NOT THE PERSON WHO KNOWS MYSELF BEST.
AND BECAUSE OF THAT, SOMETIMES I WORRY THE PEOPLE AROUND ME.
SAKURA ...
I WISH...
...I HAD A MIRROR.

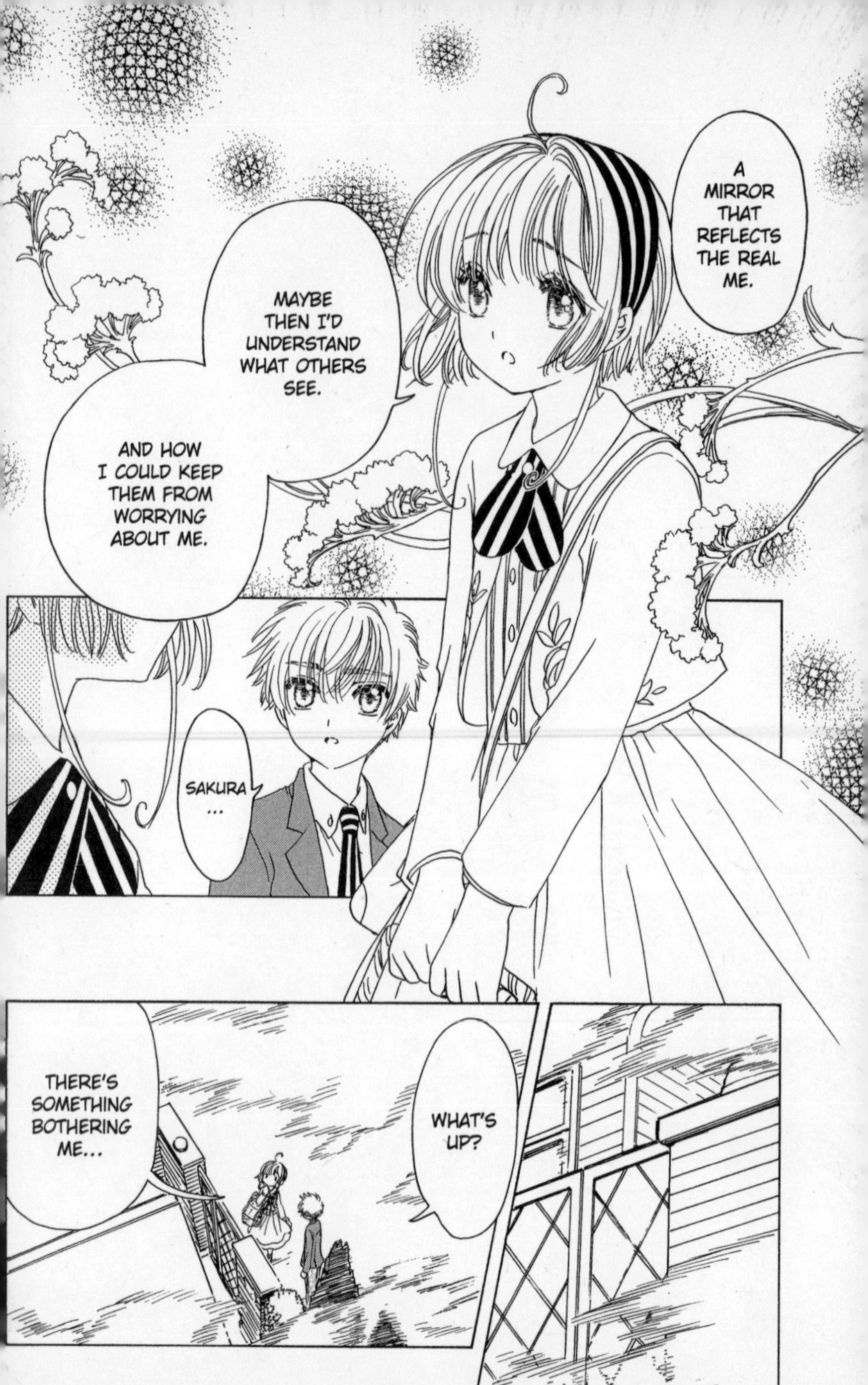
A MIRROR THAT REFLECTS THE REAL ME.
MAYBE THEN I'D UNDERSTAND WHAT OTHERS SEE.
AND HOW I COULD KEEP THEM FROM WORRYING ABOUT ME.
SAKURA ...
WHAT'S UP?
THERE'S SOMETHING BOTHERING ME...

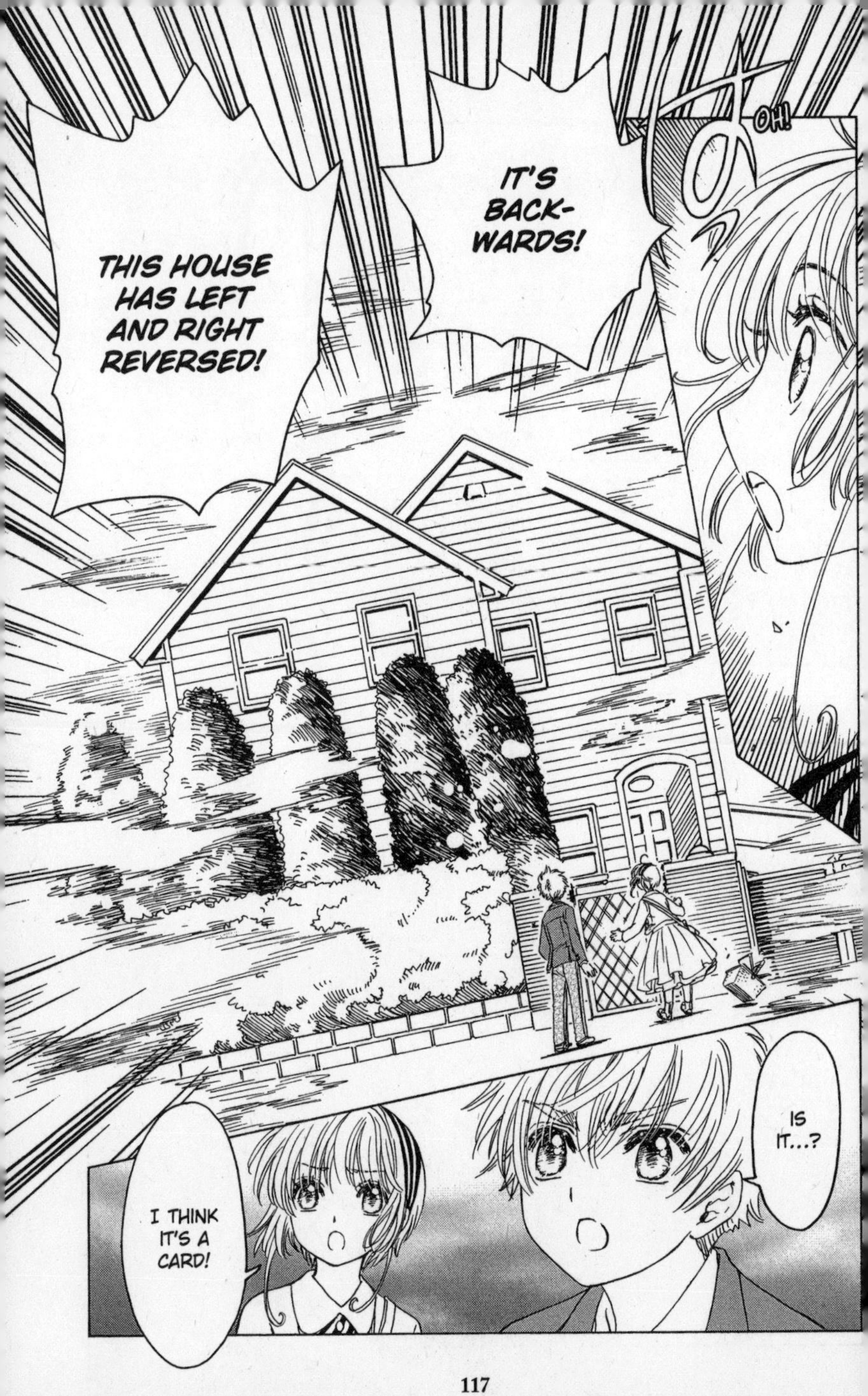
OH!
IT'S BACKWARDS!
THIS HOUSE HAS LEFT AND RIGHT REVERSED!
IS IT...?
I THINK IT'S A CARD!

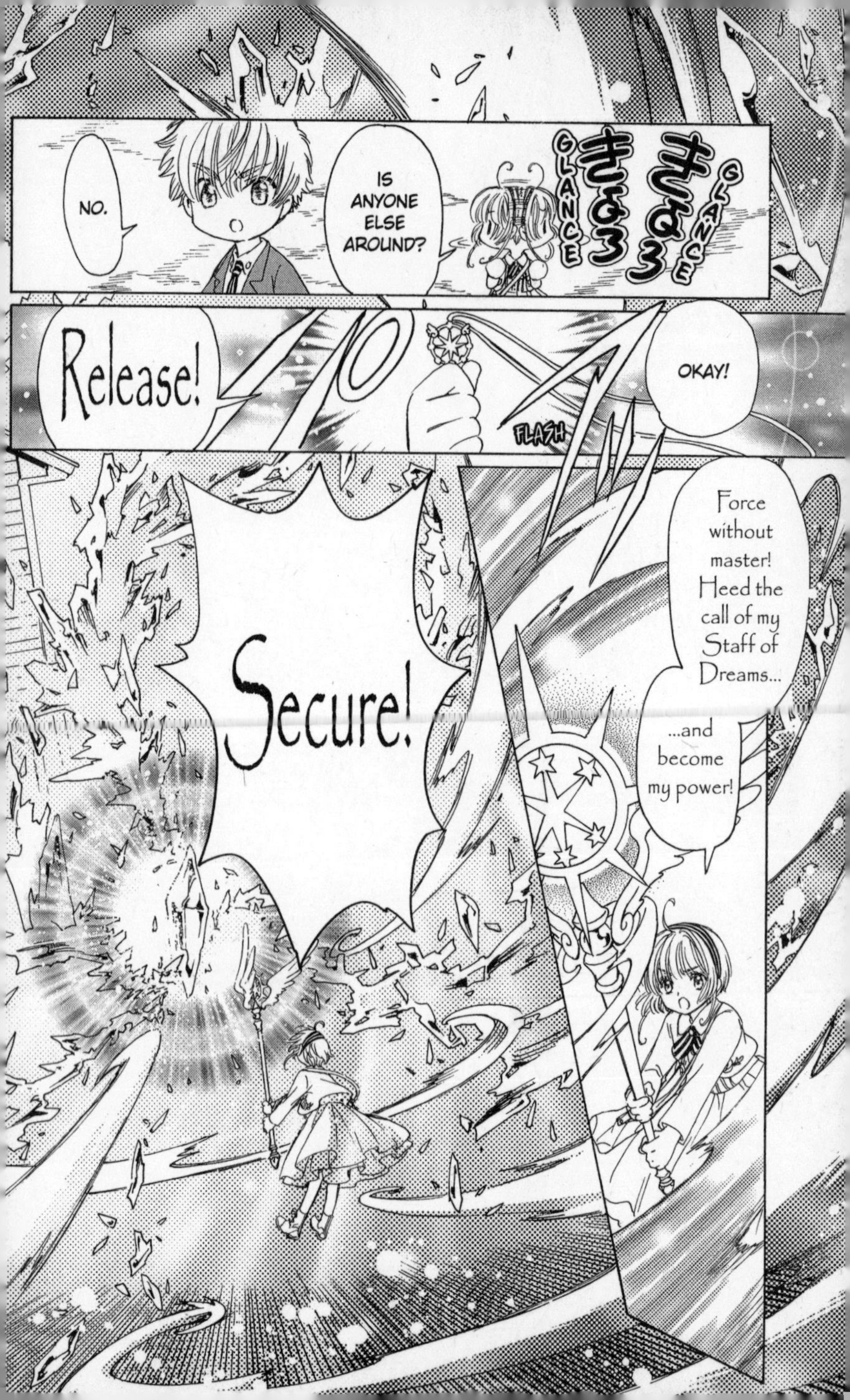
GLANCE
GLANCE
IS ANYONE ELSE AROUND?
NO.
OKAY!
FLASH
Release!
Force without master! Heed the call of my Staff of Dreams...
...and become my power!
Secure!

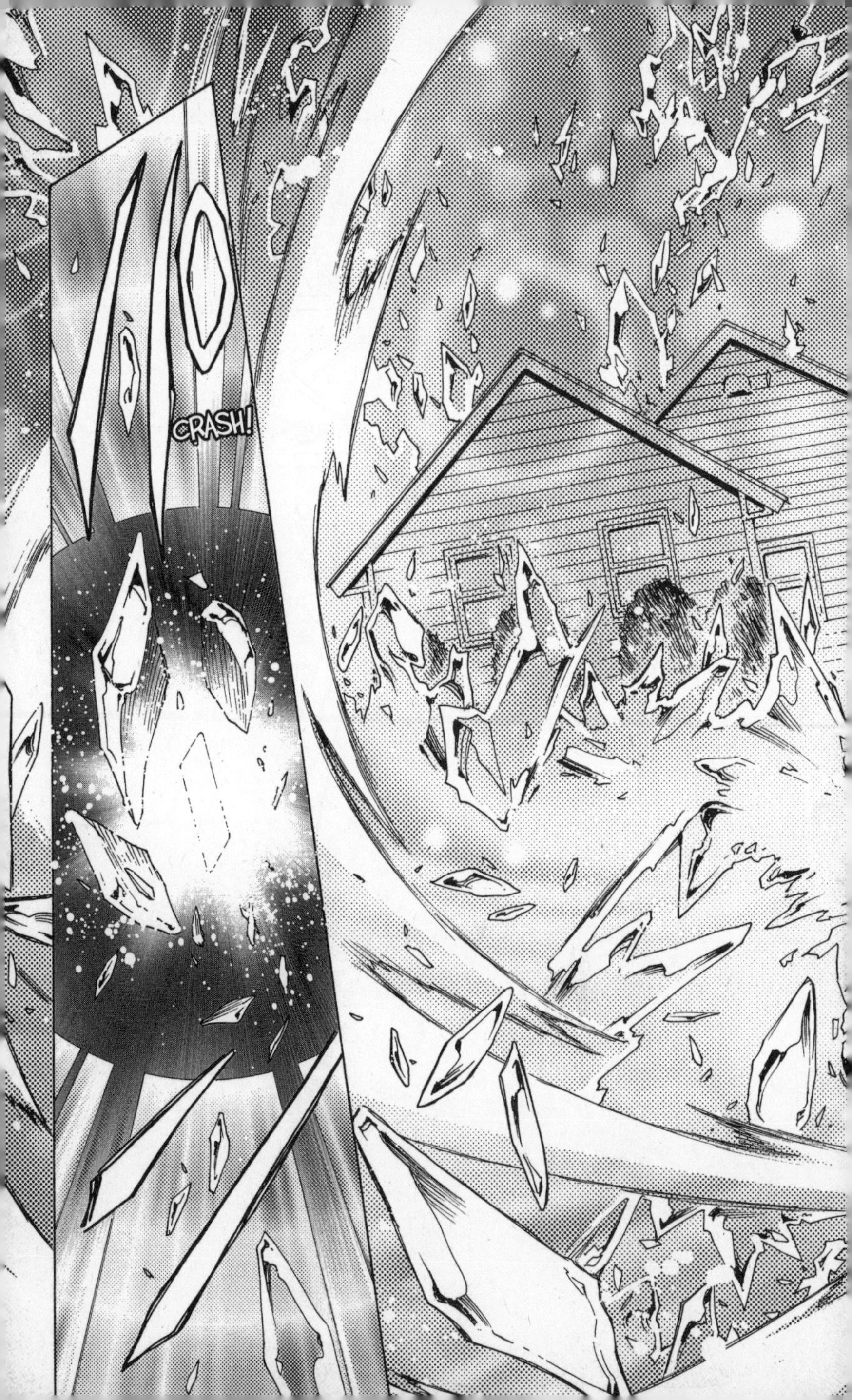
CRASH!

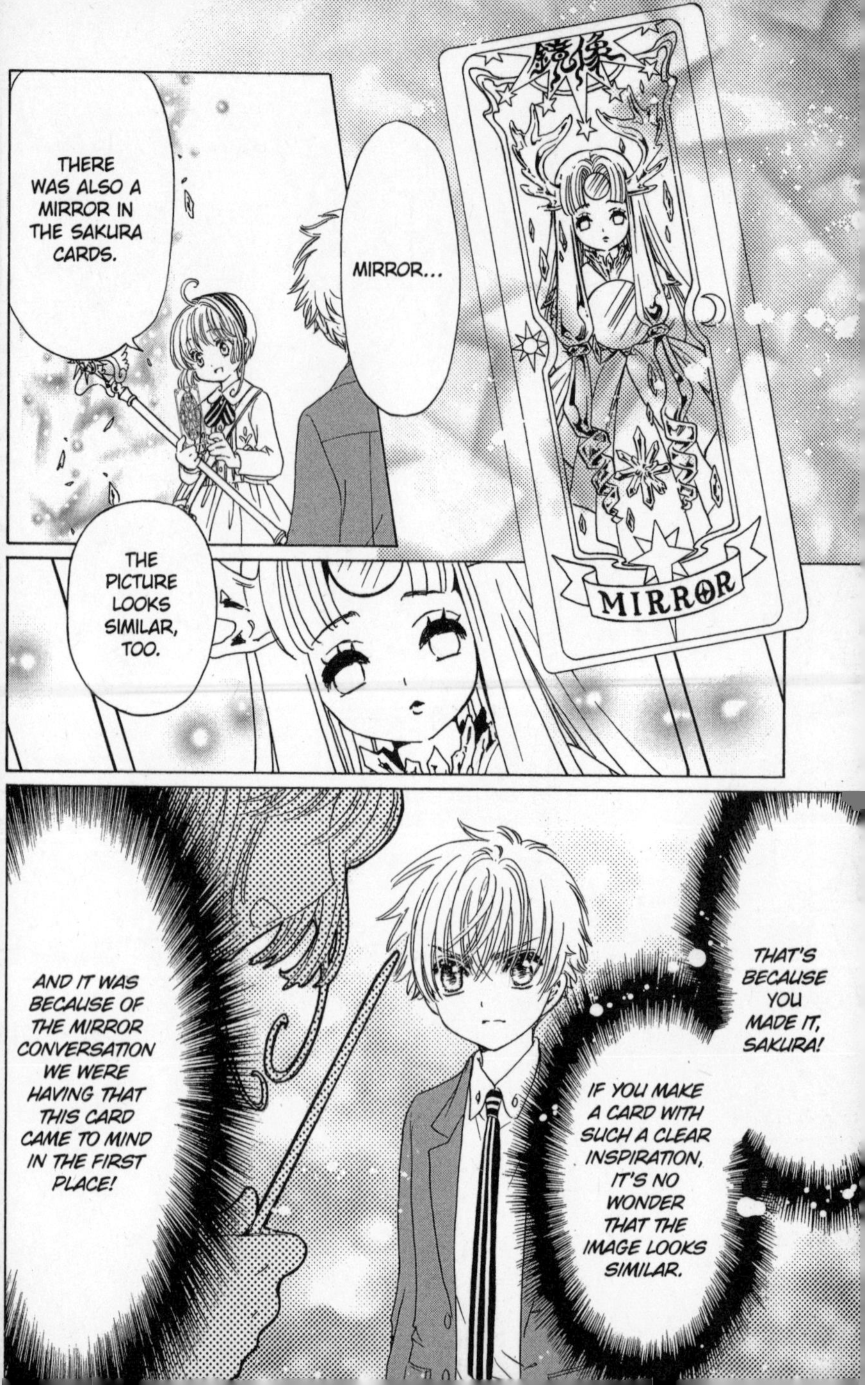
鏡像
MIRROR
MIRROR...
THERE WAS ALSO A MIRROR IN THE SAKURA CARDS.
THE PICTURE LOOKS SIMILAR, TOO.
THAT'S BECAUSE YOU MADE IT, SAKURA!
IF YOU MAKE A CARD WITH SUCH A CLEAR INSPIRATION, IT'S NO WONDER THAT THE IMAGE LOOKS SIMILAR.
AND IT WAS BECAUSE OF THE MIRROR CONVERSATION WE WERE HAVING THAT THIS CARD CAME TO MIND IN THE FIRST PLACE!

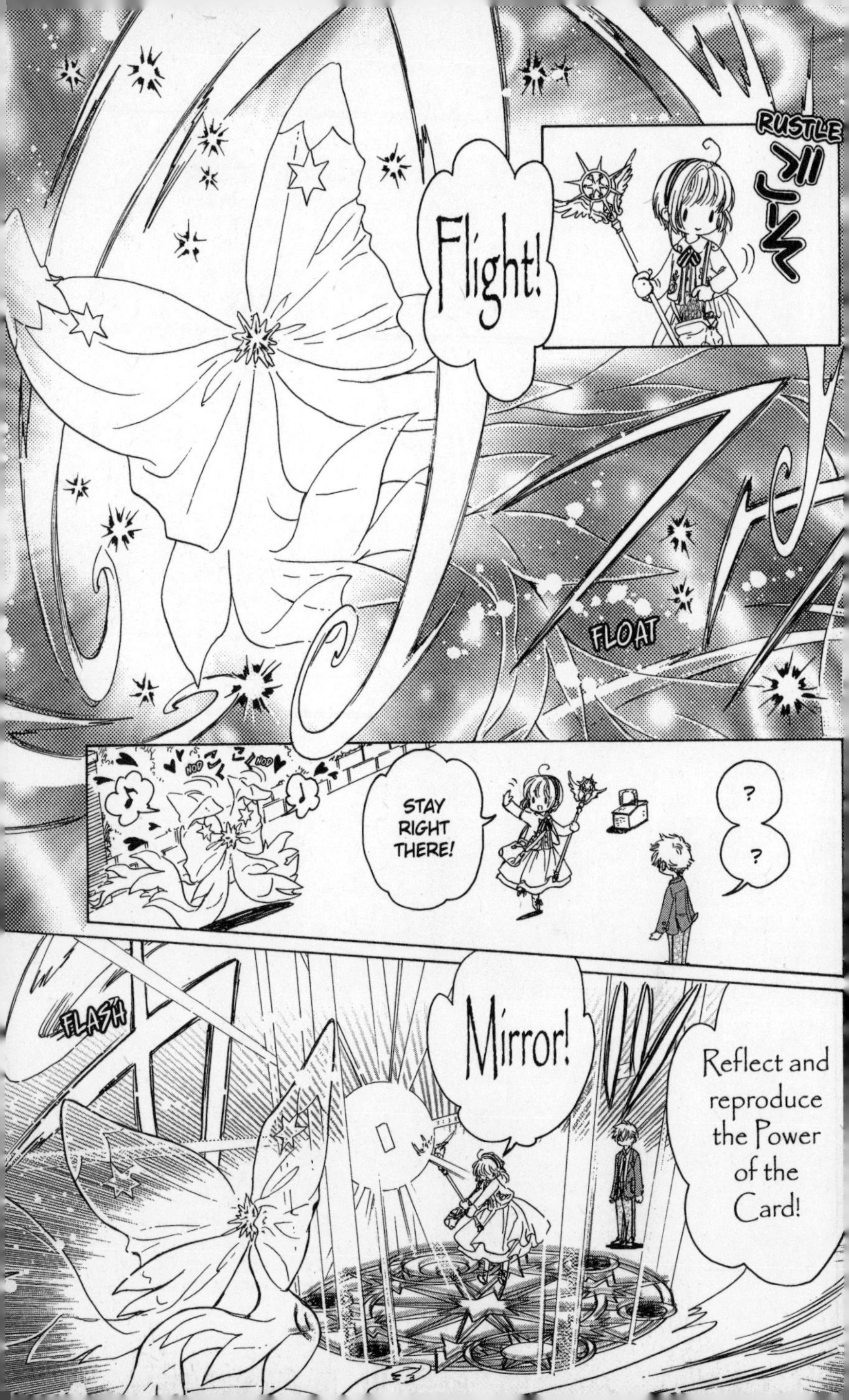
RUSTLE
Flight!
FLOAT
?
?
STAY RIGHT THERE!
NOD
NOD
Reflect and reproduce the Power of the Card!
Mirror!
FLASH

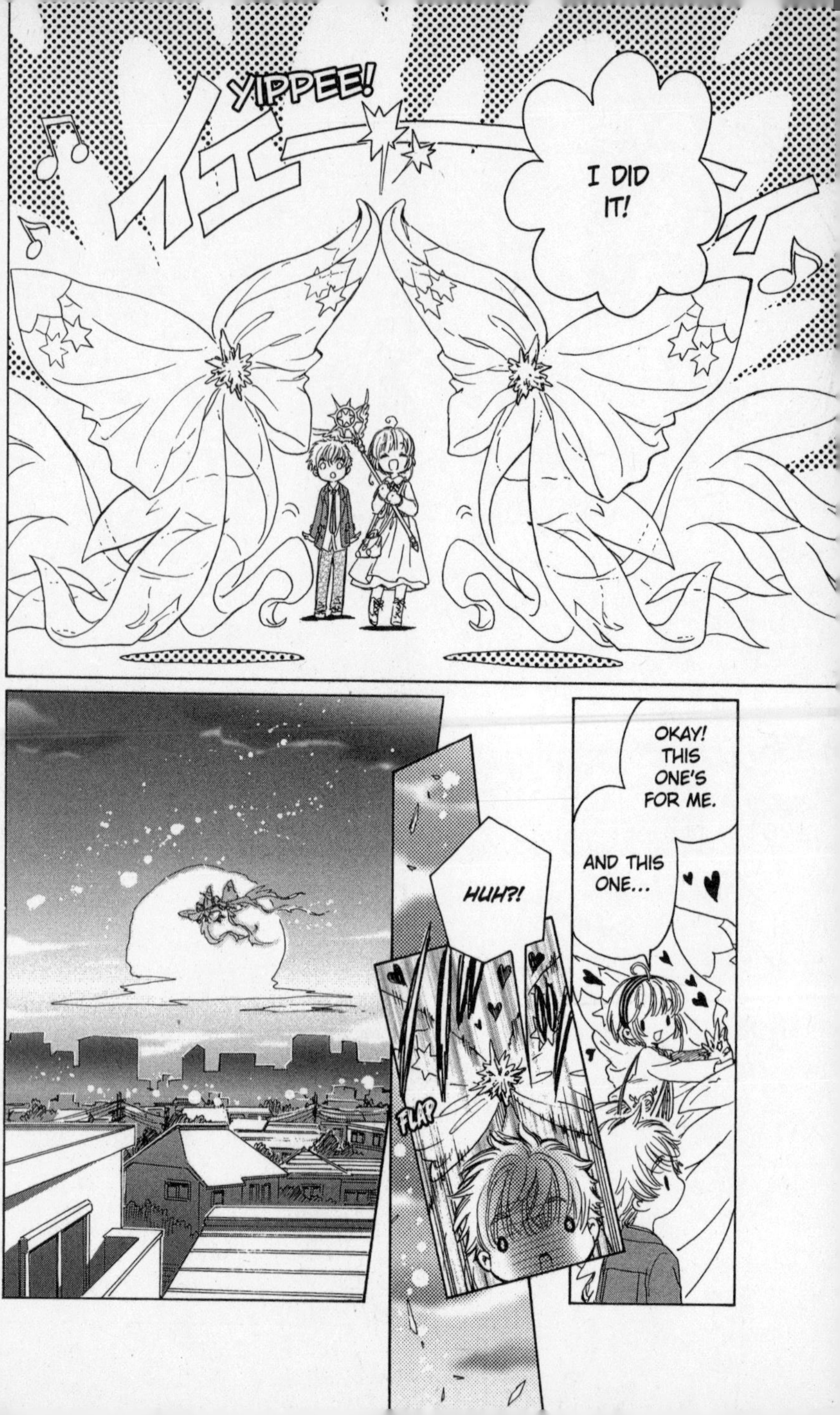
YIPPEE!
I DID IT!
OKAY! THIS ONE'S FOR ME.
AND THIS ONE...
HUH?!
FLAP

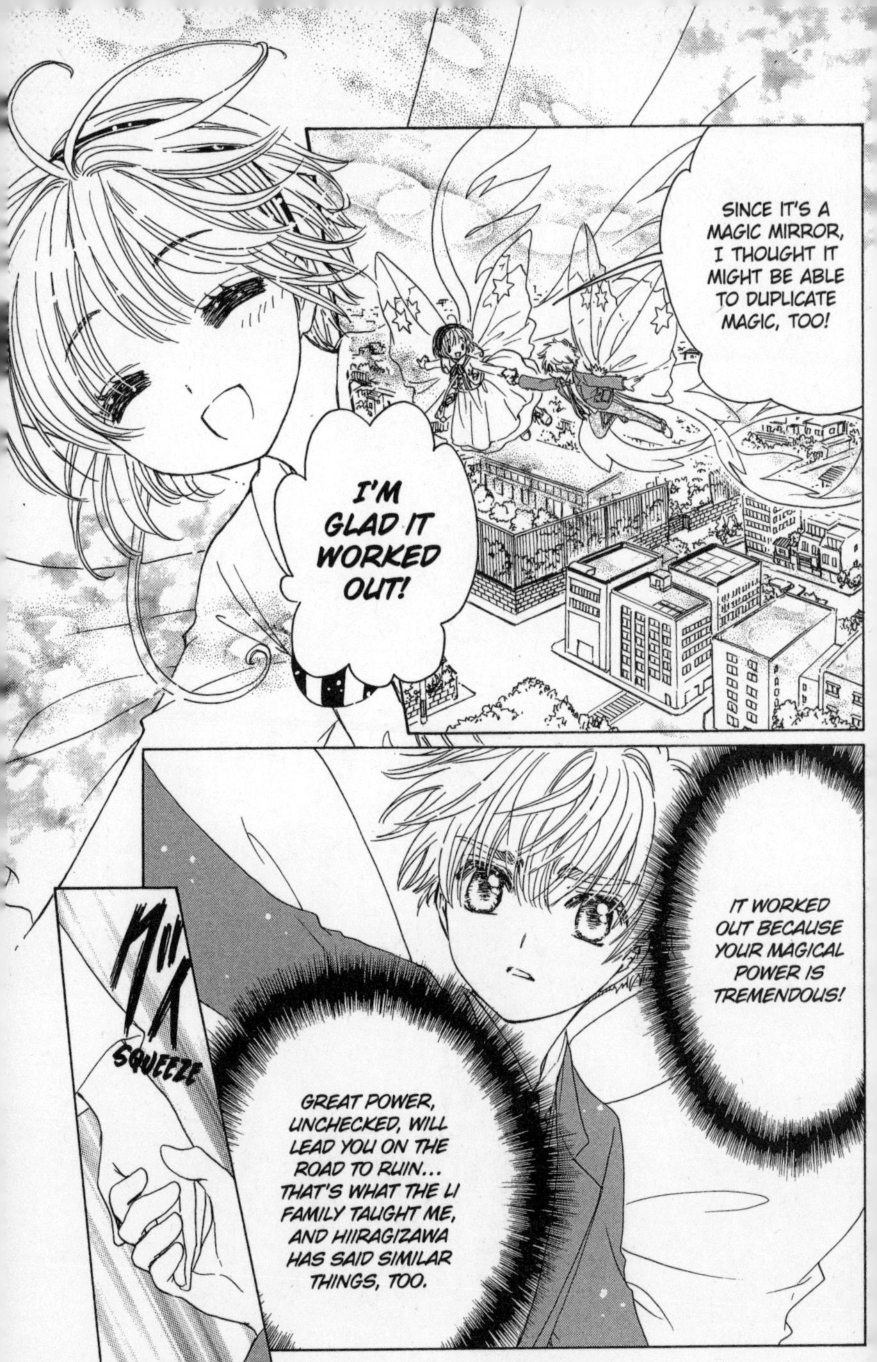
SINCE IT'S A MAGIC MIRROR, I THOUGHT IT MIGHT BE ABLE TO DUPLICATE MAGIC, TOO!
I'M GLAD IT WORKED OUT!
IT WORKED OUT BECAUSE YOUR MAGICAL POWER IS TREMENDOUS!
GREAT POWER, UNCHECKED, WILL LEAD YOU ON THE ROAD TO RUIN... THAT'S WHAT THE LI FAMILY TAUGHT ME, AND HIIRAGIZAWA HAS SAID SIMILAR THINGS, TOO.
SQUEEZE

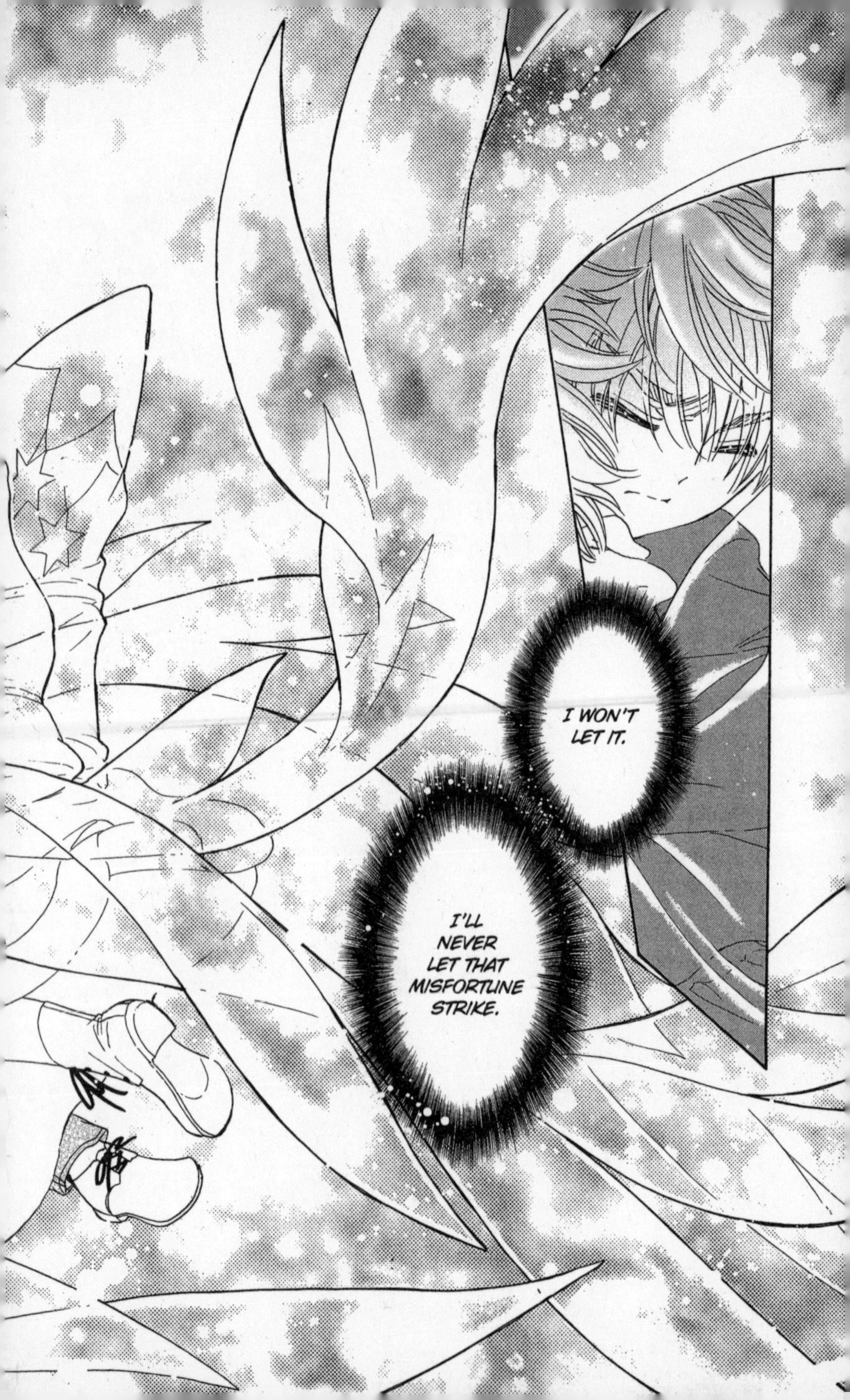
I WON'T LET IT.
I'LL NEVER LET THAT MISFORTUNE STRIKE.

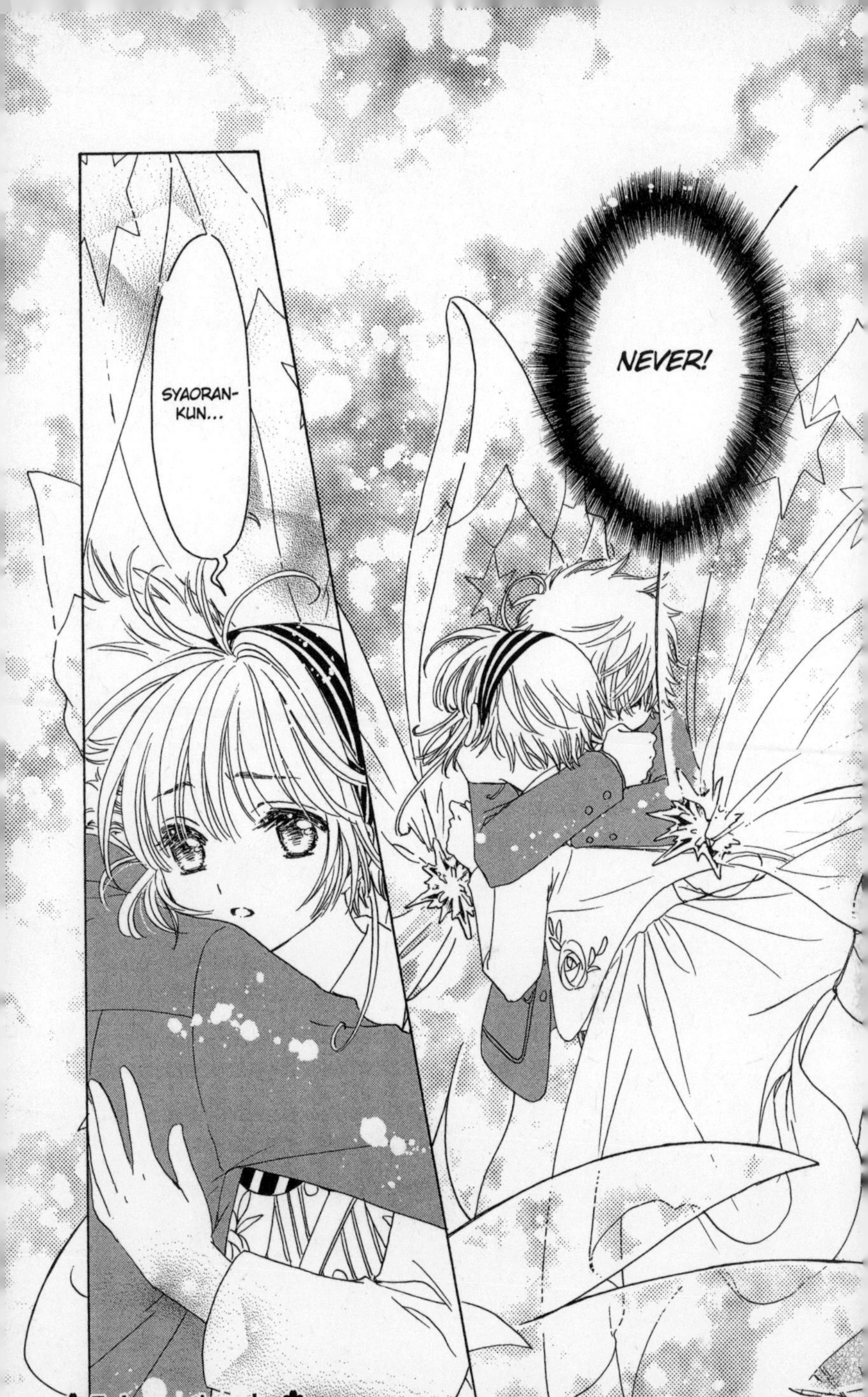
NEVER!
SYAORAN-KUN...

✿ To be continued... ✿

Cardcaptor Sakura

CLEAR CARD

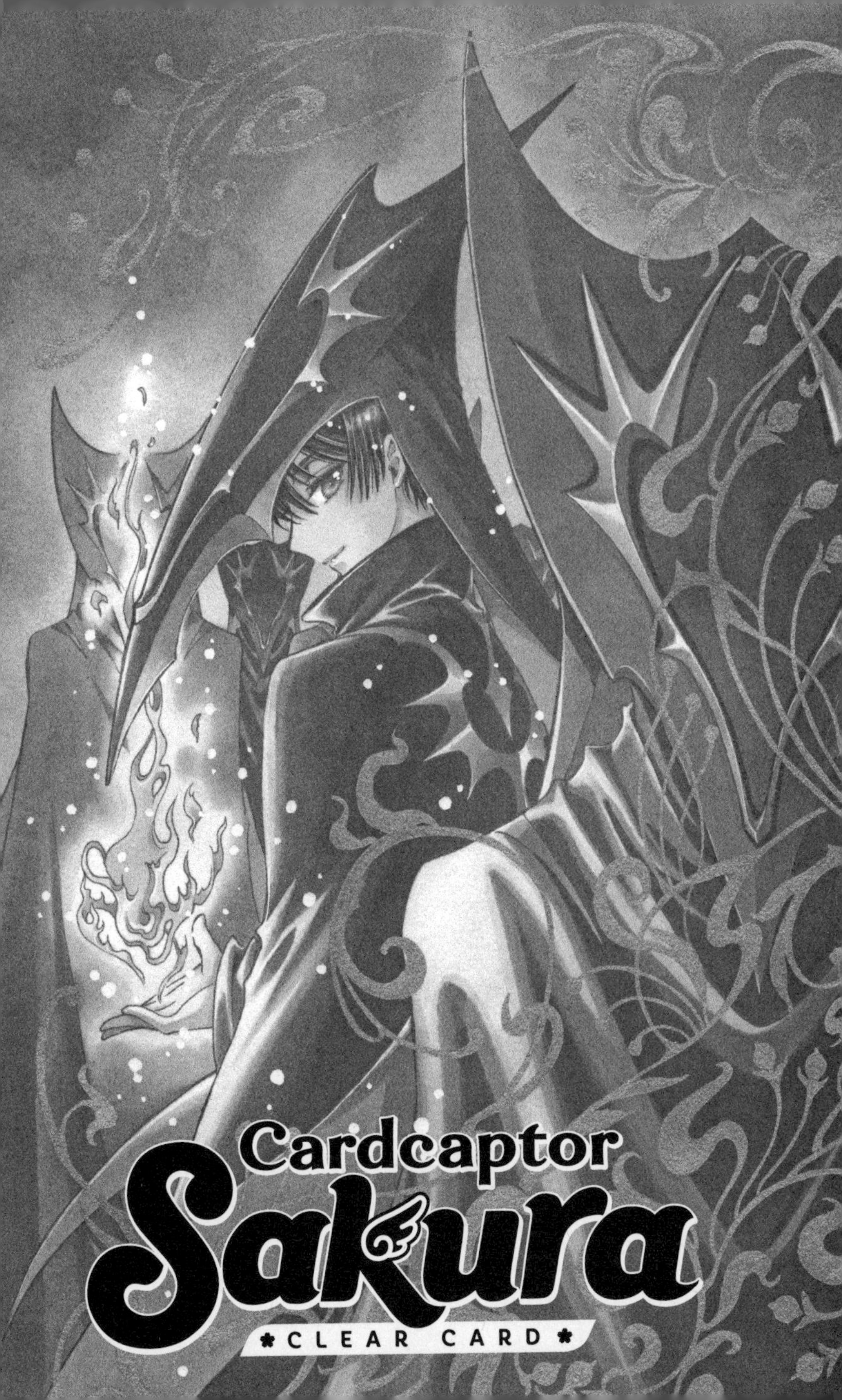
Cardcaptor
Sakura
CLEAR CARD

Cardcaptor Sakura
CLEAR CARD

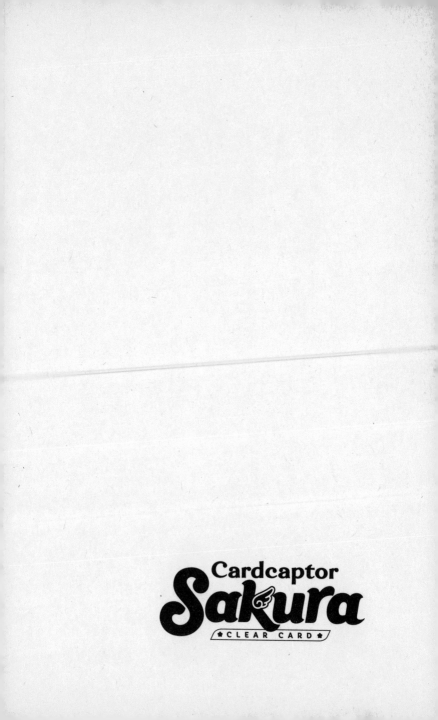

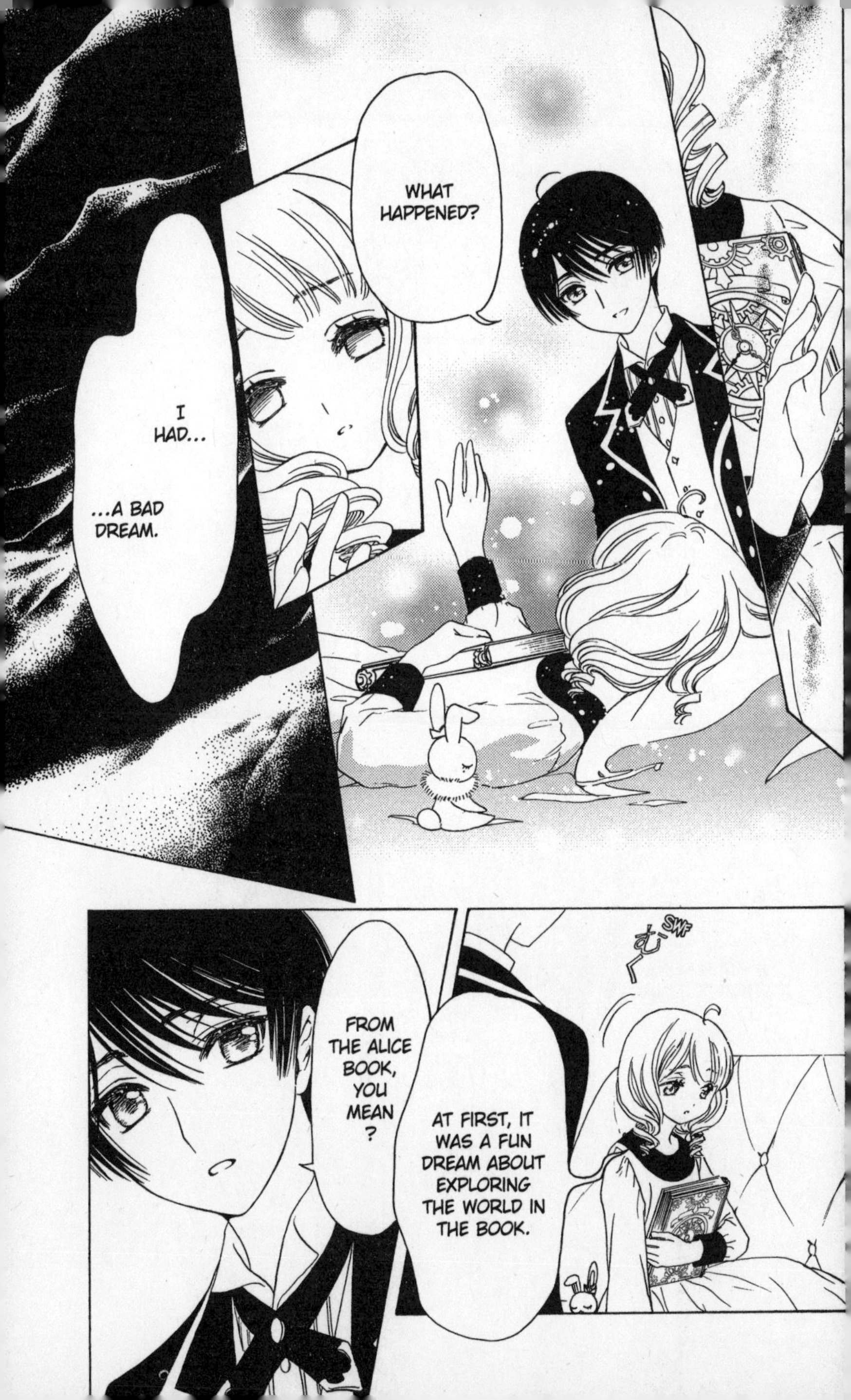
WHAT HAPPENED?
I HAD...
...A BAD DREAM.
SWF
FROM THE ALICE BOOK, YOU MEAN?
AT FIRST, IT WAS A FUN DREAM ABOUT EXPLORING THE WORLD IN THE BOOK.

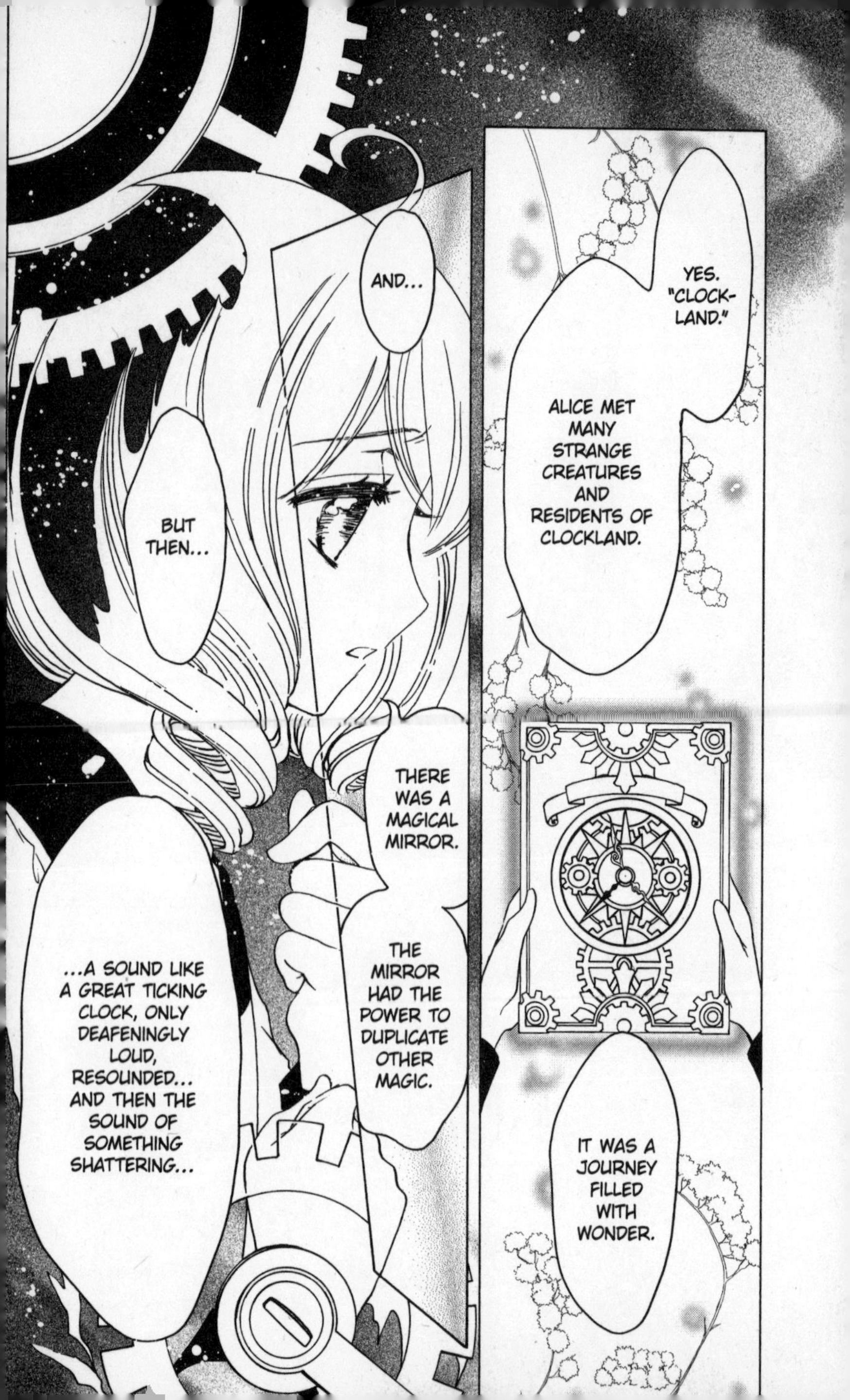
YES. "CLOCK-LAND."
ALICE MET MANY STRANGE CREATURES AND RESIDENTS OF CLOCKLAND.
IT WAS A JOURNEY FILLED WITH WONDER.
AND...
THERE WAS A MAGICAL MIRROR.
THE MIRROR HAD THE POWER TO DUPLICATE OTHER MAGIC.
BUT THEN...
...A SOUND LIKE A GREAT TICKING CLOCK, ONLY DEAFENINGLY LOUD, RESOUNDED... AND THEN THE SOUND OF SOMETHING SHATTERING...

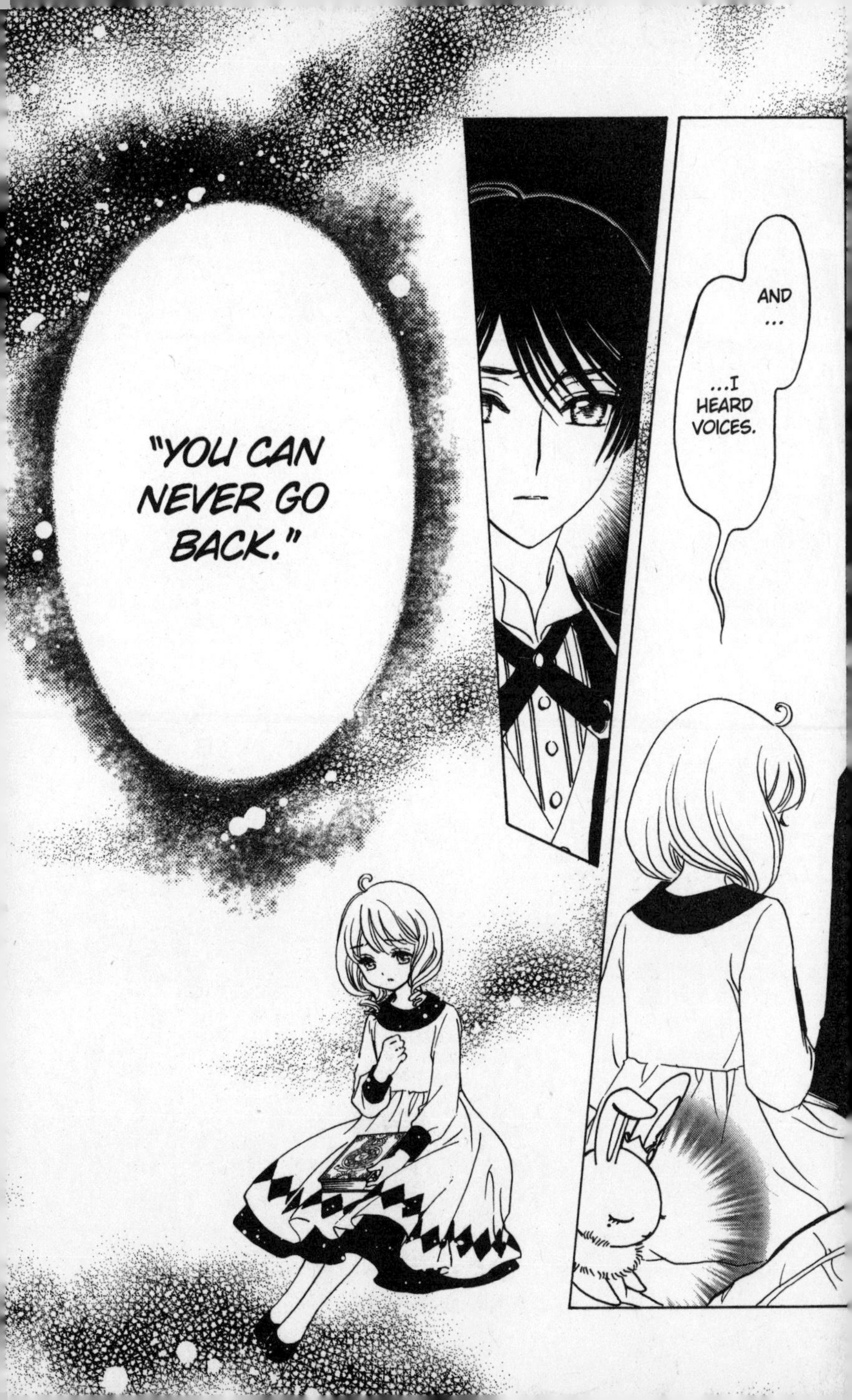
AND ...
...I HEARD VOICES.
"YOU CAN NEVER GO BACK."

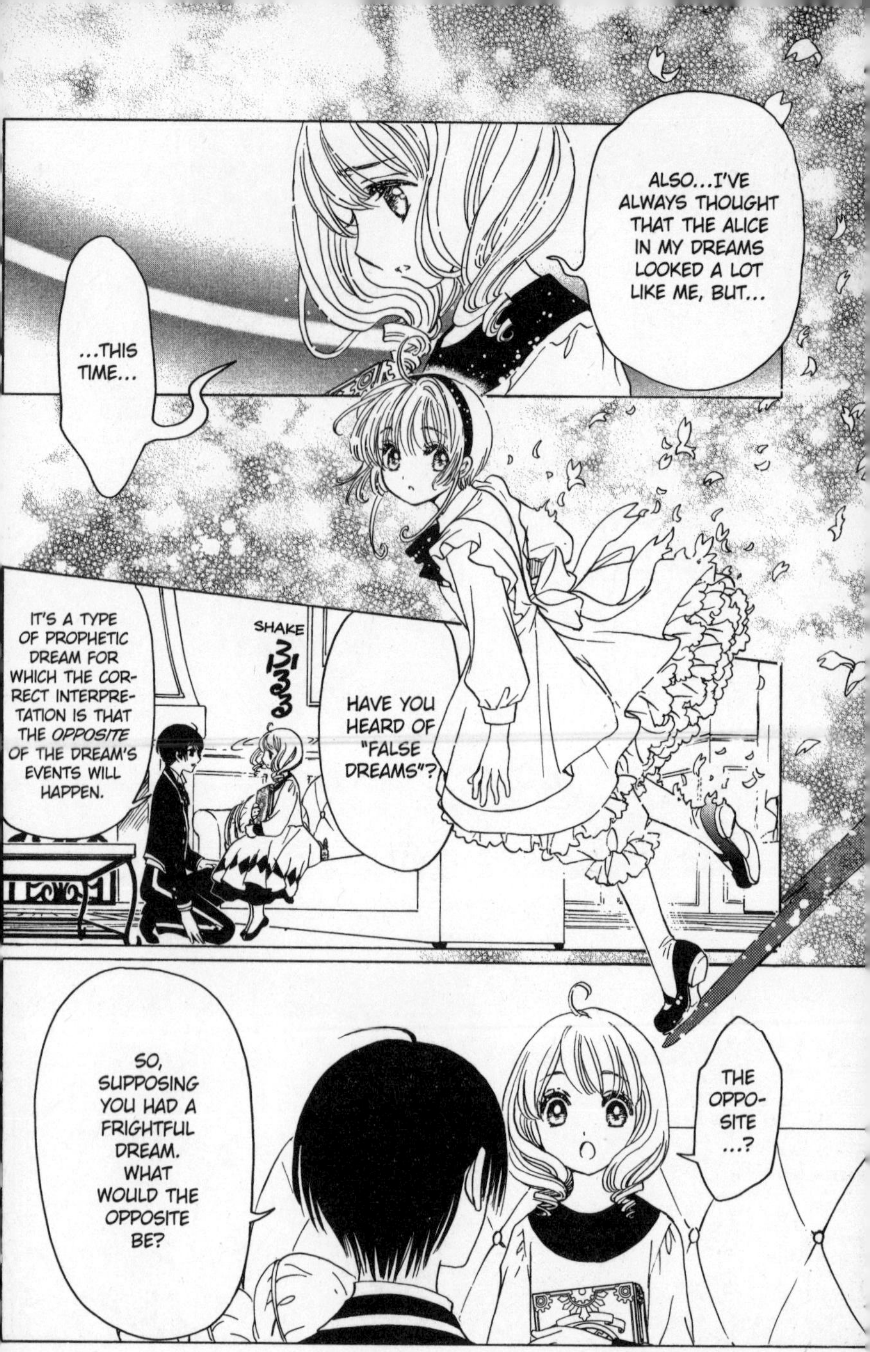
ALSO...I'VE ALWAYS THOUGHT THAT THE ALICE IN MY DREAMS LOOKED A LOT LIKE ME, BUT...
...THIS TIME...
HAVE YOU HEARD OF "FALSE DREAMS"?
SHAKE
IT'S A TYPE OF PROPHETIC DREAM FOR WHICH THE COR-RECT INTERPRE-TATION IS THAT THE *OPPOSITE* OF THE DREAM'S EVENTS WILL HAPPEN.
THE OPPO-SITE ...?
SO, SUPPOSING YOU HAD A FRIGHTFUL DREAM. WHAT WOULD THE OPPOSITE BE?

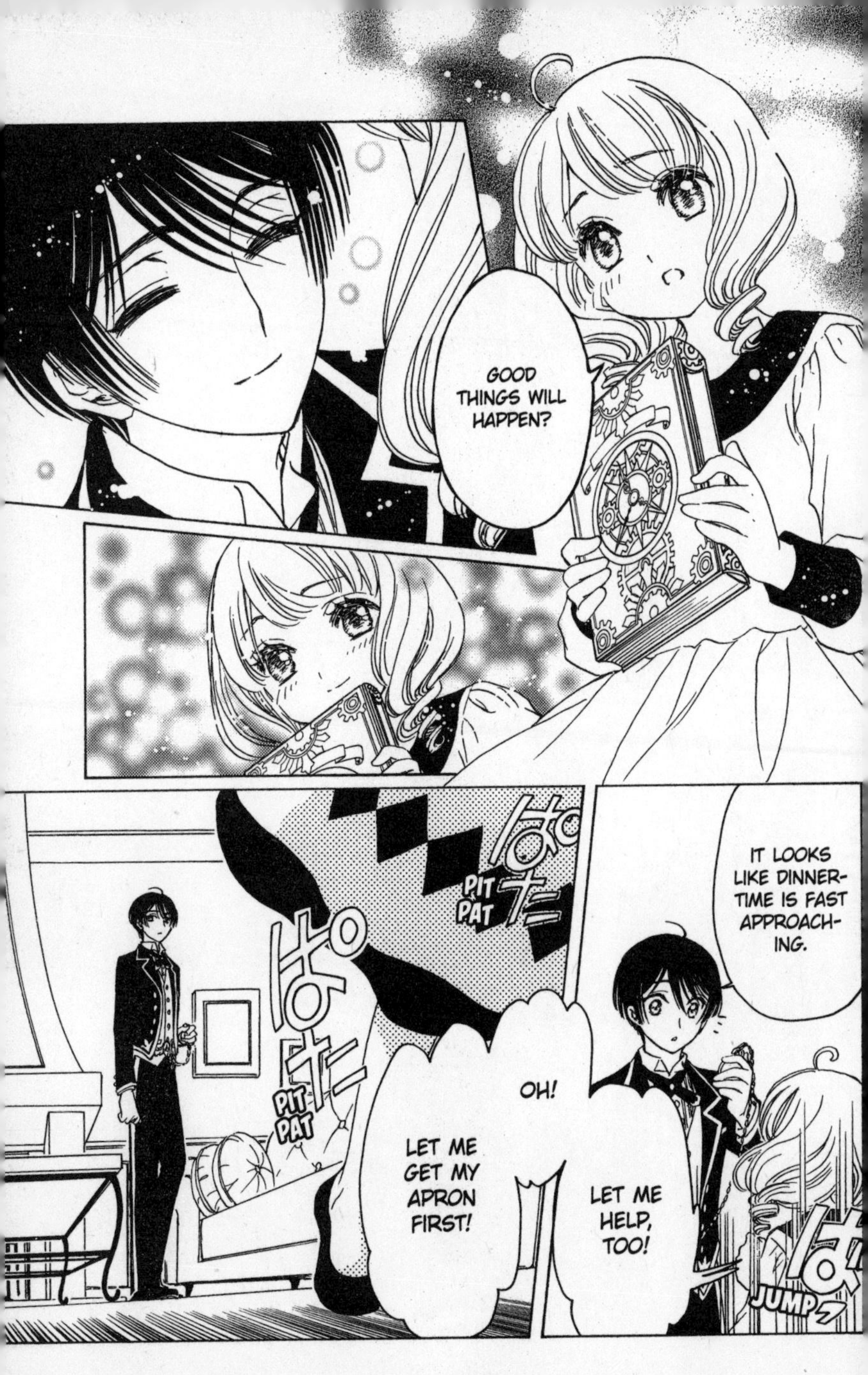
GOOD THINGS WILL HAPPEN?
IT LOOKS LIKE DINNER-TIME IS FAST APPROACHING.
JUMP
OH!
LET ME HELP, TOO!
LET ME GET MY APRON FIRST!
PIT PAT
PIT PAT

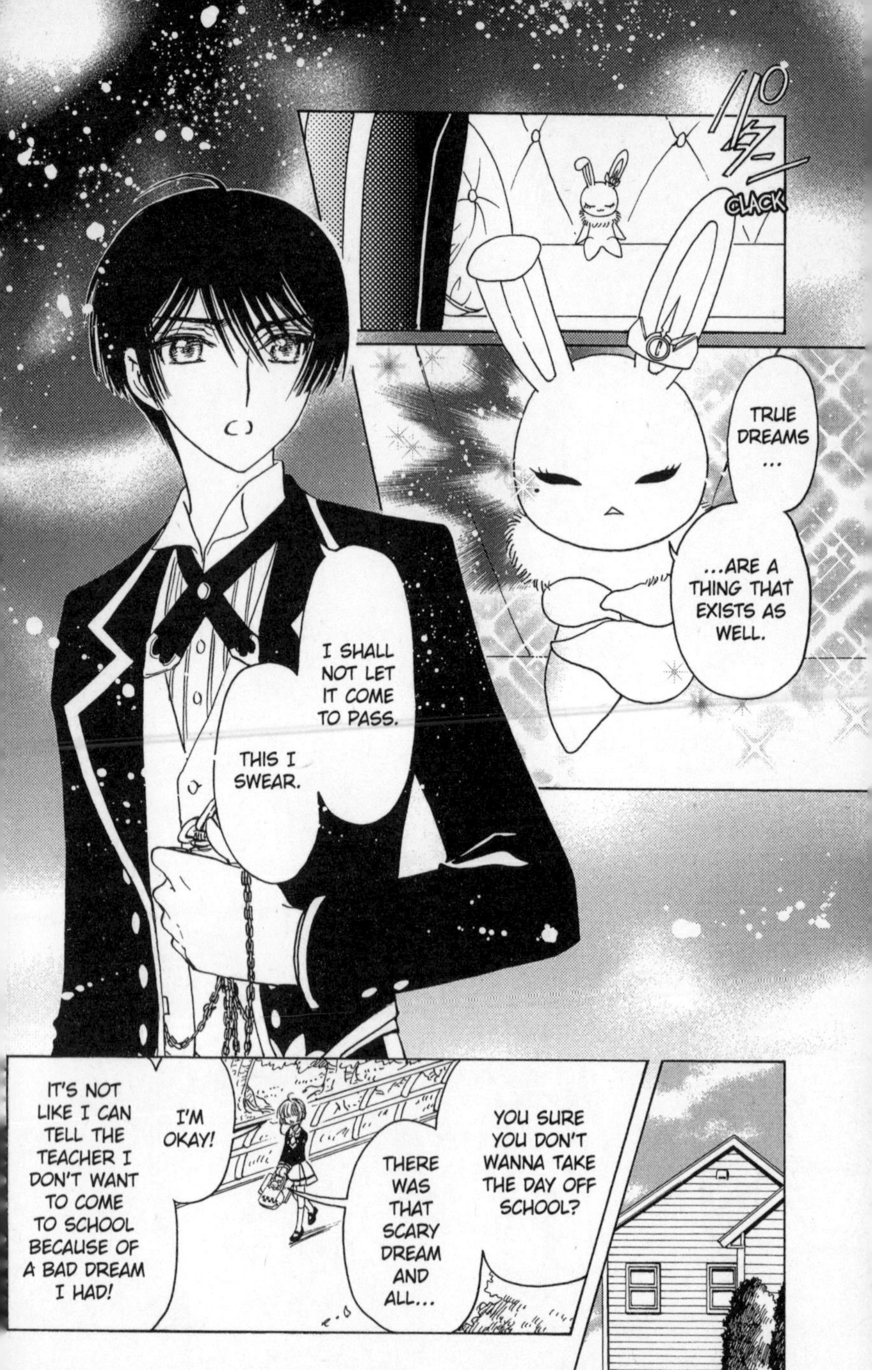
CLACK
TRUE DREAMS...
...ARE A THING THAT EXISTS AS WELL.
I SHALL NOT LET IT COME TO PASS.
THIS I SWEAR.
YOU SURE YOU DON'T WANNA TAKE THE DAY OFF SCHOOL?
THERE WAS THAT SCARY DREAM AND ALL...
I'M OKAY!
IT'S NOT LIKE I CAN TELL THE TEACHER I DON'T WANT TO COME TO SCHOOL BECAUSE OF A BAD DREAM I HAD!

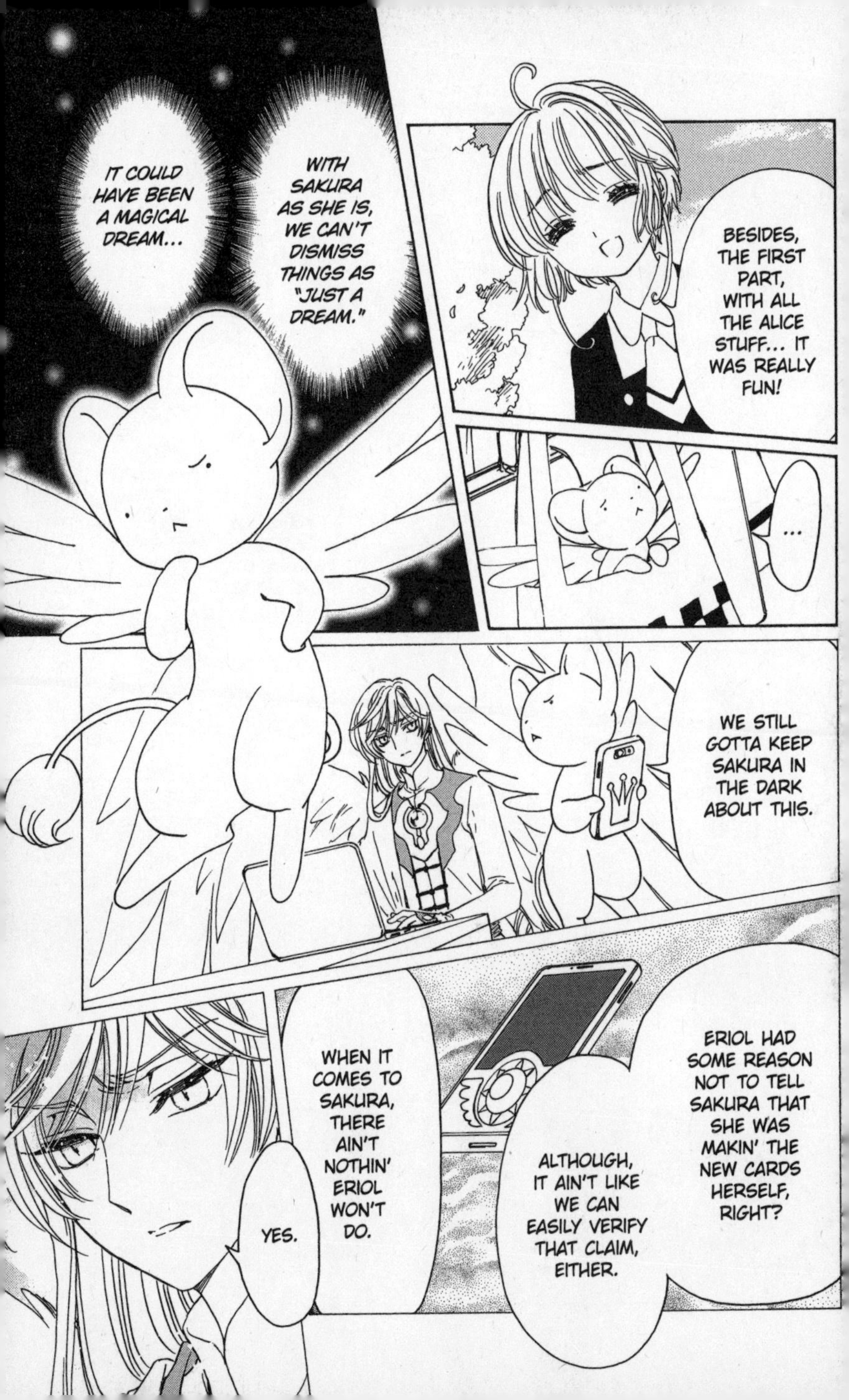
BESIDES, THE FIRST PART, WITH ALL THE ALICE STUFF... IT WAS REALLY FUN!
...
WITH SAKURA AS SHE IS, WE CAN'T DISMISS THINGS AS "JUST A DREAM."
IT COULD HAVE BEEN A MAGICAL DREAM...
WE STILL GOTTA KEEP SAKURA IN THE DARK ABOUT THIS.
ERIOL HAD SOME REASON NOT TO TELL SAKURA THAT SHE WAS MAKIN' THE NEW CARDS HERSELF, RIGHT?
ALTHOUGH, IT AIN'T LIKE WE CAN EASILY VERIFY THAT CLAIM, EITHER.
WHEN IT COMES TO SAKURA, THERE AIN'T NOTHIN' ERIOL WON'T DO.
YES.

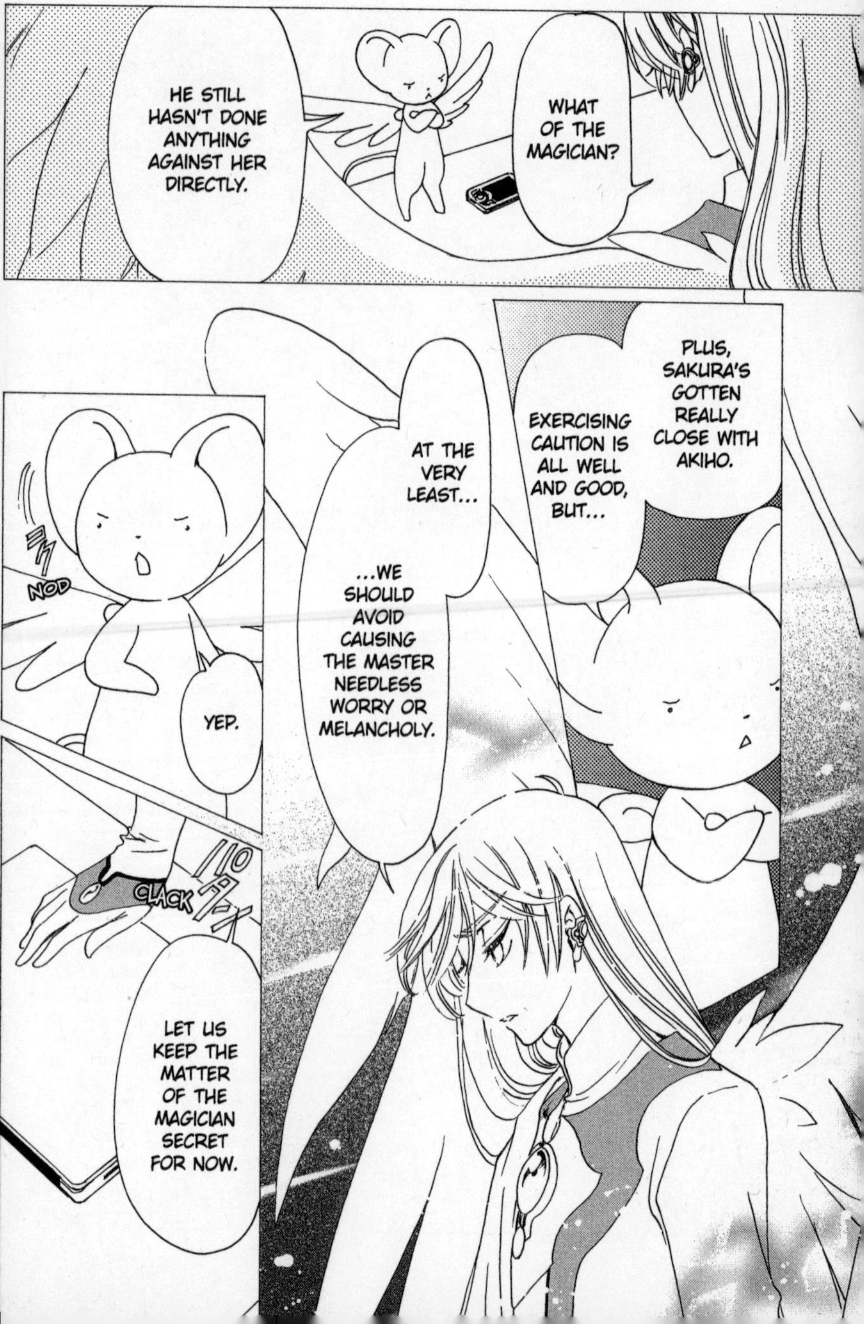
WHAT OF THE MAGICIAN?
HE STILL HASN'T DONE ANYTHING AGAINST HER DIRECTLY.
PLUS, SAKURA'S GOTTEN REALLY CLOSE WITH AKIHO.
EXERCISING CAUTION IS ALL WELL AND GOOD, BUT...
AT THE VERY LEAST...
...WE SHOULD AVOID CAUSING THE MASTER NEEDLESS WORRY OR MELANCHOLY.
NOD
YEP.
CLACK
LET US KEEP THE MATTER OF THE MAGICIAN SECRET FOR NOW.

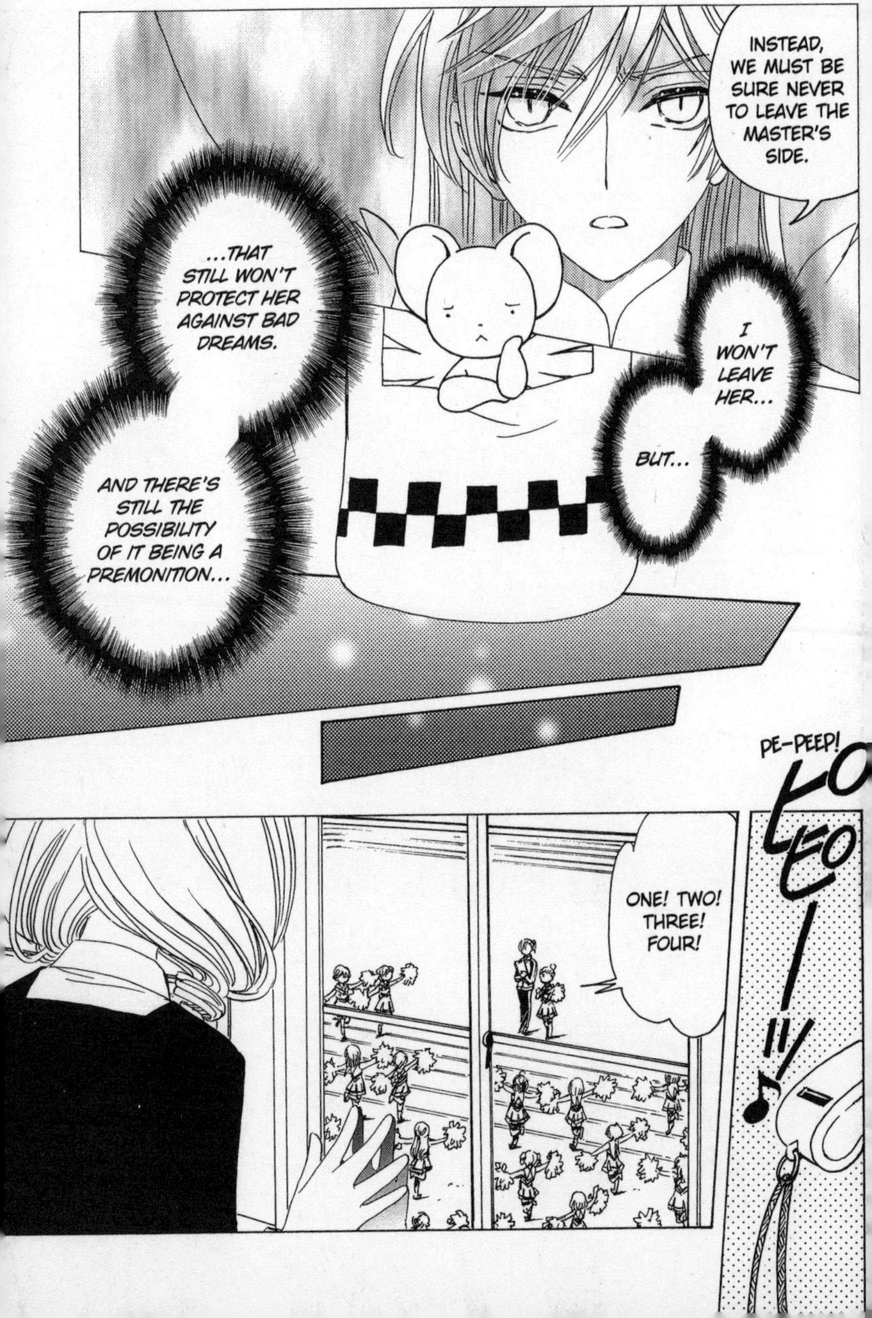
INSTEAD, WE MUST BE SURE NEVER TO LEAVE THE MASTER'S SIDE.
I WON'T LEAVE HER...
BUT...
...THAT STILL WON'T PROTECT HER AGAINST BAD DREAMS.
AND THERE'S STILL THE POSSIBILITY OF IT BEING A PREMONITION...
PE-PEEP!
ONE! TWO! THREE! FOUR!

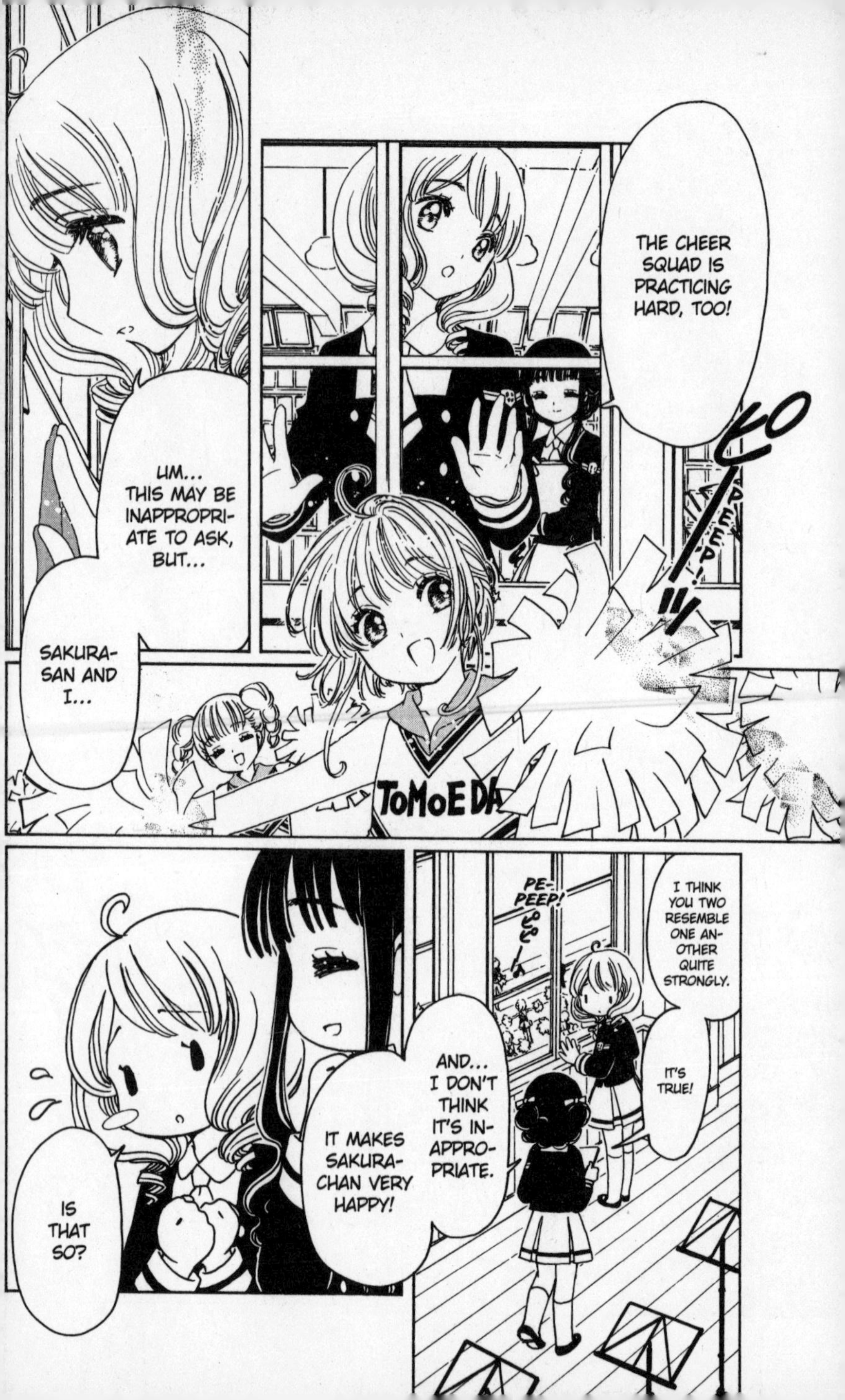
THE CHEER SQUAD IS PRACTICING HARD, TOO!
PEEP!!
UM... THIS MAY BE INAPPROPRI-ATE TO ASK, BUT...
SAKURA-SAN AND I...
TOMOEDA
PE-PEEP!
I THINK YOU TWO RESEMBLE ONE AN-OTHER QUITE STRONGLY.
IT'S TRUE!
AND... I DON'T THINK IT'S IN-APPRO-PRIATE.
IT MAKES SAKURA-CHAN VERY HAPPY!
IS THAT SO?

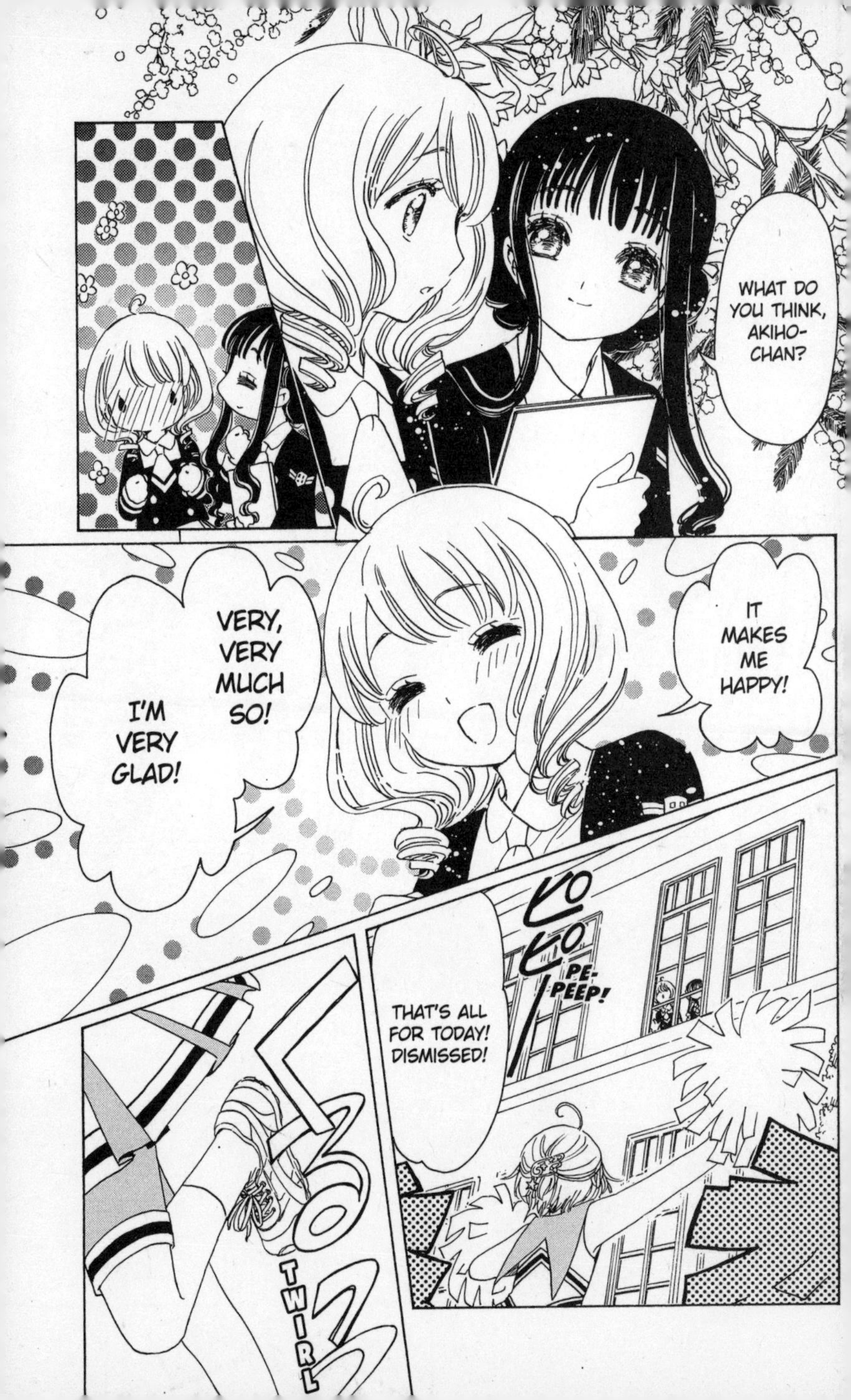
WHAT DO YOU THINK, AKIHO-CHAN?
IT MAKES ME HAPPY!
I'M VERY GLAD!
VERY, VERY MUCH SO!
PE-PEEP!
THAT'S ALL FOR TODAY! DISMISSED!
TWIRL

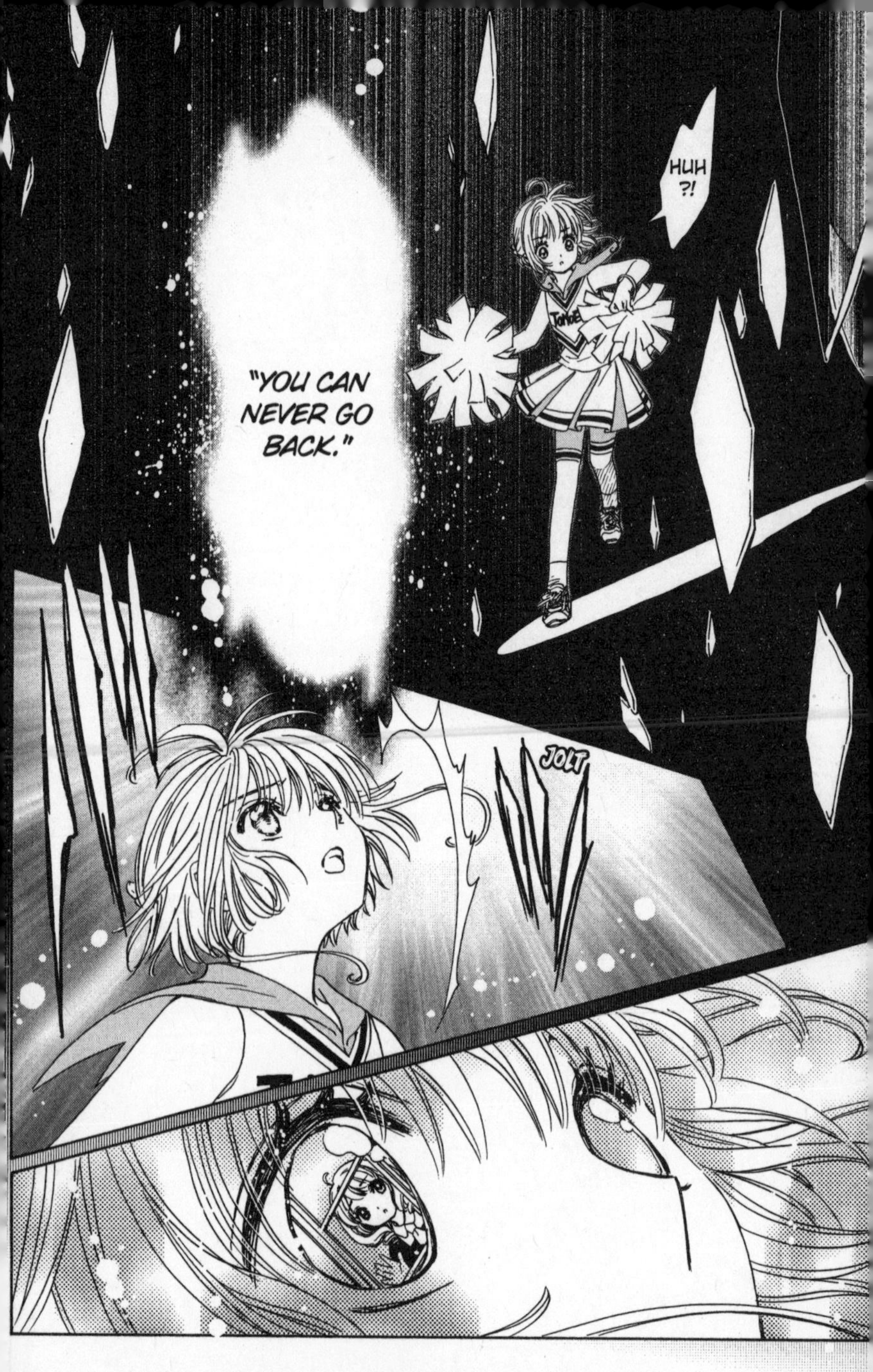
HUH ?!
"YOU CAN NEVER GO BACK."
JOLT

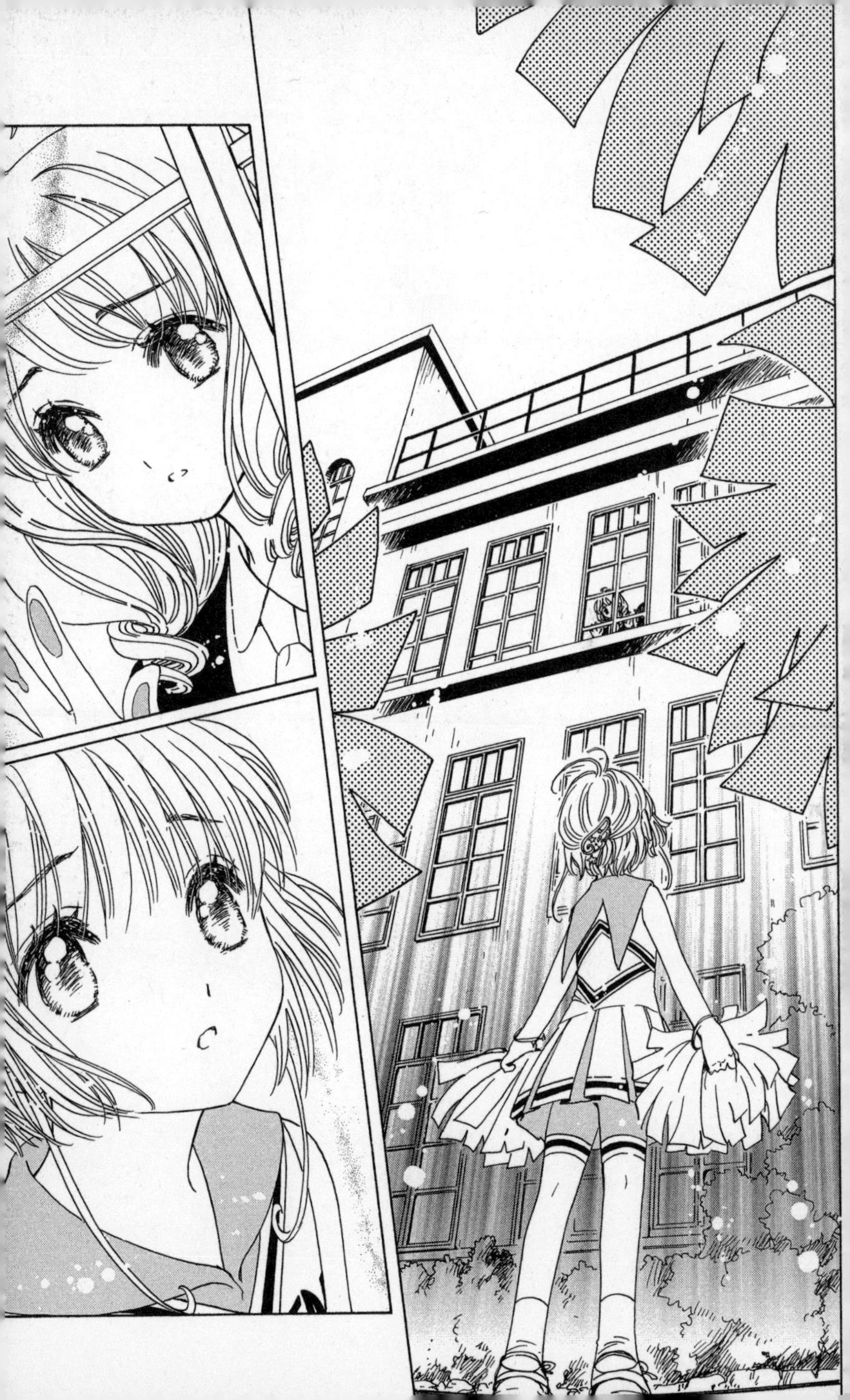

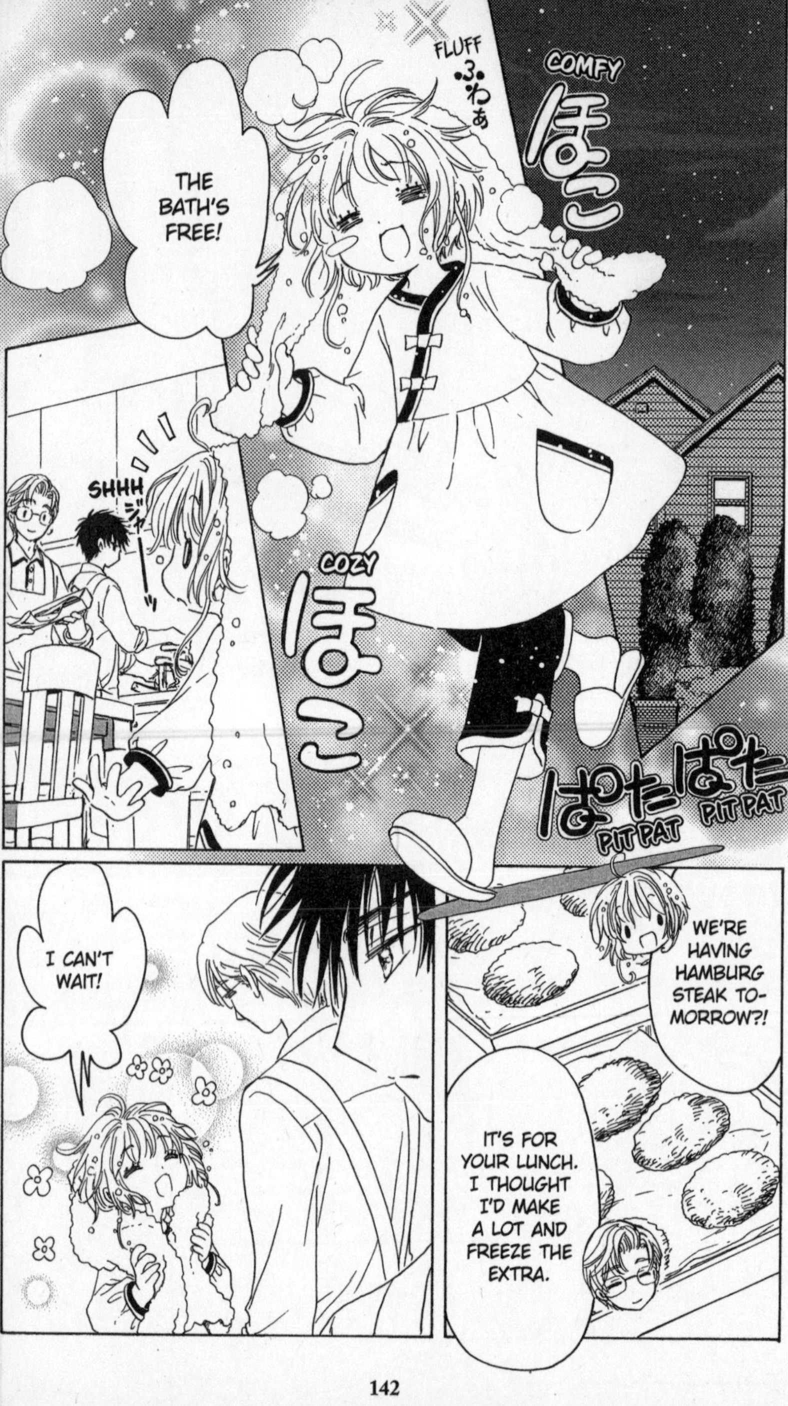
COMFY
ほこ
FLUFF
ふわぁ
THE BATH'S FREE!
COZY
ほこ
ぱたぱた
PIT PAT PIT PAT
SHHH
ジャーッ
WE'RE HAVING HAMBURG STEAK TO-MORROW?!
IT'S FOR YOUR LUNCH. I THOUGHT I'D MAKE A LOT AND FREEZE THE EXTRA.
I CAN'T WAIT!

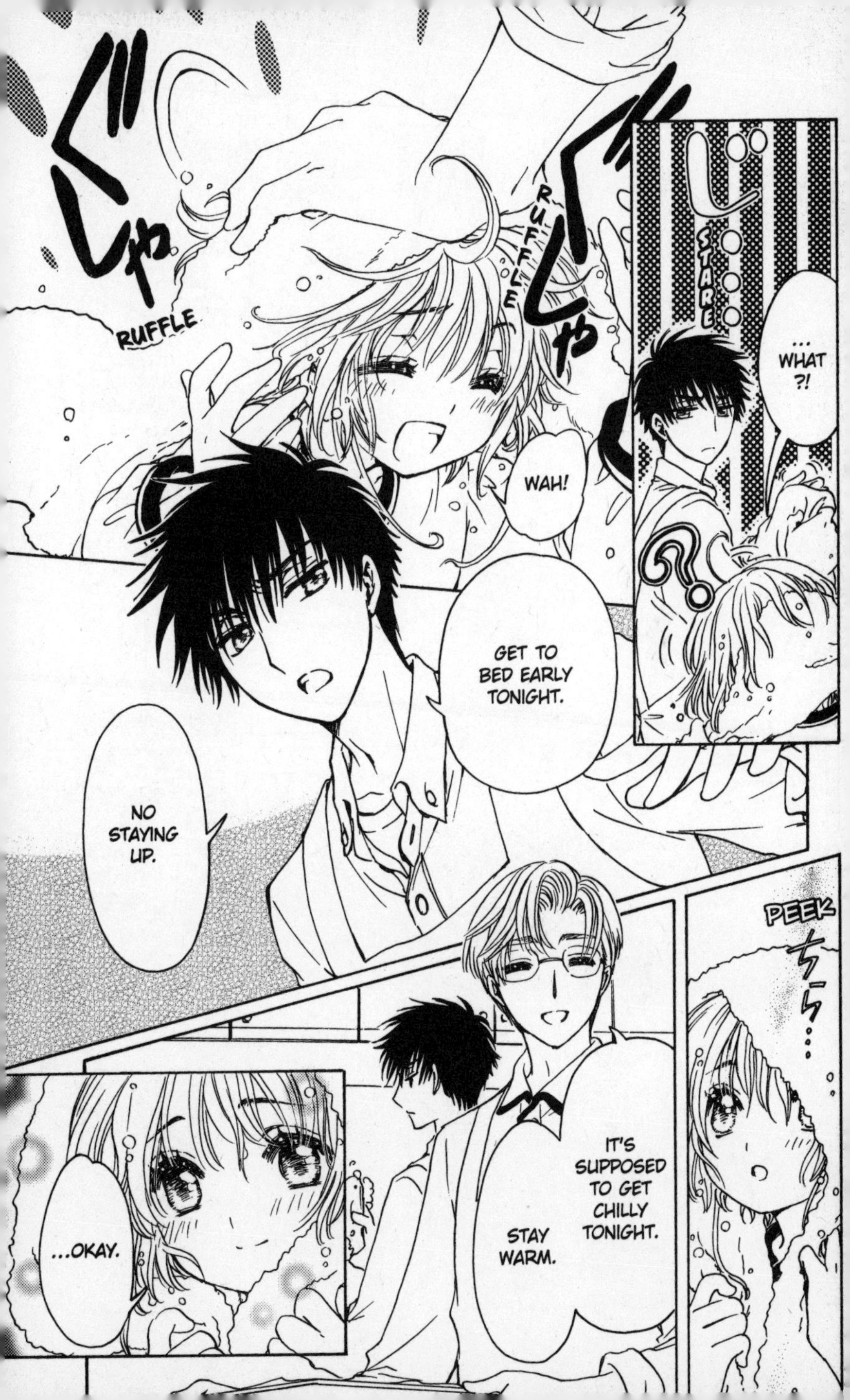
ぐしゃ
RUFFLE
ぐしゃ
RUFFLE
WAH!
じ…
STARE
...WHAT?!
GET TO BED EARLY TONIGHT.
NO STAYING UP.
ちら…
PEEK
IT'S SUPPOSED TO GET CHILLY TONIGHT.
STAY WARM.
...OKAY.

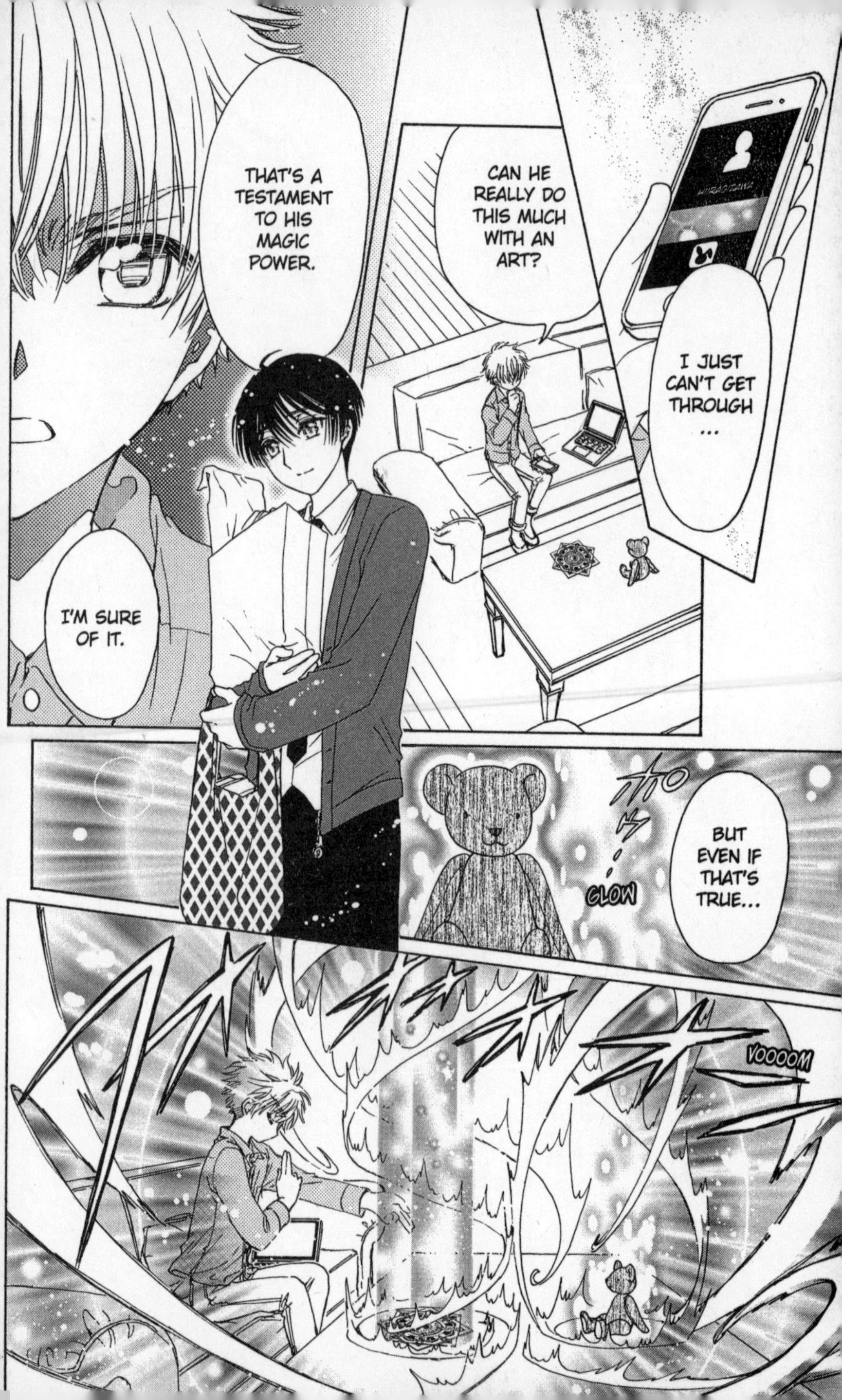
I JUST CAN'T GET THROUGH ...
CAN HE REALLY DO THIS MUCH WITH AN ART?
THAT'S A TESTAMENT TO HIS MAGIC POWER.
I'M SURE OF IT.
BUT EVEN IF THAT'S TRUE...
GLOW
VOOOOM

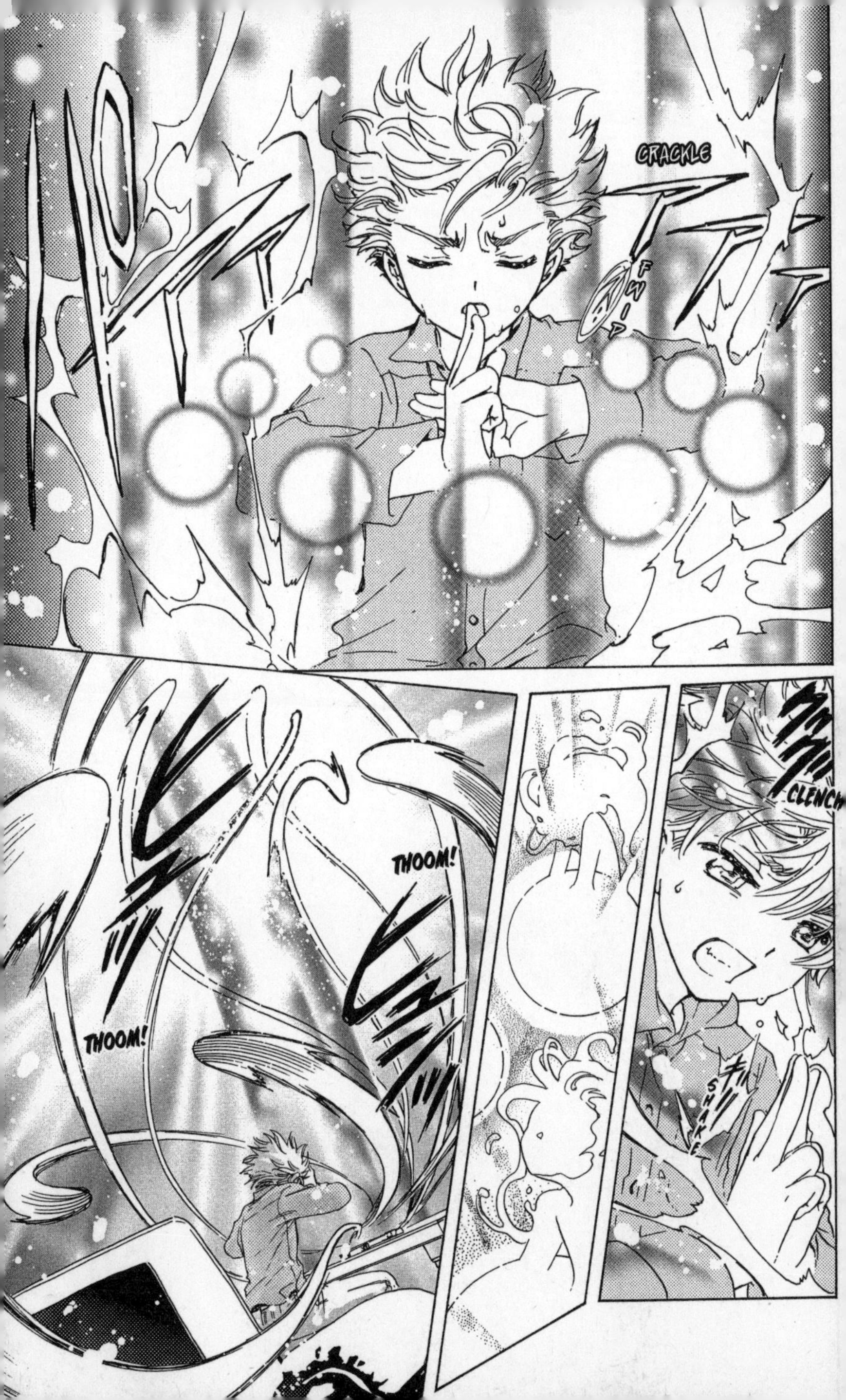
CRACKLE
FWIP
CLENCH
SHAKE
THOOM!
THOOM!

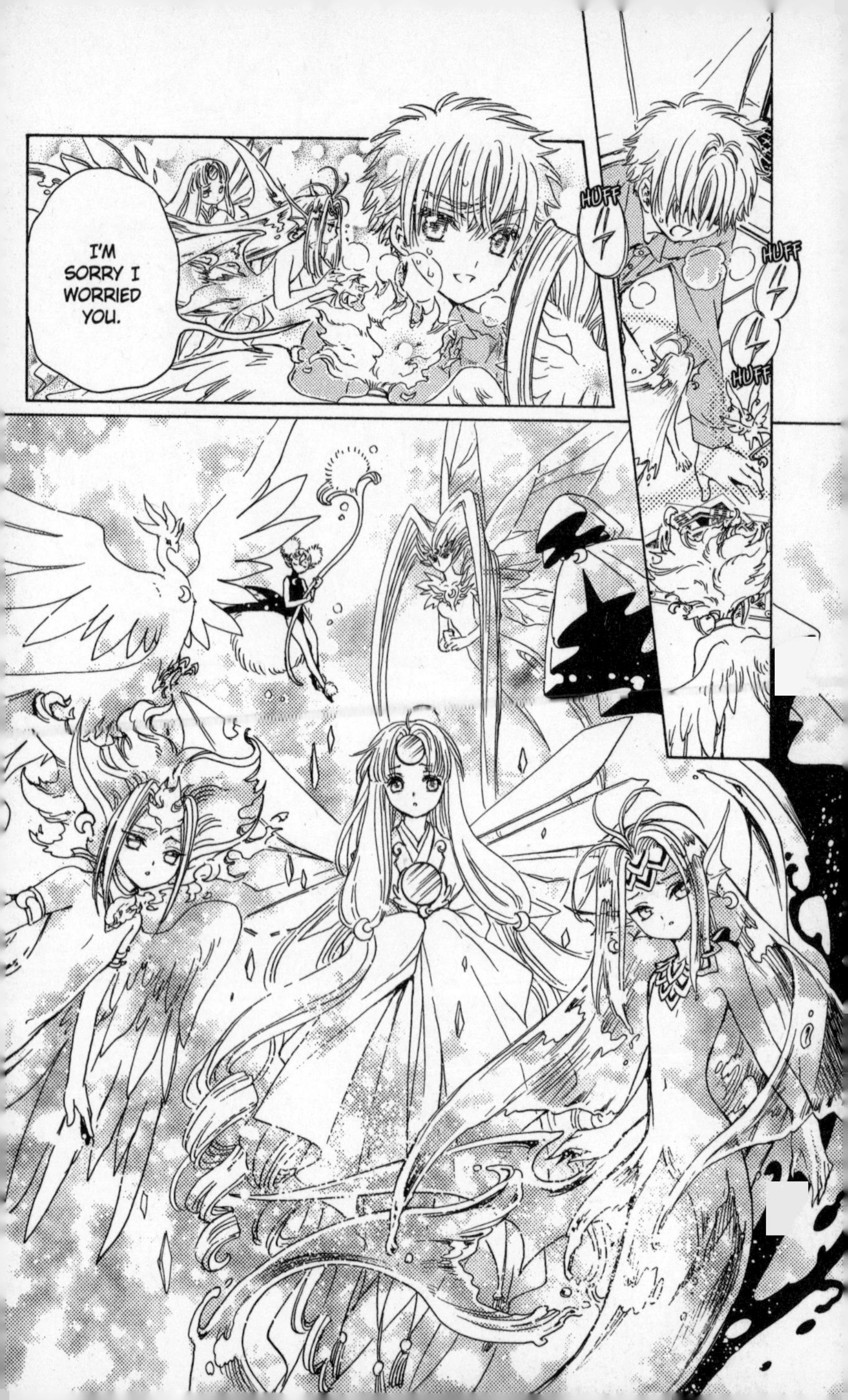
HUFF
HUFF
HUFF
I'M SORRY I WORRIED YOU.

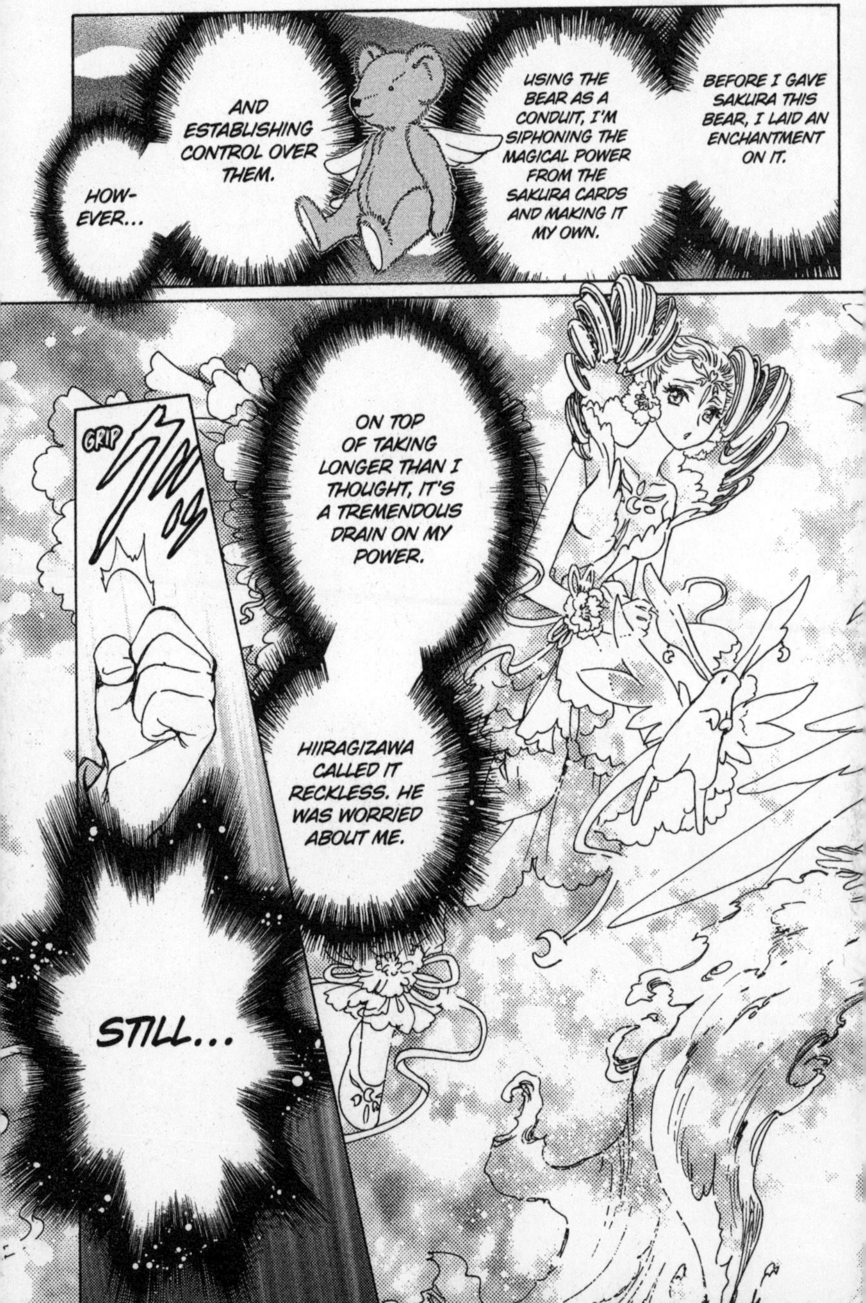
BEFORE I GAVE SAKURA THIS BEAR, I LAID AN ENCHANTMENT ON IT.
USING THE BEAR AS A CONDUIT, I'M SIPHONING THE MAGICAL POWER FROM THE SAKURA CARDS AND MAKING IT MY OWN.
AND ESTABLISHING CONTROL OVER THEM.
HOW-EVER...
ON TOP OF TAKING LONGER THAN I THOUGHT, IT'S A TREMENDOUS DRAIN ON MY POWER.
HIIRAGIZAWA CALLED IT RECKLESS. HE WAS WORRIED ABOUT ME.
GRIP
STILL...

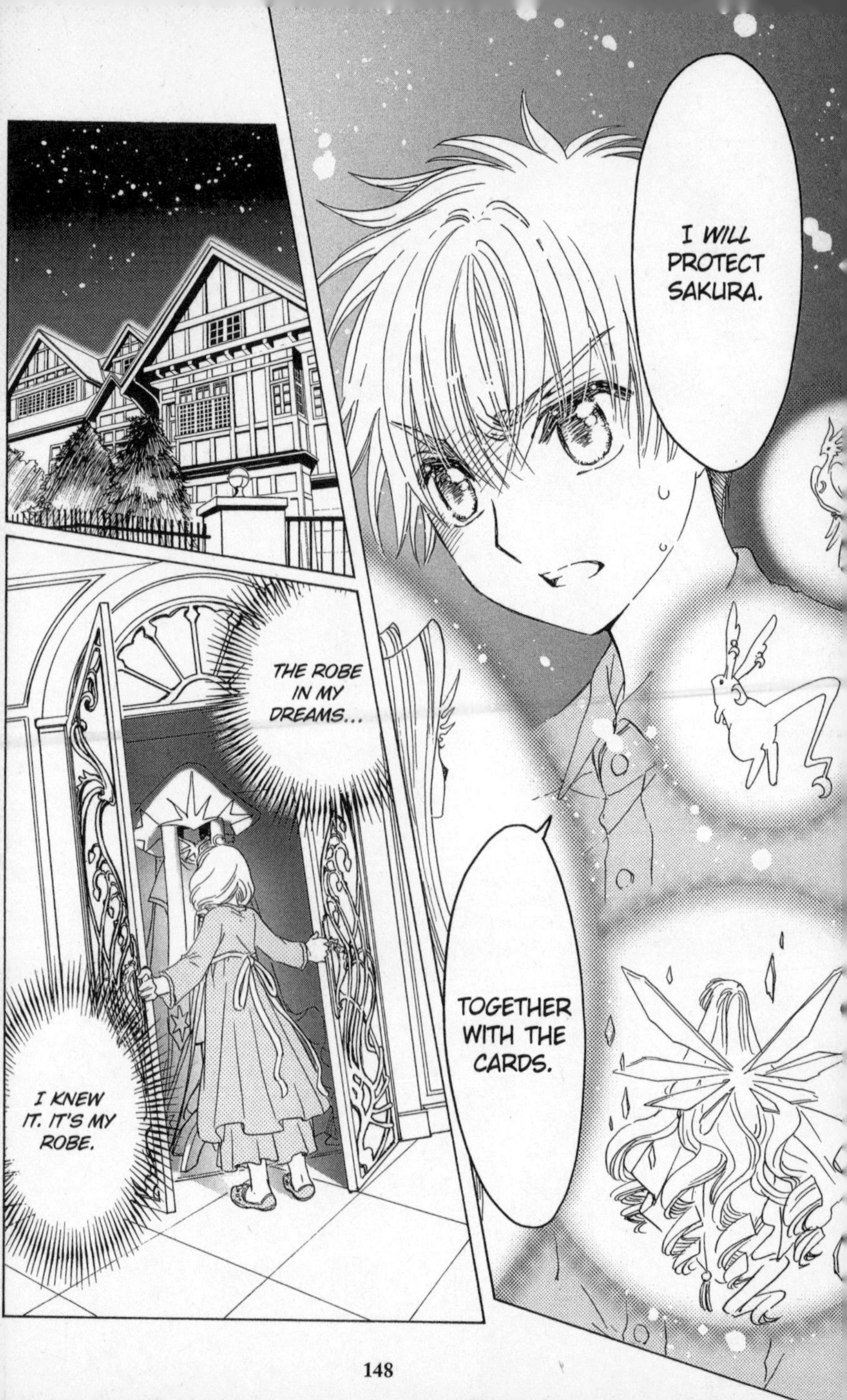
I WILL PROTECT SAKURA.
TOGETHER WITH THE CARDS.
THE ROBE IN MY DREAMS...
I KNEW IT. IT'S MY ROBE.

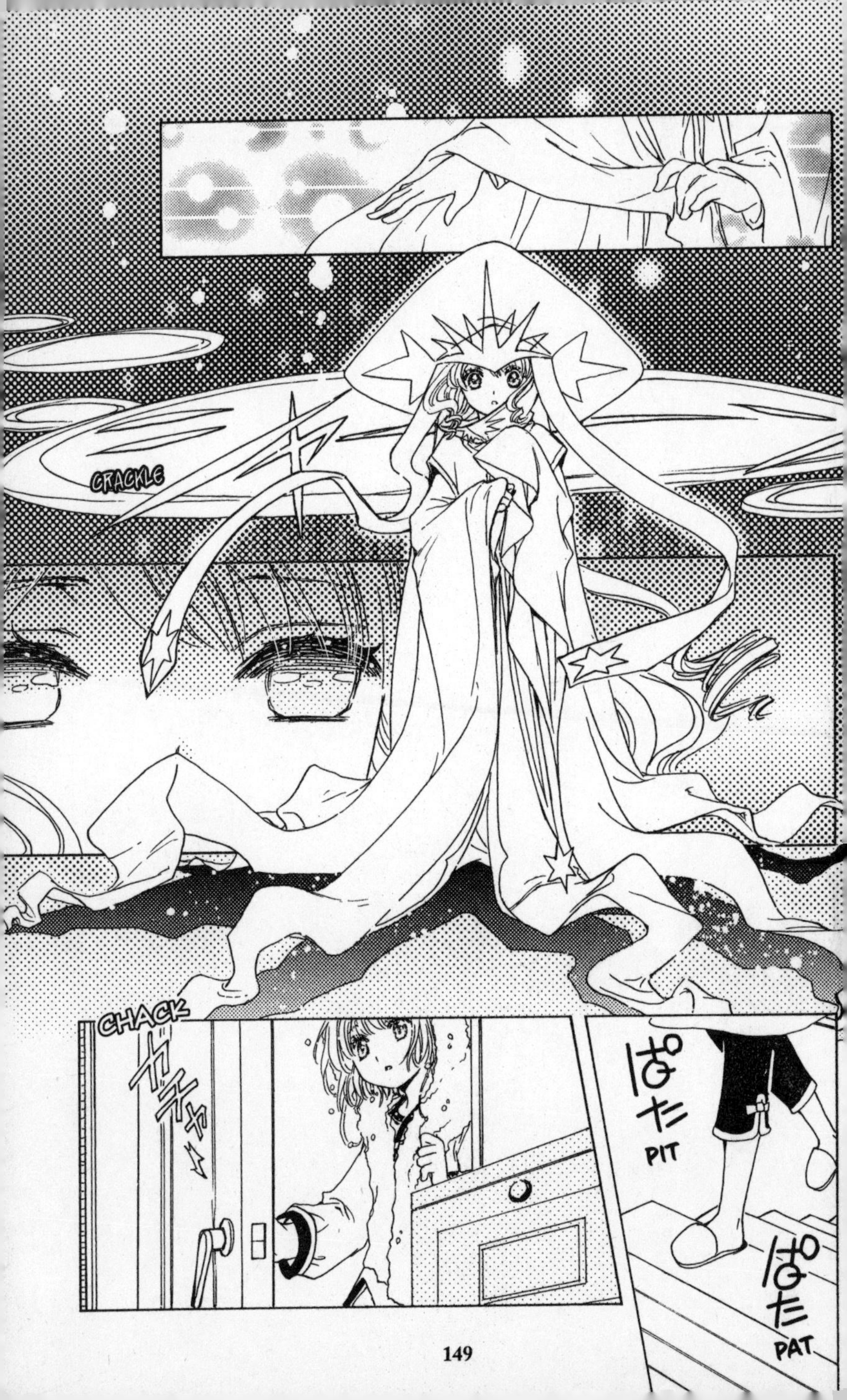
CRACKLE
ぱた
PIT
ぱた
PAT
CHACK
ガチャ

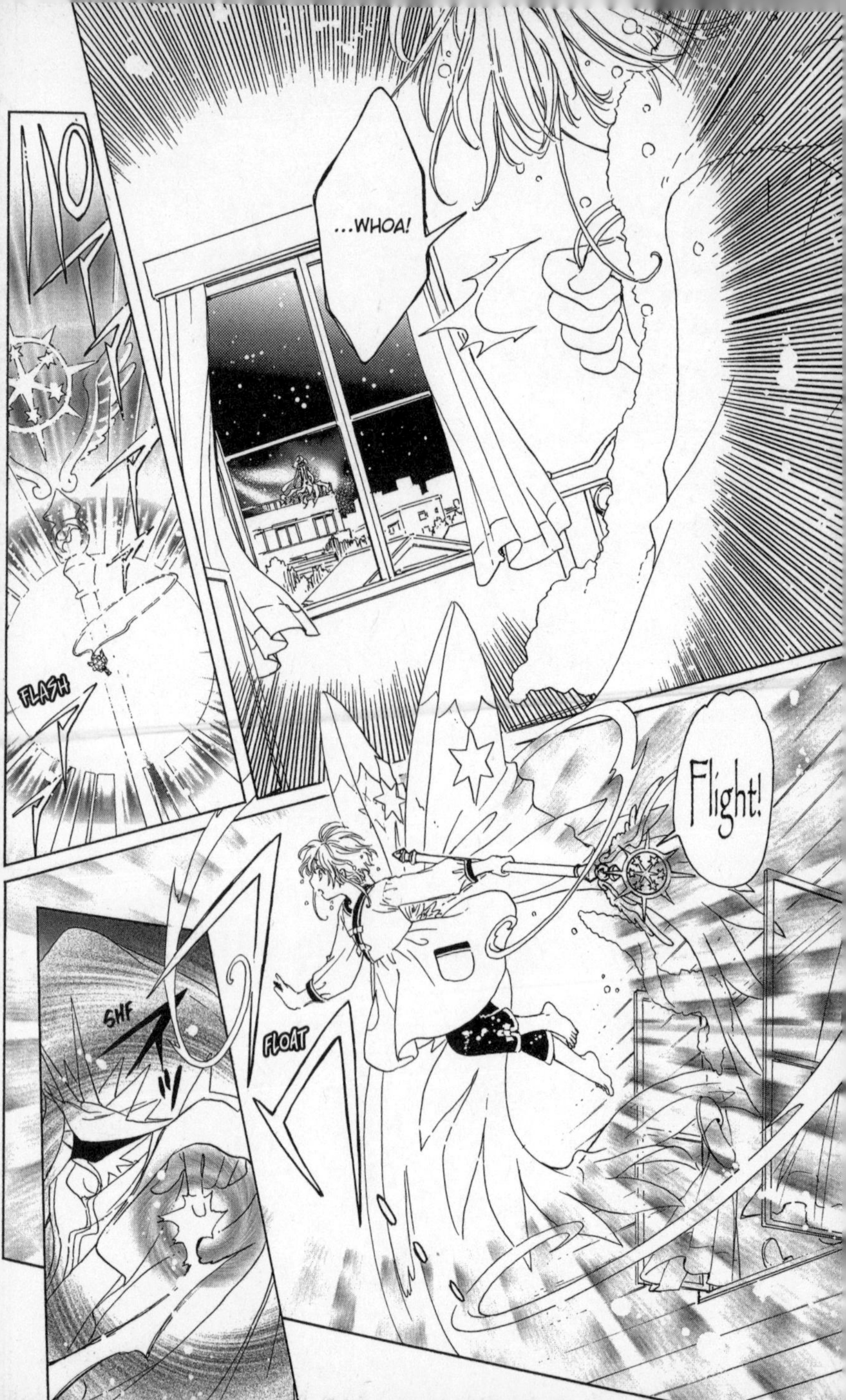
...WHOA!
FLASH
Flight!
FLOAT
SHF

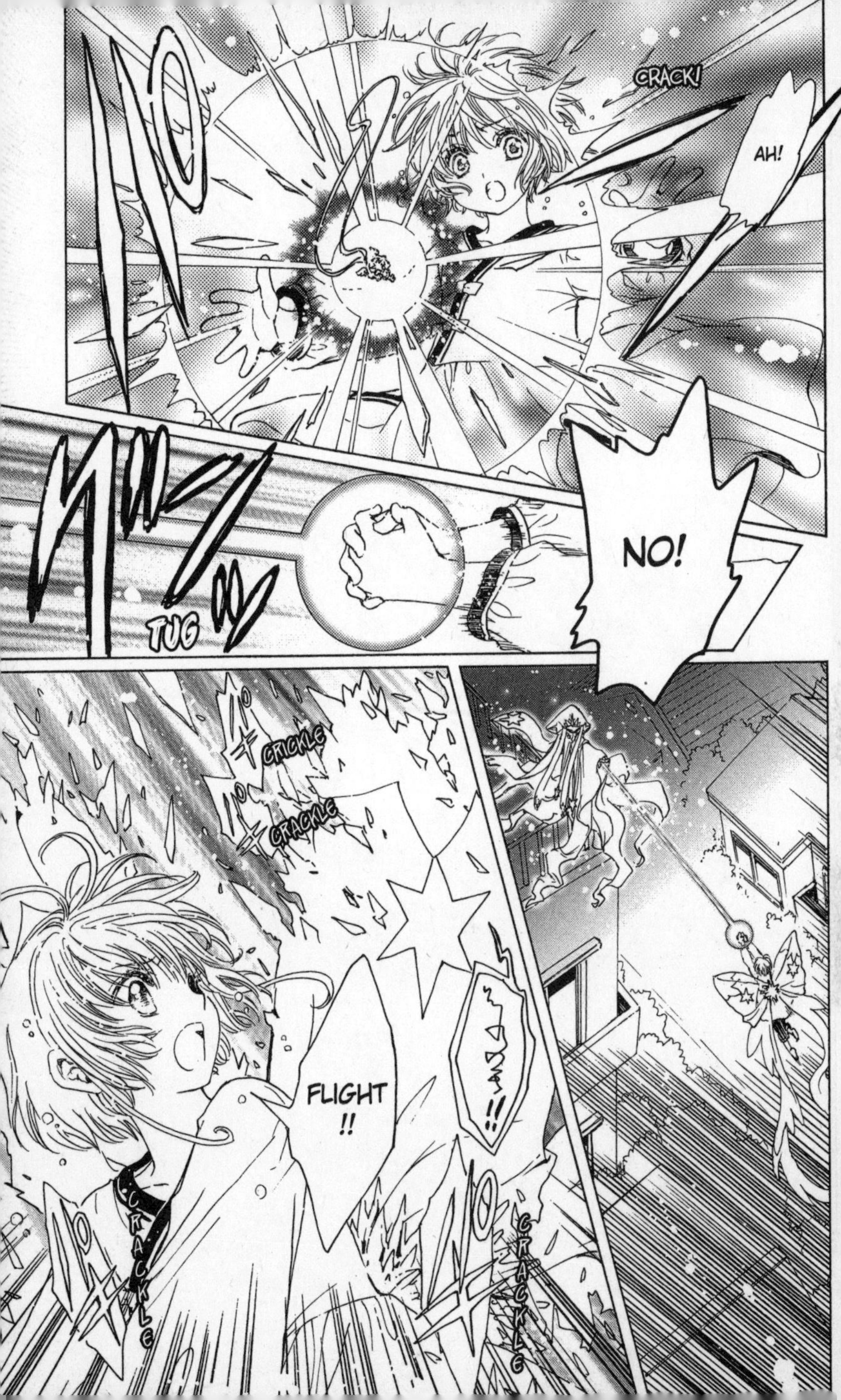
CRACK!
AH!
NO!
TUG
CRICKLE
CRACKLE
FLIGHT!!
CRACKLE
CRACKLE

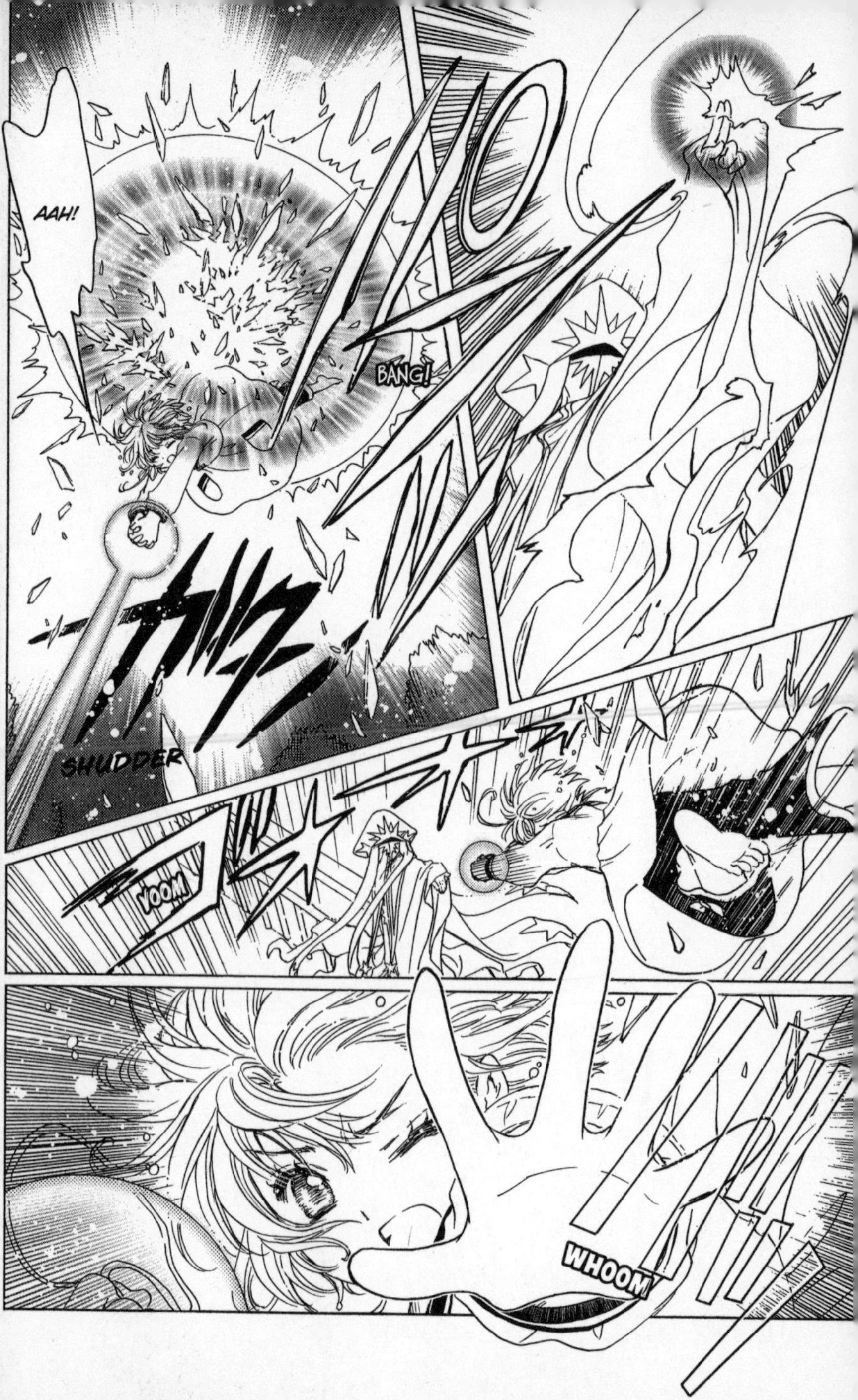
AAH!
BANG!
SHUDDER
VOOM
WHOOM

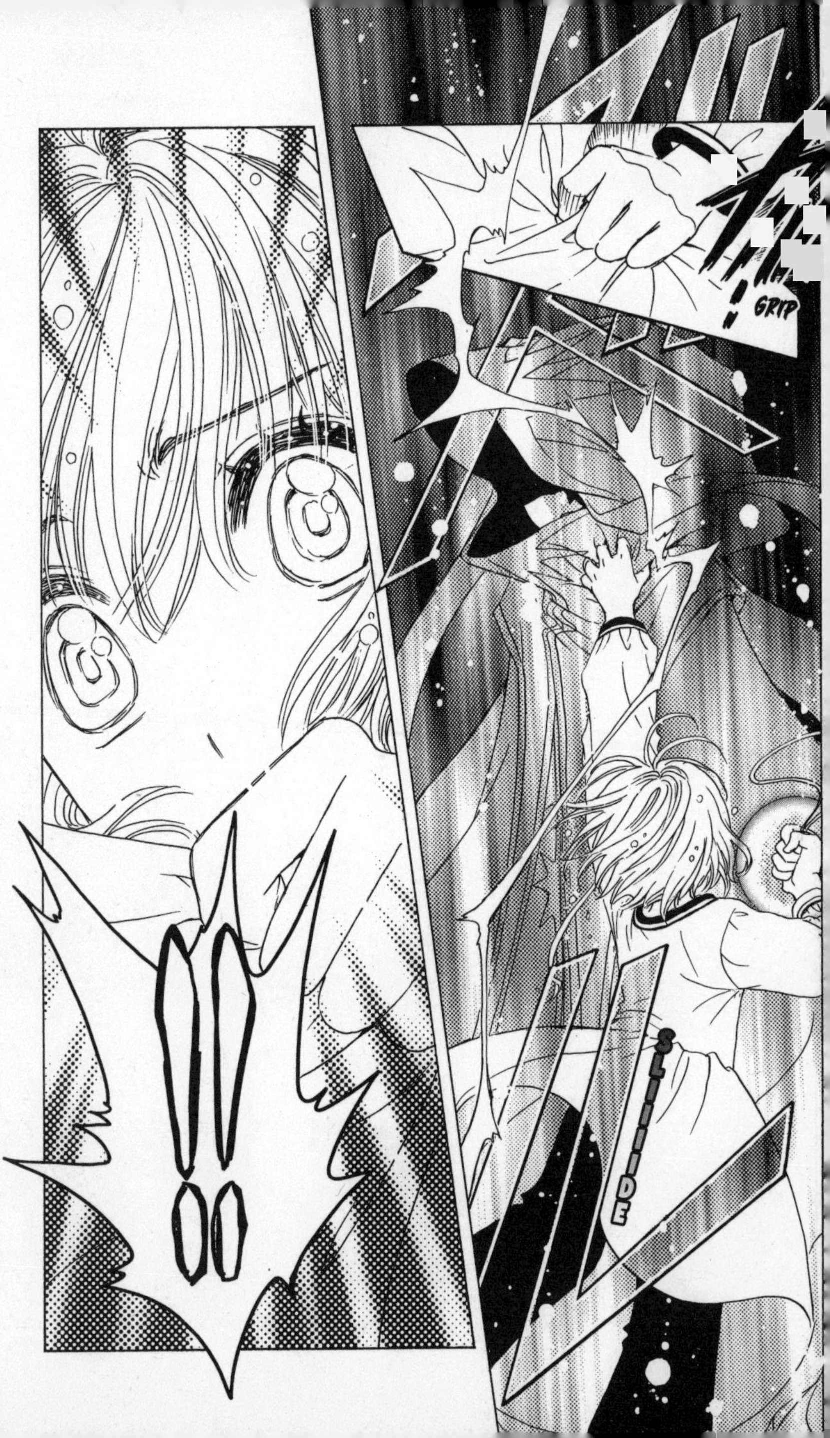
GRIP
SLIIIIDE
!!

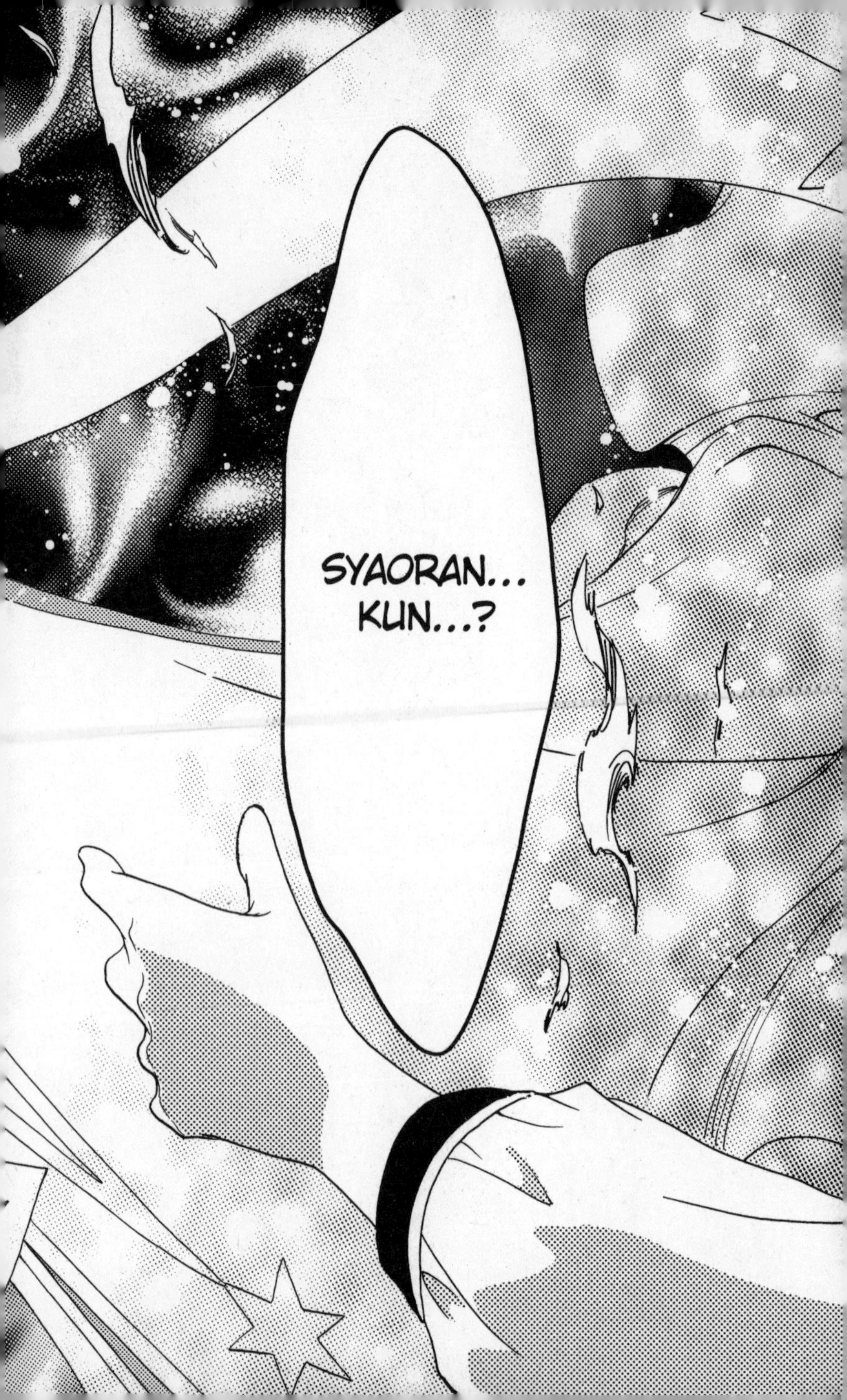
SYAORAN...
KUN...?

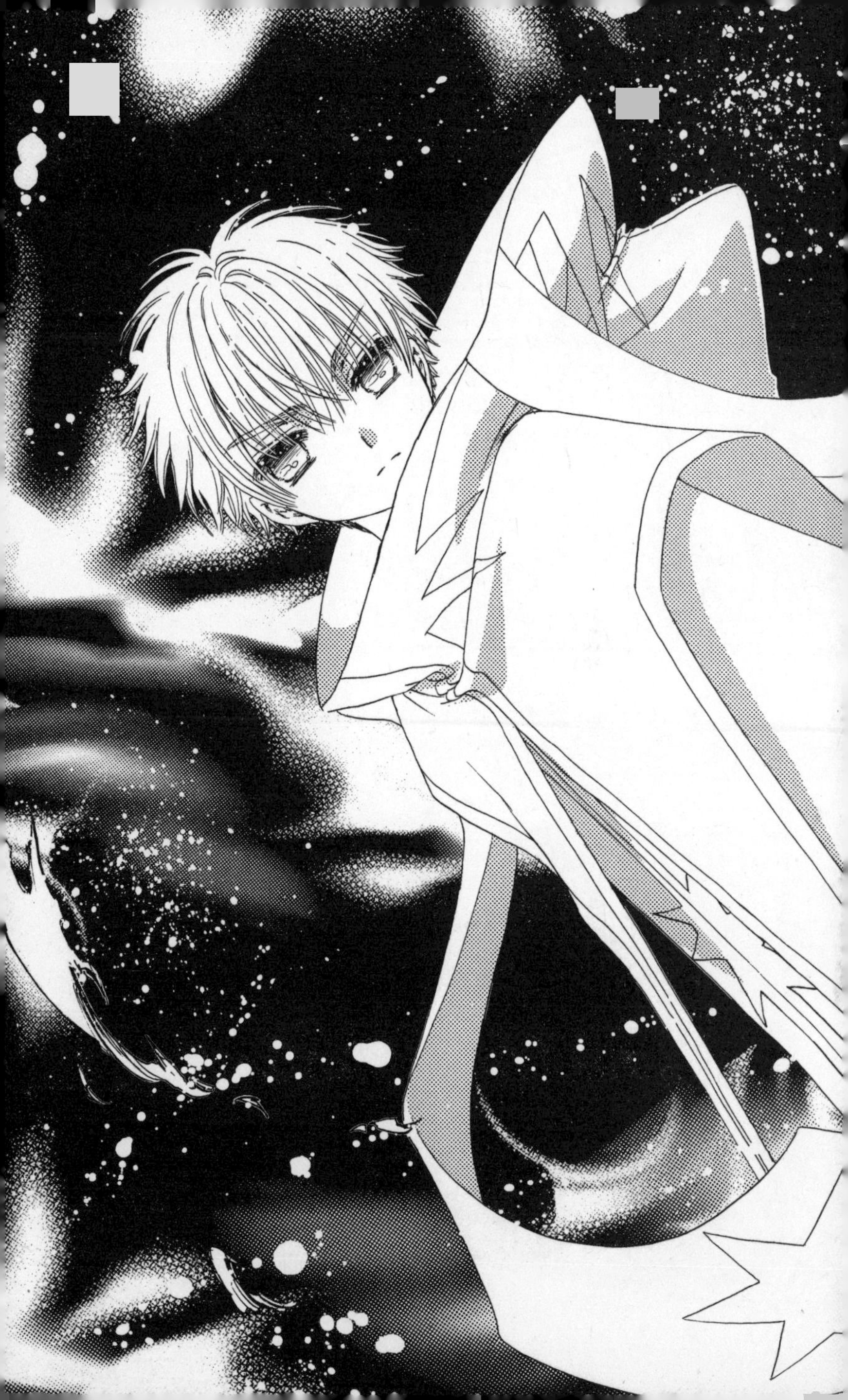

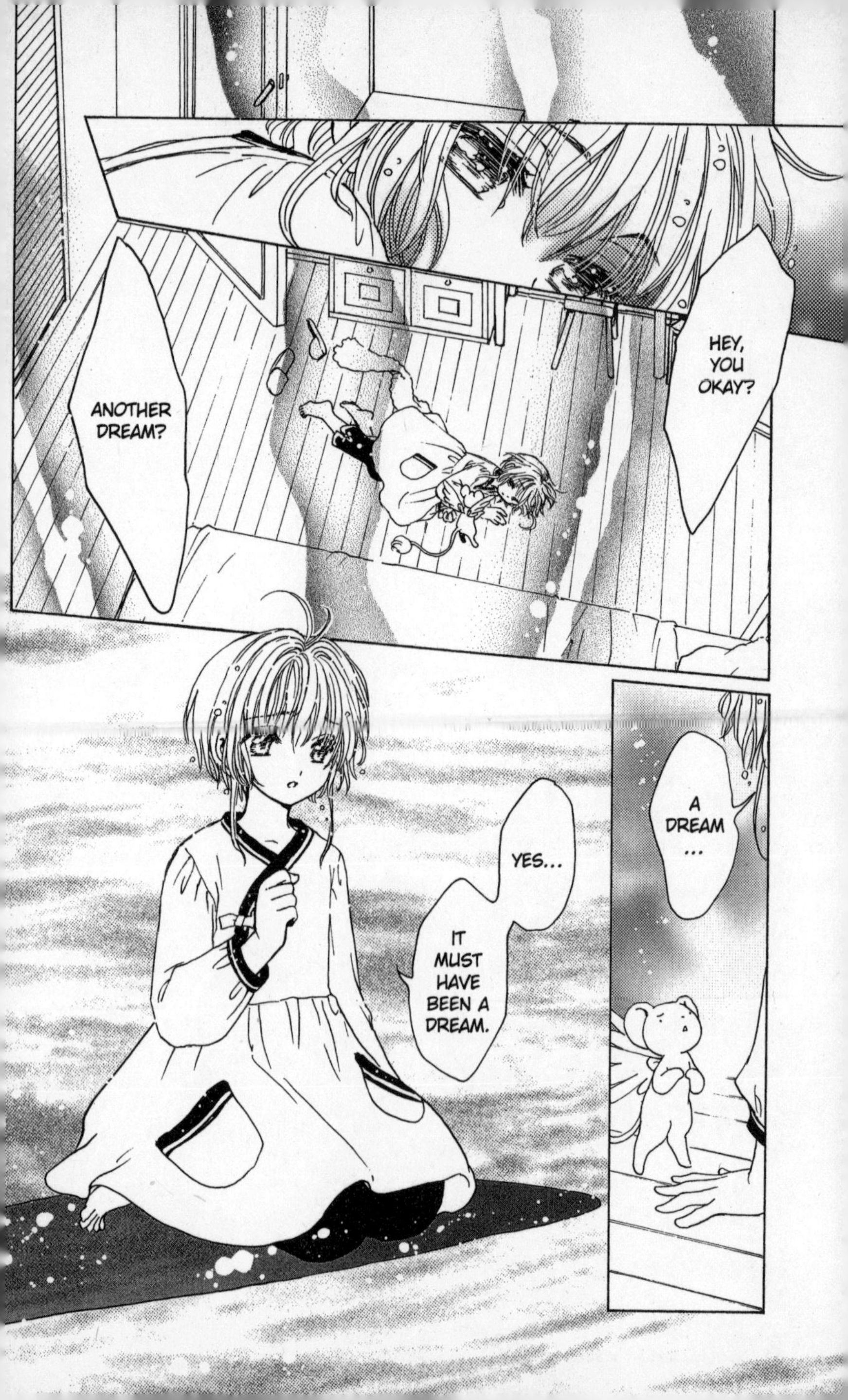
HEY, YOU OKAY?
ANOTHER DREAM?
A DREAM ...
YES...
IT MUST HAVE BEEN A DREAM.

♣ Continued in Volume 6 ♣

WAITING FOR SPRING

A sweet romantic story of a soft-spoken high school freshman and her quest to make friends. For fans of earnest, fun, and dramatic shojo like *Kimi ni Todoke* and *Say I Love You.*

KISS ME AT THE STROKE OF MIDNIGHT

An all-new Cinderella comedy perfect for fans of *My Little Monster* and *Say I Love You!*

LOVE AND LIES

Love is forbidden. When you turn 16, the government will assign you your marriage partner. This dystopian manga about teen love and defiance is a sexy, funny, and dramatic new hit! Anime now streaming on Anime Strike!

YOUR NEW FAVORITE ROMANCE MANGA IS WAITING FOR YOU!

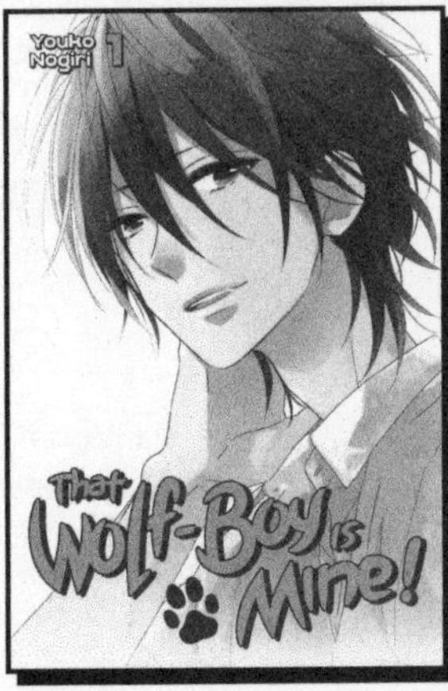
Youko Nogiri
1
That Wolf-Boy is Mine!

THAT WOLF-BOY IS MINE!

A beast-boy comedy and drama perfect for fans of *Fruits Basket*!

"A tantalizing, understated slice-of-life romance with an interesting supernatural twist."

- Taykobon

WAKE UP, SLEEPING BEAUTY

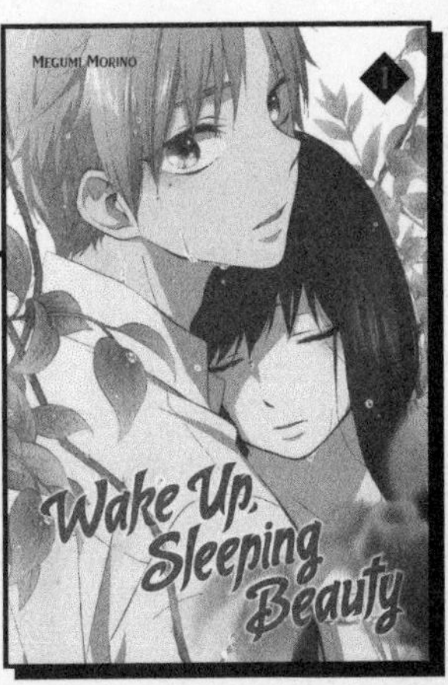
MEGUMI MORINO
1
Wake Up, Sleeping Beauty

This heartrending romantic manga is not the fairy tale you remember! This time, Prince Charming is a teenage housekeeper, and Sleeping Beauty's curse threatens to pull them both into deep trouble.

CardCaptor Sakura Clearcard volume 5 is a work of fiction. Names, characters, places, and incidents are the products of the author's imagination or are used fictitiously. Any resemblance to actual events, locales, or persons, living or dead, is entirely coincidental.

A Kodansha Comics Trade Paperback Original.

Published in the United States by Kodansha Comics,
an imprint of Kodansha USA Publishing, LLC, New York.

Publication rights for this English edition arranged through Kodansha Ltd., Tokyo.

First published in Japan in 2018 by Kodansha Ltd., Tokyo, as
Kaadokyaputaa Sakura Kuriakaado Hen volume 5.

ISBN 978-1-63236-659-7

Printed in the United States of America.

www.kodanshacomics.com

9 8 7 6 5 4 3 2 1

Translation: Devon Corwin
Lettering: Erika Terriquez
Editing: Paul Starr
Kodansha Comics edition cover design: Phil Balsman